Power and Political Economy from Thatcher to Blair

T0311875

This book investigates the policies of the Thatcher, Major and Blair governments and their approaches towards concentration of economic and political power.

The 1979–2007 British governments have variously been described as liberal or, to use a political insult and a favourite academic label, neoliberal. One of the stated objectives of the Thatcher, Major and Blair governments—albeit with differing focal points—was to disperse power and to empower the individual. This was also a consistent theme of the first generation of neoliberals, who saw monopolies, vested interests and concentration more generally as the 'great enemy of democracy'. Under Thatcher and Major, Conservatives sought to liberalize the economy and spread ownership through policies like Right to Buy and privatisation. New Labour dispersed political power with its devolution agenda, granted operational independence to the Bank of England and put in place a seemingly robust antitrust framework. All governments during the 1979–2007 period pursued choice in public services. Yet our modern discourse characterises Britain as beset by endemic power concentration, in markets and politics. What went wrong? How did so-called neoliberal governments, which invoked liberty and empowerment, fail to disperse power and allow concentration to continue, recur or arise?

The book will be of interest to students and scholars of contemporary British history, political economy and politics, as well as specific areas of study such as Thatcherism and New Labour.

Robert Ledger has a PhD in political science from Queen Mary University of London. He currently lives and works in Frankfurt am Main, Germany. He is the author of *Neoliberal Thought and Thatcherism: "A Transition From Here to There?"*

British Politics and Society

Social change impacts not just upon voting behaviour and party identity but also the formulation of policy. But how do social changes and political developments interact? Which shapes which? Reflecting a belief that social and political structures cannot be understood either in isolation from each other or from the historical processes that form them, this series examines the forces that have shaped British society.

Inside the Welfare State
Foundations of Policy and Practice in Post-War Britain
Virginia A. Noble

British Military Intervention and the Struggle for Jordan
King Hussein, Nasser and the Middle East Crisis, 1955–1958
Stephen Blackwell

The Permanent Under-Secretary for Foreign Affairs, 1854–1946
Keith Neilson and T.G. Otte

The Western European Union
International Politics Between Alliance and Integration
Sally Rohan

Windrush (1948) and Rivers of Blood (1968)
Legacy and Assessment
Edited by Trevor Harris

Power and Political Economy from Thatcher to Blair
The Great Enemy of Democracy?
Robert Ledger

For more information about this series, please visit: https://www.routledge.com/British-Politics-and-Society/book-series/BRITPOL

Power and Political Economy from Thatcher to Blair

The Great Enemy of Democracy?

Robert Ledger

Routledge
Taylor & Francis Group

LONDON AND NEW YORK

First published 2021
by Routledge
2 Park Square, Milton Park, Abingdon, Oxon OX14 4RN

and by Routledge
52 Vanderbilt Avenue, New York, NY 10017

Routledge is an imprint of the Taylor & Francis Group, an informa business

British Library Cataloguing-in-Publication Data
A catalogue record for this book is available from the British Library

Library of Congress Cataloging-in-Publication Data
Names: Ledger, Robert, author.
Title: Power and political economy from Thatcher to Blair: the great enemy of democracy? / Robert Ledger.
Description: 1 Edition. | New York: Routledge, 2021. | Series: British politics and society | Includes bibliographical references and index.
Identifiers: LCCN 2020042899 (print) | LCCN 2020042900 (ebook) | ISBN 9780367857677 (hardback) | ISBN 9781003014959 (ebook)
Subjects: LCSH: Great Britain–Economic policy–21st century. | Neoliberalism–Great Britain–History–20th century. | Conservatism–Great Britain–History–20th century. | Power (Social sciences)–Great Britain–History–20th century. | Thatcher, Margaret–Influence. | Great Britain–Politics and government–1979-1997.
Classification: LCC HC256.7 .L43 2021 (print) | LCC HC256.7 (ebook) | DDC 330.941/085–dc23
LC record available at https://lccn.loc.gov/2020042899
LC ebook record available at https://lccn.loc.gov/2020042900

ISBN: 978-0-367-85767-7 (hbk)
ISBN: 978-1-003-01495-9 (ebk)

Typeset in Times
by Deanta Global Publishing Services, Chennai, India

Contents

Acknowledgements

I would like to thank a number of people who helped develop my thinking on several of this book's themes: Dr. Torsten Riotte, Dr. Andreas Fahrmeir and the history seminar at Goethe University, Frankfurt am Main; the organisers of and participants at the *Rethinking British Neoliberalism* conference at UCL, London, in September 2017; and the staff and students at Schiller University, Heidelberg.

I would also like to thank my family for their support, and Richard Morris, Martin Longstaff and Peter Finn for their input and help over the years.

Most of all, I would like to thank my wife, Rebecca, for her enduring support and encouragement.

Introduction

Concentration, of power and wealth, is one of the key issues of our times. Despite the somewhat academic framing of concentration, inequality or market power, the themes and trends they represent are at the core of recent British political history. Numerous writers, including this one, have described the economic and political paradigm in Britain since 1979 as one dominated by 'neoliberalism', or a resurgence of economic liberalism. Although the very notion of neoliberalism has been contested, in so far as it was a coherent set of principles or policies, the prevailing economic model was seriously shaken by the 2007–08 financial crisis. In the decade since, we have seen economic liberal principles attempt to reassert themselves, for instance through austerity and public spending cuts, while simultaneously being challenged by groups on the left and right seeking to overturn the status quo, often in a more collectivist direction. At the root of neoliberal thinking is a notion that its proponents have failed to adequately address. In the early years of the renewal of economic liberalism, from the 1930s, neoliberals, notably from the United States and Germany, identified concentration of power as a danger to a functioning society and a threat to both economic and political liberty. In this way, neoliberals proposed mechanisms and institutions to prevent concentration in the economic sphere, accompanied by a rather technocratic approach to politics. We saw some of these principles put into practice, albeit with significant contingencies, from the mid-1970s in Britain. The paradox of the neoliberal approach, however, was that the economy and democratic model it encouraged were singularly incapable of preventing concentration. In fact, concentration of economic and political power has soared during the so-called neoliberal era. The forces this concentration, and this approach more generally, have unleashed increasingly manifested themselves during the 2010s.

In recent years, there has been growing discussion about concentration of power. In particular, on the left, this has centred around analysis of long-run inequality, while many on the right have focused on sovereignty. One of the core points of convergence for both approaches has been a critique of globalisation. Distribution of power, within the globalised economy as well as at the political level, has also been discussed. Nevertheless, there have been few in-depth investigations into the processes and decisions that led to the current situation in terms of concentration. A number of themes raised in our current debates require further investigation, especially against the backdrop of contemporary political history. The rationale for this book builds upon the author's previous work on neoliberalism and Thatcherism.[1] In particular, early neoliberals were wary of concentration of power and its deleterious impact on individual freedom and, ultimately, democratic institutions and accountability. These early neoliberals, therefore, stated as one of their objectives a greater distribution of power, using the language of freedom and liberty. Although the priorities of neoliberals shifted over the following decades, this kind of rhetoric was seized upon by Margaret Thatcher and her government. The language of individual freedom and choice, as well as competition, continued under Thatcher's successors. Many modern accounts of British politics, however, as well as identifying neoliberalism as a pervasively malign influence, outline a growing accumulation of economic and political power.[2] This analysis has manifested itself in the debate around inequality, monopolies and cartels as expressions of market power, the corruption of government by vested interests and a globalised economy that politically disempowers the individual. Clearly, there is a disconnect between a string of supposedly neoliberal governments that failed to implement, or even ignored, one of neoliberalism's main tenets.

This book will look at how British governments, from Thatcher to Blair, actually responded to, or encouraged, concentration of power. The story is more nuanced than the 'market fundamentalist' yet 'pro-big business' narrative that has emerged around Thatcherism and New Labour. Archival evidence shows how the Thatcher government was more animated about competition in its later privatisations than in its earlier efforts, demonstrated by its different approach to regulation. More famously, it attempted to spread ownership of capital, the Right to Buy scheme being perhaps the best-known example. John Major's government was less radical in office, but even his, at the time much maligned, Citizen's Charter policy was an attempt to empower the individual. It was New Labour that implemented the 1998 Competition Act, which seemed more in keeping with the 'social market economy' model and proved the most significant piece of UK antitrust legislation in the post-war period. The Blair government also initiated political devolution that dispersed power within the UK, transforming the British constitutional settlement. It also granted operational independence to the Bank of England in monetary policy.

In some respects, recent UK governments have been surprisingly bold in giving away power from the centre. Nevertheless, there is significant evidence that market power increased at several points in the privatised industries, as well as the deregulated post-Big Bang financial and banking services sectors. The power of trade unions, meanwhile, was significantly reduced under the Thatcher and Major governments, without seeing a significant reversal under New Labour. The contemporary literature shows, in the aggregate, a growing increase in market power. Meanwhile, wealth has increasingly concentrated amid soaring inequality, particularly during the Thatcher years. In certain respects, power left the centralised nation state, owing to a more globalised economy as well as initiatives such as devolution. Many of today's discontents appear unhappy at the way power was realigned during the neoliberal era and beyond. This is the broad rationale for the book. The objective of this project is to better understand the years from 1979 until the 2007–08 financial crash as a discrete historical period and, specifically, to analyse what British governments have done to address the challenges posed by concentration of power.

Methodology

This study will primarily use qualitative methods, focused on analysis of neoliberal thinkers and recent political history. The insights of neoliberals themselves will be used to show how neoliberalism can be viewed on its own terms—that is to say, how neoliberals would view so-called neoliberal governments. Some quantitative methods are also employed to gauge market power. A number of measures of economic concentration, including the Herfindahl–Hirschman Index, will be used to demonstrate how competitive particular markets have been over time. Likewise, a range of measures help determine wealth inequality.

The book will look for the most part at the political and economic history of the 1979–2007 period. There are a number of reasons for this. First, from a historian's perspective, it allows some distance to analyse the events of these decades more dispassionately, although, admittedly, the New Labour era is still fresh enough that here we are dealing with contemporary history. Second, the Thatcher, Major and Blair governments have sometimes been grouped together as neoliberal. Using this timeframe allows some interrogation of the claim. Third, the 1979–2007 period is almost a discrete one in terms of financial liberalisation. The Thatcher government removed exchange controls soon after taking office, and the financial crisis that took hold in 2007 to some extent marked the end of an era for lightly regulated finance capital. Nevertheless, the narrative will inevitably pre-date 1979 at times and, in the exploration of British competition policy, by some decades. Similarly, several of the themes covered in this book have been included with post-2007 events in mind. Therefore, there will be some discussion of concentration trends after Tony Blair left office.

Broadly speaking, this study attempts to answer a number of questions. Most generally, how and why did power accumulate during the 1979–2007 period, if indeed that is the case? Related to this, the book intends to investigate the extent to which British governments during this era attempted to disperse economic and political power. Political economy, including neoliberal theory, will be employed to try and explain the actions of governments in relation to concentration, as well as related trends. Finally, this study aims to tentatively answer how trends in concentration have informed, and are informing, the post-2007 narrative of British politics.

Literature review

A number of works examine concentration of power, although investigations into the subject more generally are relatively rare. One exception is Frank Bealey's book, *Power in Business and the State: An Historical Analysis of its Concentration*.[3]

Even in 2001, Bealey outlined the growing concentration of economic and political power. The book also discussed increasing managerialism in politics. This current study will also look at how politics came to be viewed as technocratic during the so-called neoliberal era, in particular under New Labour, and how the 2010s have seen the emergence of the antithesis of technocracy: populism. In addition, Bealey described UK governments' attempts at decentralising power and how, in general, they overpromised and underdelivered in this area. Several other books and articles have investigated elements of concentration, some of which are discussed below. One more recent work, however, *Power in Economic Thought*, edited by Manuela Mosca, includes a history of economic concentration, based on economic theory, in a number of European states over the space of two centuries.[4] A UK-centric approach to concentration, based more on political history and government policy from the mid to late 20th century, however, is not covered in the literature.

Market power

Core themes of this study include market power, economic regulation and competition. A number of books trace the history of antitrust in the UK during various phases and different ideological settings. Tony Freyer, for instance, outlines the history of competition policy in the US and UK from the late 19th century until the Thatcher and Reagan era, in *Regulating Big Business: Antitrust in Great Britain and America; 1880–1990*.[5] Freyer describes how Britain trailed the US in antitrust after the 1890 Sherman Act and how Britain subsequently developed its own idiosyncratic form of regulation. In more recent decades, Britain's competition framework has been more influenced by the development of the European Union (EU), as described in Angus MacCulloch and Barry J. Rodger's book *Competition Law and Policy in the EU and UK*.[6] A particularly detailed and definitive account of Britain's competition policy and its history is found in Andrew Scott's "The Evolution of Competition Law and Policy in the United Kingdom".[7] Along with other authors, Scott highlights the significance of the 1998 Competition Act in the development of antitrust in the UK, as well as the importance of the EU in formalising a British competition regime. This is developed further in Gregory Baldi's article "Europeanising Antitrust: British Competition Policy Reform and Member State Convergence".[8]

A number of studies look specifically at market power, the strategies used by firms, and regulators' responses, such as Chiara Fumagalli et al.'s *Exclusionary Practices: The Economics of Monopolisation and Abuse of Dominance*.[9] The idea of market power is disputed by Chicago School neoliberals themselves, including by George Stigler and Milton Friedman. Perhaps the best-known challenge to antitrust is Robert Bork's work, notably his 1978 book *The Antitrust Paradox*.[10]

Rent-seeking

The concept of rent-seeking is closely linked with market power, setting out how particular firms or industries exert excessive power over the political process and, as a result, extract favourable conditions and subsidies from governments and regulators. Public choice theory was influential in developing the concept of rent-seeking. Although initially targeted at the public sector, it is perhaps more apt as a critique of markets and business. For instance, Guy Standing, in his book *The Corruption of Capitalism: Why Rentiers Thrive and Work Does Not Pay*, outlines how big business is often subsidised and extracts rent from the taxpayer, as well as more corrupt practices within the modern economy.[11] Other authors have described collusion within the British economy, particularly after the 2007–08 financial crash, as well as concepts such as 'regulatory capture', where business interests manage to orientate regulatory decisions towards their own agenda, rather than the public interest or that of consumers.[12]

Inequality

A topic that has garnered much attention in recent years, wealth inequality entered the spotlight in particular thanks to the work of French economist Thomas Piketty.[13] Using a huge amount of data, Piketty shows how income inequality fell during the mid-20th century and then started to increase at the start of the neoliberal era, from the late 1970s. As well as wealth inequality, this current study will investigate regional disparities in the UK, with implications for both regional policy and devolution, as well as Britain's uncodified constitution. Regional changes were important for shifts in power during the 1979–2007 period. A number of these issues, and how they pertain to the New Labour governments, are analysed in Carole Thornley and Dan Coffey's *Globalization and Varieties of Capitalism: New Labour, Economic Policy and the Abject State*, in particular Labour's approach to workers.[14]

Structural changes

Several of the trends examined in this book have been swept along by major changes and structural shifts in the global economy. First among these has been accelerating globalisation. Dani Rodrik identifies 'hyperglobalization', in his book *The Globalization Paradox: Democracy and the Future of the World Economy*, as exerting a pernicious impact on democratic accountability, outlining how the costs and benefits of the process need realigning.[15] The work of Keith Cowling and Philip R. Tomlinson has also identified some of the trends surrounding globalisation and concentration, arguing these have "met the wider interests of the global community" and "contributed to a series of 'strategic failures' throughout the world economy".[16] Cowling and Tomlinson also outline the shifts in relative power between states and large firms, describing how, "At a national and global level, the growth in corporate power also has implications for relationships with governments and labour".[17] A number of these themes will be explored in detail in this current study.

Chapter summary

This book is broadly divided into four parts: approaches to concentration, economic concentration, political concentration, and trends and consequences. The first chapter will outline the key theoretical views of political and economic power concentration. In particular, there will be a focus on neoliberalism. The broad – often pejorative – term neoliberalism is posited into three key strands, which inform our contemporary perspective: German Ordoliberalism, the Austrian School and the Chicago School. Each neoliberal strand has a different approach to concentration of power and, crucially, its relationship with democracy. The title of the book stems from one of the early neoliberals, Henry Simons, who wrote that monopolies—the ultimate manifestation of economic concentration—were the "great enemy of democracy". This sentiment was shared by European neoliberals, particularly the German Ordoliberals, but clashed with the later interpretation that neoliberal thinkers, such as Milton Friedman and Friedrich Hayek, were wary of democracy. The ideological perspectives explored in this chapter will be compared with political debates in Britain, particularly during the period directly predating Thatcherism.

Chapter 2 will examine the history of competition policy in the UK. Limited before the Second World War, it was the Attlee government that first introduced significant legislation to restrain monopolies, cartels and anti-competitive behaviour. The model put in place in the late 1940s, of a fair trading body and monopolies commission, was broadly pursued into and beyond the Thatcher era. Indeed, competition policy was one area where we can see some degree of bipartisan consensus in the post-1945 era. Crucially, politicians retained enough discretion over the process to undermine the credibility of British competition policy. It would be the 1998 Competition Act, introduced by New Labour, that put in place a more robust antitrust framework.

Economic concentration is looked at across two chapters. Chapter 3 explores the structural changes that took place in the British economy between 1979 and 2007 and led to shifts in economic concentration. This includes the changes within the national economy itself, such as the rise of services and decline of heavy industry and manufacturing. Finance will be given particular attention as a sector that became crucial, and in some respects divisive, for Britain during these decades. Regional inequalities will be examined, sitting alongside changes in ownership in the British economy as well as different approaches to skills and education, fuelling shifts in concentration. The trends explored in this chapter, importantly, all took place against the backdrop of accelerating globalisation. Chapter 4 looks at UK competition policy in more detail during the Thatcher, Major and Blair years. This will be explored in terms of sectoral case studies, in energy markets and in the media, as well as more generally. Without almost constant regulation, markets in Britain will be shown to tend towards concentration.

The third part of the book looks at the distribution of political power in Britain under Thatcher, Major and Blair, in terms of the nation-state. The key trend here is devolution from the centre under the Blair government, a move resisted by its Conservative predecessors. Chapter 5 will examine the thinking behind devolution and its political, electoral and ideological considerations. At the same time, other trends will be explored that reduced the ability of central government to legislate effectively, or at least created that perception, owing to factors such as globalisation of trade and pooling of sovereignty at the supranational level, most notably the acceleration of the European project after the 1986 Single European Act. Chapter 6 will further examine the relationship between politics and power, including the notion that the executive accumulated growing clout in the 1979–2007 period. A number of trends will also be explored that appear to show declining trust in both government and institutions, from failure to broach income inequality to collusion in the form of 'regulatory capture' and the apparent increase in national scandals. These developments have aided the rise of populism.

The final section will look at how developments concerning the concentration of political and economic power have impacted upon contemporary events. Populists on both the left and right owe their rise, in part, to a critique of many of these trends: state-managed but partial economic liberalisation, the increase in global trade as a proportion of the total, the rise of supranational projects, policy-making that fails to live up to the rhetoric of power dispersal, and an incapability or unwillingness to prevent growing wealth inequality. The results manifested themselves after the 2007–08 financial crisis in the ascendency of political collectivism, reflected by nationalism and more radical left-wing ideas. Nevertheless, although populists have seen success at the ballot box, the rise of the new tech giants operating in a rapidly changing economy, with huge implications for the nature of work, suggest that concentration continues its inexorable march.

Notes

1 Robert Ledger, *Neoliberal Thought and Thatcherism: "A Transition from Here to There?"* (Abingdon: Routledge, 2017).
2 This is a consistent theme of *The Economist* newspaper. See Chapter 1 for more details.
3 Frank Bealey, *Power in Business and the State: An Historical Analysis of Its Concentration* (Abingdon: Routledge, 2001).
4 Manuela Mosca, *Power in Economic Thought: Palgrave Studies in the History of Economic Thought* (Basingstoke: Palgrave Macmillan, 2018).
5 Tony Freyer, *Regulating Big Business: Antitrust in Great Britain and America; 1880–1990* (Cambridge: Cambridge University Press, 1992).
6 Angus MacCulloch and Barry J. Rodger, *Competition Law and Policy in the EU and UK* (Abingdon: Routledge, 1999).
7 Andrew Scott, "The Evolution of Competition Law and Policy in the United Kingdom", LSE Working Papers 9/2009, 13, http://eprints.lse.ac.uk/24564/1/WPS2009-09_S cott.pdf [accessed 30 July 2020]. This paper was subsequently printed as a chapter in Pradeep S. Mehta, ed, *Evolution of Competition Laws and Their Enforcement: A Political Economy Perspective* (London: Routledge, 2012).
8 Gregory Baldi, "Europeanising Antitrust: British Competition Policy Reform and Member State Convergence", *British Journal of Politics and International Relations*, 8:1 (2006), 503–518.
9 Chiara Fumagalli, Massimo Motta and Claudio Calcagno, *Exclusionary Practices: The Economics of Monopolisation and Abuse of Dominance* (Cambridge: Cambridge University Press, 2018).
10 Robert Bork, *The Antitrust Paradox* (New York: Free Press, 1978).
11 Guy Standing, *The Corruption of Capitalism: Why Rentiers Thrive and Work Does Not Pay* (London: Biteback, 2016).

12 J.R. Branston, Keith Cowling and Philip R. Tomlinson, "Profiteering and the Degree of Monopoly in the Great Recession: Recent Evidence from the US and the UK", *Journal of Post Keynesian Economics*, 37:1 (2014), 135–162; Keith Cowling and Philip R. Tomlinson, "Globalisation and Corporate Power", *Contributions to Political Economy*, 24:1 (2005), 33–54.
13 Thomas Piketty, *Capital in the Twenty-First Century* (Cambridge: Harvard University Press, 2014).
14 Carole Thornley and Dan Coffey, *Globalization and Varieties of Capitalism: New Labour, Economic Policy and the Abject State* (Basingstoke: Palgrave Macmillan, 2009).
15 Dani Rodrik, *The Globalization Paradox: Democracy and the Future of the World Economy* (New York: W.W. Norton, 2011).
16 Cowling and Tomlinson, "Globalisation and Corporate Power", 33.
17 Ibid., 44.

1 The ideological perspective

How power is concentrated and dispersed in Britain—and other democratic states—may sound like a rather abstract subject, something to animate academics, and even then, only a few political scientists. Yet the principle of power concentration, both economic and political, is at the heart of politics and political discourse. The subject is intertwined with political and economic rhetoric, campaign promises and day-to-day policymaking. Hardly any British political leader fails to promise greater opportunity, freedom or fairness than existed previously. But these terms can stimulate, in practice, vastly different policies. Equality of opportunity or outcome, freedom of choice or from the state, reducing inequality or increasing the possibilities to improve one's circumstances. How these apparently benign questions are broached can lead political practitioners in vastly different directions. In the December 2019 UK General Election, the Conservatives pledged that a "Shared Prosperity Fund will be used to bind together the whole of the United Kingdom, tackling inequality and deprivation in each of our four nations" and that, "We as Conservatives want to give you freedom—low taxes, opportunity, the chance to realise your dreams".[1] The Labour Party, meanwhile, bemoaned "regional inequality" and pledged that, if it was elected, "Sectoral collective bargaining will increase wages and reduce inequality", and it would "create a National Education Service to provide support and opportunity throughout your life".[2] In short, Britain's political parties—even in these brief examples— offer vastly different measures to address issues of inequality, opportunity and the differentials in power. Looked at generically, we may expect parties of the left to legislate to spread power and opportunity, and the right to deregulate for similar ends. Yet, as authors such as Jamie Peck have outlined, even apparently liberalising and deregulatory reforms are a form of intervention and create their own consequences.[3] Likewise, the highly interventionist post-war Labour governments, during a period where it has been widely considered that economic inequality declined,[4] were heavily criticised for allowing too much power to reside with trade unions.[5]

In fact, there has been lively debate on some of these issues. With the passing of several years—and, in the case of the Thatcher and Major governments, decades—there is distance to evaluate the records of the 1979–2007 governments, invariably described as more economically liberal than their immediate predecessors. Historians have been prone to group together these governments as 'neoliberal' or somehow contiguous. New Labour has been derided by many on left and right as sanitised neoliberalism, while the Major government has been dubbed "Thatcherism with a human face".[6] The 'Thatcher & Sons' approach,[7] although having some cogency, fails to capture the differing priorities of each government, particularly that of New Labour. Nevertheless, the arguments over how similar British policymaking has been since the late 1970s encapsulates one dimension of the current debate: how and if liberal democracy can be reformed or 'fixed' rather than overhauled. Second, and related to the first, is the notion that underperforming economies such as Britain and its contemporaries have created the conditions for the populist surge of the 2010s. Although this book primarily explores the 1979–2007 period, with some discussion of the 2007–08 financial crash, it seeks, implicitly and tentatively, to examine the trends that have led to later events.

The issue regarding concentration of power that has most gained traction in recent years is that we are living through an era of rising inequality. A rare example of an economist who cuts through to the mainstream is Thomas Piketty, whose bestseller, *Capital in the Twenty-First Century*, accompanied by extensive data published online, demonstrates broad trends in income and wealth inequality.[8] To generalise a dense work, inequality in Britain—as well as its contemporaries— broadly declined between the early 1930s and the late 1970s, before rising, concentrating ever more capital in the wealthiest 1% of society. This narrative was seized on by the left, as well as by parts of the mainstream political parties, during the 2010s. For the purposes of this book, Piketty's trend conveniently starts to change, in the mid to late 1970s, around the start of the first Thatcher government. That inequality increased under Conservative governments was perhaps unsurprising. More interesting is how the sharp increase in inequality marked a change from the post-war period and how it has persisted after Thatcherism, with some minor periods of exception.

After growing inequality, the second economic theme that has increased in salience—even if it has not necessarily had much impact on the policymaking agenda—and is relevant to this book is economic competition and monopolies. Issues that more easily cut across the political spectrum such as monopolies, cartels and economic competition—perhaps better summarised as problems of market power—can seem somewhat technocratic but, similarly to inequality, were prevalent in the 2020 Democratic primary campaign in the US, in particular in the rhetoric of Massachusetts Senator Elizabeth Warren. Apart from left-wing critiques of market power, there are a number of concurrent, often similar, diagnoses made by what we would consider keepers of the liberal economic flame. For instance, *The Economist* newspaper has railed for much of the 2010s against growing market power, including in Britain, predicting dire consequences if Western countries cannot reverse the trend.[9] That favourite target of the anti-capitalist left, the International Monetary Fund (IMF), even articulated its concerns over the rise of corporate power in its April 2019 World Economic Outlook.[10] Meanwhile, market power and economic concentration are regular themes of more centrist writers and think-tanks, for instance the British-based Resolution Foundation[11] and the Social Market Foundation.[12]

Some questions of market power will be addressed in this book, such as the broad trends put in motion between 1979 and 2007—the shifting approach to antitrust regulation and certain sectors including finance and banking, energy and other privatised utilities and broadcasting. Others, highly relevant for the 2010s and 2020s such as the big tech companies of a 21st-century 'Gilded Age', will only be lightly touched upon owing to the location of these industries as predominantly post-2007 issues. Nevertheless, some of the themes posited in the 1979–2007 period will be extrapolated into the post-2008 crash era, which has seen its own particular trends.

Both inequality and market power play into ideas that, in many countries, including the UK, politics and economics are not played on a level playing field, that power is concentrated and becoming increasingly so. The final trend that can be linked with this book is the rise of populism. Whereas income inequality and lack of economic competition can seem academic and relatively dry themes, populism and its practitioners seek emotional targets. Populists—defined as claiming to represent the (ordinary) 'people' in opposition to an elite establishment that attempts to block the will of said people—of both left and right, as well as their many variants, loudly complain how the economic "game is rigged", and that political corridors of power are "closed to outsiders".[13] Many of these arguments, insofar as they are coherent, are linked to ever greater concentration of economic power. This book will tentatively attempt to analyse the link between accumulated power and the concurrent rise of populist politics.

This chapter will look at a number of theoretical interpretations of power concentration and distribution by examining several key philosophical paradigms. It will begin with neoliberalism, a term used to broadly describe the resurgence of economic liberal thought in the mid-20th century and sometimes to describe British governments from Margaret Thatcher's administration onwards. We will then move on to look at a range of other positions, from socialism to corporatism. Many of these theoretical views contain contradictory positions regarding power, seeming to offer both liberating and accumulating elements.

Defining market power

Before we move on to how theory views concentration of power, it is worth first defining what is meant by the terms frequently used in this book. Market power incorporates a number of principles that impede economic competition, including economic 'rents', formation of cartels and monopolies, as well as state aid.

In practice, market power is gauged slightly differently from country to country, as well as in a particular period. These variations are a recurring theme in this book. Nevertheless, one of the arbiters of market power and economic competition in the 1979–2007 period, Britain's Office of Fair Trading (OFT), broadly defined market power in 2004:

> Market power is not an absolute term but a matter of degree, and the degree of market power will depend on the circumstances of each case.

In assessing whether an undertaking has substantial market power, it is helpful to consider whether and the extent to which an undertaking faces competitive constraints. Those constraints might be existing competitors, potential competitors and other factors such as strong buyer power from the undertaking's customers.[14]

For economic theorists, debates around market power and competition often start with a preferred view of an ideal market. A broad estimation of a hypothetical 'perfect' free market might be the presence of a large number of producers and consumers, 'perfect' information for market participants and no barriers to entry. Of course, a situation such as this is never likely to be achieved in practice, yet most instances of market power, indeed of accumulation of economic power itself, involve impeding one of these pillars of an ideal market.[15] In addition, anti-competitive behaviour can also be linked to another economics concept, that of 'rent-seeking'. The topic of rent-seeking was popularised in economics and politics debates from the 1960s by public choice theorists, often associated with the University of Virginia, such as James Buchanan and Gordon Tullock. For instance, these theorists defined rent-seeking as seeking payment "over and above that which resources could command in any alternative use" and a "diversion of value from consumers generally to the favoured rent seeker".[16] Whereas this school of thought primarily directed its energies towards state bureaucracy, becoming somewhat of a 'New Right' political favourite in the process, rent-seeking is perhaps better employed in the analysis of companies and market power.[17] Indeed, as we shall see, many of the case studies examined in this book demonstrate rent-seeking to one extent or another.

Market power, unlike concentration of political power, is a concept that can be quantified. A number of measurements are used in different settings and favoured by different academics. The Lerner Index can be used to indicate the degree of monopoly,[18] as well as measures such as the four-firm or eight-firm concentration ratio (CR_4 and CR_8, respectively).[19] The Herfindahl–Hirschmann Index (HHI) was sometimes used by UK regulators after the 1998 Competition Act, which was introduced by the newly elected Labour Party.[20] We will explore these measures and how they apply to the British economy in later chapters.

Economic liberals differ quite markedly over how to deal with market power, from those who think any interference in a market only serves to distort it further, to those who believe regulation should be targeted at rent-seeking and competition-stifling tactics. Then there is the problem of which level of market power to use in deciding on regulation. For a discipline that appears concerned with numbers, market power can prove a decidedly slippery subject. The OFT, for instance attempted to categorise unfair market behaviour in its 2004 report, as:

a position of economic strength enjoyed by an undertaking which enables it to prevent effective competition being maintained on the relevant market by affording it the power to behave to an appreciable extent independently of its competitors, customers and ultimately of consumers.[21]

Defining concentration of political power

Even more subjective is how to define accumulated political power. This book will look at the topic from a number of angles. First, and related to the previous section, we shall look at how economic power asserts itself through the political process. Although presented sometimes in conspiratorial terms, attempting to influence the political process has been completely normalised in Britain and similar countries. One could also say that other, non-business groups try similar tactics, whether unions, pressure groups or other collectives. One of the primary arguments of this book is that the so-called neoliberal era enthusiastically attempted to reduce the influencing potential of non-business vested interests on political decisions, while doing much less to tame the influence of business.

Political power may accumulate within the government itself. This is particularly relevant in Britain owing to the country's lack of a written constitution. Theoretically, governments, and prime ministers, with stable parliamentary majorities—such as those led by Margaret Thatcher and Tony Blair—can wield huge amounts of power. At several stages during the 1979–2007 period, critics were concerned that too much power was concentrated within the executive, that unelected advisors were over mighty and that collective decision-making—or cabinet government—was on the wane. Although not primarily a study about the inner workings of government, this book will nevertheless touch upon this theme within the British polity, arguing that it is, in fact, much less significant than usually claimed.

Another specifically British theme during the Thatcher–Major–Blair era has been how power is distributed across the country, its regions and nations. Despite the Conservative governments sometimes being labelled as liberal, and therefore seeking to disperse power, it was during this era that local power appeared to become more centralised. Regional power too was drawn to London and South East England. Tony Blair's government, on the other hand, took a different view of regional policy, initiating a sweeping devolution agenda, reviving the Northern Irish assembly and establishing assemblies in Cardiff and Edinburgh. The concerns that power (and wealth) was becoming ever more concentrated in London, however, continued apace during the New Labour years. Devolution is included as an example of the different approaches taken by the three governments to distribution of regional power in Britain during the 1979–2007 period. In addition, issues around regional power appear to have had a long-term impact on the rise of populism in the UK.

Finally, political power will be gauged in this book through the exercise of ideology. Although more abstract and problematic to gauge, the so-called dominant ideological framework in Britain during this era—neoliberalism—has been the subject of endless academic studies and political slurs. An apparent consensus emerged in the 1980s over Britain's neoliberal policy agenda. What this meant in practice will be examined in detail during this book. What relationship, though, do political and economic ideas have with power? As outlined by political scientists such as Peter A. Hall, dominant ideologies often set the parameters within which the political debate takes place and produce a range of politically possible policy ideas.[22] These ideas are transmitted through networks, the media, academia and education. So, when a significant number of more economically liberal-minded politicians and decision-makers were in office in Britain, for instance in the 1980s and 1990s, this had an impact on how power was distributed. To provide one example, when Gordon Brown swiftly moved to give operational independence to the Bank of England in May 1997, he did so against a backdrop of broad support from the press, academic thinking and his own New Labour coterie, whereas, just a generation before, the move would have been considered politically impossible.

Although this book will look at economic and then political power across several, separate chapters, it is worth pointing out here that, clearly, the two are often interdependent. In particular, we shall look at the relationship with how economic interests—including, but not solely, companies and economic sectors more broadly—exert influence. For instance, one section of the book will explore the role of 'the City', that is to say the British financial services sector, which has come to play a significant role in politics as, essentially, a pressure group. The same could be said for industry groups such as the Confederation of British Industry (CBI), as well as trade unions. We will not solely look at economic interests that exert political influence, but the two are obviously not mutually exclusive; to quote a headline in *The Economist* from 2016, "Political power follows economic power".[23]

Neoliberalism

Shortly after Labour's calamitous performance in the 2019 UK General Election, Tony Blair lambasted the current state of his party and its direction since the demise of 'New Labour', particularly under the leadership of Jeremy Corbyn:

> if we denounce our own government's record, don't be surprised if the people conclude we shouldn't be put back into power. The constant assertion by the Labour leadership that Britain's problems were the product of 40 years of 'neoliberalism', as if the policies of the Thatcher era were the same as the last Labour government, was a hideous combination of bad politics and worse history.[24]

The passage captures a well-entrenched narrative that Blair was clearly exasperated by: that there was little difference between New Labour and its Conservative predecessors under Margaret Thatcher and John Major. The term neoliberalism has often been aligned with the Thatcher–Major–Blair period and virtually always as a means of criticism. Taylor Boas and Jordan Gans-Morse outlined how the term morphed in the 1990s into the ultimate, yet somehow increasingly nebulous, political insult.[25] In its current, all-encompassing critical form, we can perhaps best summarise the term as a synonym for 'market fundamentalism', a turbo-charged pro-market approach somehow supported by sympathetic governments, global business elites and the inner logic of the neoliberal system itself.

Discussions of neoliberalism are never too far from conspiratorial world views. Yet the developing historical debates surrounding neoliberalism are more interesting than these caricatures. To understand neoliberalism's—the resurgence of economic liberalism during the 20th century—relationship with power, we must first go back to the 1930s.

As this is primarily a study of British political economy between 1979 and 2007, it may seem a little beyond its scope to delve into 1930s German thought. However, we will briefly look at this period and the key insights of German economic liberals, and other likeminded thinkers, because they acted as a catalyst for the development of neoliberalism. Perhaps more importantly, this foundational neoliberal phase will offer a number of key insights that will inform other sections of this book, particularly the approach to concentration of power.

The early historical accounts of the mid-20th-century resurgence of economic liberalism took a particular interest in the work of American economist Milton Friedman and others from the 'Chicago School', as well as Austrian thinker Friedrich von Hayek and the various think-tanks they inspired. This is unsurprising as Friedman specifically aimed to influence policymakers and was a gifted communicator, coming up with relatively simple soundbites such as "inflation is always and everywhere a monetary phenomenon"[26] and inspiring the 'government is the problem'[27] mantra of Reagan-era conservatives in the US. Friedman and Hayek also won the Nobel Prize in the 1970s and were prominent in right-wing and libertarian circles during the period. Politicians such as Margaret Thatcher were keen to have an audience with Hayek and Friedman, although it should be pointed out that the pair often diverged on key points. As academic studies of neoliberalism proliferated, however, understanding of 20th-century economic liberalism deepened and became more contextualised. Richard Cockett was one of the first British writers to fully outline the importance of neoliberalism in the 1930s, inspiring many more books and articles on its development and giving us a picture that is much more than both the generalisations of those who use neoliberalism as a catch-all political insult and accounts that solely focus on the influence of Friedman and Hayek in the 1970s.

Neoliberalism, put simply, was a response to both government intervention in many countries during the 1930s and the reputational damage done to free market economic liberalism as a result of the 1929 Wall Street Crash and subsequent Great Depression. For this group of liberals, markets still had relevance and immense potential to transform quality of living for the better. They also appreciated that any return to a pre-1929 laissez-faire approach was neither possible nor desirable. Therefore, an immediate comparison with our modern generalisation of neoliberalism is that the approach was not one of 'market fundamentalism', or similar. The 'neo' prefix is perhaps best summarised as some role for the state— indeed, a greater and more activist role for the state than had existed up to this point. What that role should be is where we immediately see divisions between different thinkers, schools of thought and settings. Nevertheless, the early neoliberals, who we may consider a 'first generation', generally sought to use markets as a means rather than an end—in and of itself different from subsequent generations. In addition, each group of economic liberals sought responses to the problems that they experienced, as has been described by Rachel Turner.[28]

German neoliberalism

The term neoliberalism first came into use, albeit limited, in 1930s Europe, notably in Germany. For these liberals, the state should provide some parameters for markets, such as enforcing the rule of law and contracts, as well as encouraging competition by preventing, or regulating against, monopolies and cartels. This must be set against the backdrop of interwar Germany. Economic collusion was viewed as rife in the Weimar Republic, while the Nazis then snuffed out political liberalism within months of coming to power in 1933. For German neoliberals, a linkage could be made between concentration of economic power and the demise of the Weimar state. This was to be one of the prime concerns of the early neoliberals. Economic concentration gradually lost salience in the discourse around neoliberalism.

German neoliberals gathered in a number of locations and universities, including Munich and, most notably, in the southern German city of Freiburg. Constitutional economists Walter Eucken and Franz Böhm were the central figures at the Freiburg School, which has often been used as a synonym for German neoliberalism, as well as the quintessentially German term Ordoliberalism (*Ordoliberalismus* in German), or ordered liberalism. This was perhaps best captured by German thinker Alexander Rüstow, whose 1932 essay "Free Economy— Strong State" introduced the term neoliberalism. An activist state seeking to enforce competition and limit inflation was the central plank of Ordoliberal thinking. Eucken and Böhm were particularly interested in how the law, and constitution, could act to further these goals. Indeed, Eucken was prominent in formulating the post-war German Federal Republic's constitution in 1949, the "Basic Law".

Perhaps the most interesting member of the German neoliberals from this era was Wilhelm Röpke. Not a Freiburg academic, Röpke moved around institutions and went into exile in Turkey and then Switzerland soon after the Nazis came to power. Röpke engaged with the social and moral elements of economics and was also keen to promulgate his ideas, including to audiences in the English-speaking world.[29] Röpke's economic work incorporated the promotion of free trade as well as reducing cartels and monopolies.[30] In social policy, he hit upon a theme that was familiar to British Conservatives dating back to the 1920s—what Röpke inelegantly termed "proletarianization".[31] Governments should, according to Röpke, aim to avoid proletarianization, prevent 'alienation' of the working class and diminish class consciousness more generally. The obvious example of de-proletarianisation was the wider ownership of capital, in particular housing. Taken together, Röpke described his ideas as a "Third Way", a term that, in a different guise, would be a key part of New Labour's programme in the 1990s.[32] Moreover, triangulation—a favourite New Labour tactic—also fits with another of the key themes to come from German neoliberalism, outlined by theorist and politician Alfred Müller-Armack: social market economy.[33] This became a consistent rhetorical focal point for post-war German governments and is particularly associated with Ludwig Erhard, finance minister and then chancellor, himself connected with, and advised by, the Ordoliberals.[34]

To summarise, German neoliberals were particularly focused on the themes that had caused—as they saw it—so much damage to Weimar Germany: high inflation and concentration of economic power. Their ideas helped construct the new constitution and politics of post-war Germany. These two pillars would continue to loom large in German political economy for decades, although liberal critics—including Röpke himself—thought that their ideas became diluted over time.[35] There is also some evidence to show that Ordoliberal ideas regarding market power became embedded in the European Economic Community's (EEC) competition authority.

A re-evaluation of economic liberalism was not only taking place in Germany. As documented in Philip Mirowski and Dieter Plehwe's collection, *The Road from Mont Pelerin*, other European countries contained budding neoliberal movements during this period, some as unlikely as France and Italy.[36] Contrary to the later impression of turbo-capitalist libertarianism, American liberals were also developing ideas along similar lines. Indeed, as described in Daniel Stedman-Jones's *Masters of the Universe*, the 'first' Chicago School took a number of positions quite different from the better-known later, 'second', version led by Milton Friedman and George Stigler.[37] One of the leading thinkers in this first Chicago School was Henry Simons, who took a particular interest in economic and political concentration of power. The title of this current study derives from Simons's statement in 1934 that "political and economic power must be widely dispersed and decentralised in a world that would be free", and that concentration of power was the "great enemy of democracy".[38] Although not usually associated with later neoliberals, the first generation were acutely aware of how economic concentration was a threat to liberal democracy and political liberty more generally.

A number of the early neoliberals would convene in 1938 at the Colloque Walter Lippmann, named in honour of the well-known American political scientist and journalist Walter Lippmann, whose book *The Good Society* included enough liberal ideas to excite both the participants of the conference and a significant number of liberal politicians after the war.[39] The conference, which was a forum to discuss what were then considered relatively niche ideas, was the brainchild of Friedrich von Hayek. Although Hayek was in the unusual position of having some involvement with a variety of neoliberal groups, he was from the 'Austrian School', which is considered less interventionist and more puritanically free market than other economic liberals of the era. Indeed, some historians have identified a split between more laissez-faire and interventionist neoliberals even at the Paris meeting.[40] Nevertheless, Hayek had enough in common with the Ordoliberals to be close to the likes of Wilhelm Röpke. The neoliberal get-togethers would be interrupted by the Second World War, before re-emerging as the Mont Pelerin Society (MPS), which first gathered in Switzerland in April 1947. Hayek had harnessed funding from benefactors after the war to start the MPS, a feat Röpke had singularly failed to do when he tried to tap the same businessmen, such as Albert

Hunold, to launch an international liberal economic journal.[41] The Hayek–Röpke rivalry can also be seen as a metaphor for how the Ordoliberals gradually lost influence within the neoliberal 'movement', such as it was. Other thinkers rose to prominence in the MPS, such as a young Milton Friedman. A more hands-off approach to regulation proliferated under Friedman's watch, including a new theoretical framework for competition and monopolies that—as we shall see—came to dominate policymaking further down the line.

Returning to the early neoliberals, it is important to set out their views on concentration of power. Although incorporating a number of different thinkers from diverse environments, the first generation of neoliberals, in the shadow of the Great Depression and then the war, took a number of converging positions on concentration, as well as monetary policy. They were particularly energised by the need for low inflation, although the methods to obtain this were contested. Crucially, economic liberals from Germany to France to the United States— although convinced of the positive role markets could play—saw some role for the state, preventing monopoly formation and even offering some degree of social provision. In fact, taken together, the early neoliberals appeared to be proposing a moderate programme for what we would now consider a mixed economy. This generation of liberals sought to prevent concentration of power in the economy and, in so doing, would help protect against its concentration in the political sphere, which had been so disastrous in the interwar period.[42]

Post-war neoliberalism

After the war, the best-known neoliberals—many of whom had attended the 1938 Colloque Walter Lippmann—converged at the first MPS meeting in 1947. It was not a propitious moment for economic liberals. After the war, central 'planning' was popular in many countries, including Britain, and the economic ideas of John Maynard Keynes were at their pinnacle, requiring significant government involvement in the economy to maintain employment and generate demand. Nevertheless, from Mont Pelerin onwards, momentum slowly picked up for the neoliberals, particularly as the economic settlement began to falter in the early 1970s.

Historians have tended to focus on a number of trends relating to the neoliberals during this period. One, encouraged by Hayek himself, was that there was a degree of continuity among neoliberals within the MPS. Obviously, in a group of intellectuals, there would always be significant differences of opinion, but it is interesting to note how Hayek attempted to minimise intra-MPS conflict. Two significant splits, however, emerged during the MPS's early decades, which to some extent can be used as a proxy for the development of neoliberal thought itself. The first came between the Austrians and the Ordoliberals, whereby Austrian thinkers such as Ludwig von Mises (Hayek's mentor) lambasted the Ordoliberals as 'socialists', while the latter attacked Mises and Hayek as old fashioned, even commenting that the pair should be "put in spirits and placed in a museum as one of the last surviving specimen of the extinct species of liberals which caused the current [1930s'] catastrophe."[43] Subsequently, a separate split appeared, between Hayek and the Austrians, who proposed the almost complete retreat of government from economic processes, and Milton Friedman's Chicago School and its more precise policy prescriptions, such as 'monetarism'. Hayek later said he put up with Friedman's "nonsense" for the sake of the society's "unity".[44] A separate trend identified by historians of neoliberalism relates to analysis of its ideas in the post-war period. Some see a development of a 'thought collective'[45] that had some common themes, as well as a "family of neoliberalisms".[46] The former has been dominant in much literature on the subject, resulting in some nuance being lost as neoliberal thinkers and politicians became caricatured as austere, pro-globalisation market fundamentalists.[47]

Strands of neoliberalism

It is worth taking a brief look at the main neoliberal differences in approach to concentration of power, as they will have some resonance in the debates around the 1979–2007 governments. To continue the theme of how different strands of neoliberalism developed after the Second World War, these can be broadly differentiated into three schools: the Ordoliberals, the Austrian School and the Chicago School.[48] We have already looked at some of the key principles of the Ordoliberal approach and noted its influence on German economic policy after 1945 and the EEC's competition regime. Another Ordoliberal composite, the social market economy, proved more mainstream in its appeal and even exerted influence on British politicians.[49] At various points over the next decades, politicians from all three main British parties would show some interest in the social market economy.[50]

The Austrian School can be considered closest to pre-1930s economic liberalism, proposing the most minimal role for the state and being most sensitive to interventions that would 'distort' markets and the 'price mechanism', the latter a core Austrian theme. The Chicago School, meanwhile, shifted its approach under the leadership of Milton Friedman and George Stigler from the late 1940s, marking a break from Henry Simons's 'first' Chicago School. Friedman and Stigler, over the course of a number of major projects, characterised the 'second' Chicago School as somewhere between the Austrians and Ordoliberals.[51] Although less interventionist than the Ordoliberals, the Chicagoans sought to use government and the functions of the state to promote markets, create markets and generally pursue a more market-orientated direction. This would manifest itself in 'monetarist' control of the money supply to limit inflation, a break in antitrust policy— which, although more hands off, ultimately saw a role for the regulator—and even market-based social interventions such as education vouchers.[52]

Over time, the early significance of the Ordoliberals waned in neoliberal circles, particularly as Chicagoans dominated economic liberal discourse in the public sphere. The Austrian School merged in the Anglosphere with the rise of libertarianism from the 1960s, represented by intellectuals such as Murray Rothbard.[53] Future policymakers such as Alan Greenspan also derived some inspiration from libertarian writers such as the novelist Ayn Rand.[54] The different approaches, between the more policy-specific Chicago School and the Austrian libertarian Spartans, are outlined by Mark Skousen in *Vienna & Chicago: Friends or Foes?*[55] The two schools of thought differed on monetary policy, the Austrians believing in a sharp shock to return an economy to equilibrium and its 'natural' interest rate levels as soon as possible, whereas Friedman sought to control money aggregates to limit the growth of money and, therefore, inflation.[56] The two also differed on fixed and floating exchange rates.[57] It is the differences concerning competition policy and monopolies, however, that are particularly important for this current study.

The Ordoliberal School was clear in its approach to monopolies, even if putting its principles into practice proved more difficult. Ordoliberal thinkers such as Walter Eucken and Franz Böhm thought that constitutional law should restrain the accumulation of economic power. This view was shared by other German neoliberals, such as Röpke, Rüstow and Müller-Armack, as well as politicians such as Ludwig Erhard. In practice, this meant the establishment of an office to monitor and, if necessary, sanction anti-competitive behaviour, the German *Bundeskartellamt* (Federal Cartel Office). Ordoliberals also encouraged the establishment of a similar body as the EEC developed, which later became the European Commission's Competition Directorate. What this translated into in reality will be discussed in later chapters. Nevertheless, Ordoliberals saw monopolies and anti-competitive actions in general as sufficiently dangerous for both an economy and democratic institutions that they had to be rigorously policed at the state or supranational level.

Austrians took a very different view. Essentially, the more laissez-faire Austrian approach was that intervention in the economy is always harmful and leads to unintended results. Therefore, Austrian thinkers came to view antitrust actions as unnecessary.[58] For Austrians, the way to address monopolies was to improve the functioning of a market, for instance by reducing barriers to entry for competitors.

Perhaps most interesting was the approach of the Chicago School, which went on a journey that had some resonance with real-world policy, particularly in the United States. As we have seen, the 'first' Chicago School, led by Henry Simons, shared some similarities regarding competition with the Ordoliberals. This changed, however, during the 1940s and 1950s, mainly owing to the work of George Stigler and the Chicago School's long-running projects during this period, the Free Market Study Group and the Anti-Trust Project.[59] Stigler came to view large corporations with less suspicion than his predecessors at Chicago, observing how the 'competition function' could be mimicked within one large firm.[60] Simons had acted as a mentor to Friedman, who remained watchful towards concentration into the early 1950s.[61] Nevertheless, Friedman changed his mind thanks to the work of Stigler and his Chicago colleagues. In one of his most famous books, *Capitalism and Freedom*, written in 1962, Friedman outlined his new thinking on competition, saying how, in most markets, there were "giants and pygmies side by side", and that monopoly was often overemphasised.[62]

We can, therefore, see how a number of approaches emerged within neoliberalism in the mid-20th century. Ordoliberals sought to use regulation to penalise monopolies and promote competition, whereas Austrian thinkers were in favour of deregulating markets as a means to let market forces deal with competition. The Chicago School sat somewhere between the two, more relaxed about monopolies than the Ordoliberals, but not as laissez-faire as the Austrians. Most Chicagoans backed some degree of antitrust action in order to punish price fixing and prevent some mergers.[63]

Where neoliberals did agree, however, was on reducing the power of trade unions. Here we can see the development of a neoliberal approach to concentration of power more in keeping with later analysis: pro-business and anti-labour. The neoliberal critique of the British economy in particular during this period was that trade unions wielded too much power, and, as a result, markets were impeded by poor industrial relations and strikes. Interestingly, neoliberals also differed over the relationship between inflation and wage bargaining. Hayek thought that union wage demands drove inflation ever higher, whereas Friedman believed that unions were responding to increasing prices and were not the primary cause of inflation.[64] It was noticeable, however, that this approach was not extended to economic competition in the private sector.

Other approaches

How power is distributed, or concentrated, is a key concern of all economic and political ideologies. Authoritarianism is at one end of the spectrum, where power is accumulated in the hands of the state or ruler. At the other end might be anarchism or libertarianism, where there would be a minimal role for central authority. In fact, these two extremes find some resonance with the debates around neoliberalism. Some neoliberals, and the governments that were viewed as having embraced neoliberal principles, such as Margaret Thatcher's administrations, were accused of authoritarian tendencies.[65] Others, perhaps most clearly US libertarians, took more radical anti-state, anti-authority positions.

Then there are conceptual differences. Socialism seeks, at least rhetorically, to transfer power to the ordinary citizen through common ownership of the organs of the state and the levers of the economy. The founding principles of Britain's Labour Party memorably set out in its Clause IV how one of its core aims was the "common ownership of the means of production, distribution and exchange".[66] Democracy, meanwhile, also wants to empower the citizen by bringing in elected representatives responsive to the *demos* through elections and other oversight mechanisms. Democratic systems, therefore, can spread power—at least to those eligible to vote. It should be noted that neoliberals were often sceptical about socialist politics, believing that nationalisation and trade unions created blocs of concentrated power that had problematic effects on the economy as well as on political liberty. Hayek, after all, called his most famous work, a book railing against socialism and planning, *The Road to Serfdom*.[67] Nevertheless, neoliberals have also been accused of hostility towards democracy itself, in so far as some believed it encouraged vested interests to form that wielded excessive power over the economy, distorting markets and incentivising governments to pacify these groups. Hayek did express concern over "unlimited democracy",[68] while Ordoliberals also debated what they saw as the impact on civic rights of majoritarian decisions in a democracy.[69] It should also be repeated that many neoliberals did not express the same concern over accumulation of power by business or privately owned enterprises. Perhaps more telling for the 1979–2007 period was that governments pursuing even a broadly economic liberal policy agenda tended to become more managerial and technocratic. In this way, we can see how politics was subdued, as well as governments' responsiveness to democratic processes. This is perhaps best seen in the low voter turnout during the New Labour years, reaching a nadir in 2001, at 59.4%. Nevertheless, the quest to find a way to balance and even pacify competing economic and political demands is not unique to neoliberalism. Other approaches, notably corporatism, sought similar objectives.

Corporatism

In Britain, and its Western contemporaries, during the post-war period, governments of both left and right seemingly found an approach to balance demands on the economy, therefore preventing overweening power being held by unions or business, known as corporatism. This was particularly popular during the governments of Harold Macmillan and Harold Wilson. In fact, it was a Conservative Chancellor of the Exchequer, Selwyn Lloyd, who in 1961 announced "tripartite talks" between unions, industry and the government to achieve higher rates of growth.[70] As well as using fiscal policy broadly in keeping with Keynesianism— although this is open to debate—British governments sought full employment and union quiescence, alongside an expanding system of social provisions, which often came at the cost of some inflation.[71] Nevertheless, the corporatist strategy came under increasing pressure as the 1960s wore on, and particularly into the 1970s. The British state developed an ever more complex set of interventions, such as incomes policies, and bodies to coordinate this economic approach, such as the National Economic Development Council (sometimes referred to as 'Neddy').[72] This "spreading network of corporatist institutions" was something that caused disquiet for right-wing Conservative politicians of the era, such as Margaret Thatcher, over its impact on a "free economy".[73] Meanwhile, the social contract began to fray as inflation soared, unemployment crept up, and union pay demands became increasingly difficult to satisfy, and the resulting strikes ever more disruptive. Linked to these trends was the apparent weakness of the British economy in aggregate, repeated currency crises, trade deficits (balance of payments crises in the parlance of the era) and stagnating productivity. It was against this backdrop that Keynesian fiscal policy and corporatism were challenged intellectually during the 1970s and eventually rejected by Thatcherism.[74] To summarise, corporatism was part of the post-war British approach to separate competing power centres and coordinate the economic structures of the period. Although it seemed like it could be a successful approach in the early 1960s, a decade later it was in crisis, and, by the late 1970s, many no longer considered the approach viable for the stuttering British economy.

Nevertheless, there were some benefits to Britain's post-war approach, including Keynesian demand management and corporatism. In fact, many came to view these decades as somewhat of a golden age. UK GDP per capita (adjusted for inflation) increased by 34% in the 1950s, 28% in the 1960s, and 24% between 1970 and 1979.[75] The British economy grew robustly during this period, usually 2–5% per year, until the oil price hike of 1973. Unemployment hovered around 2% and was recorded in the thousands rather than the millions. Meanwhile, the Gini coefficient, one measure of inequality, had declined in the 1940s and remained steady during the immediate post-war decades, only increasing from the late 1970s. Other measures even show a decrease in inequality during this time.[76] Nevertheless, it is inflation that is the noticeable outlier during the period, with British governments consistently struggling to reduce price rises, and inflation, at times, reaching eye-wateringly high levels, peaking at almost 25% in the 1970s. At the same time, perceptions of Britain's relative economic performance troubled both policymakers and the general public, partly stimulating the push for entry into the EEC.[77]

1970s debates

By the 1970s, the economic approach of successive British governments was under strain. A number of the issues mentioned above—inflation, unemployment, poor industrial relations and a slump in international competitiveness—all appeared to become more acute during the decade. This opened the space for fierce debates on left and right about new directions for the British political economy. More radical socialist, even Trotskyist, ideas gained in popularity on the left, while the work of Friedman and Hayek received a hearing on, although not exclusively, the right. More moderate politicians, of all parties, returned to the possibilities of the social market economy, linking this with the low inflation, robust growth and more harmonious union relations in Germany. Moreover, concepts of concentration of power were also debated during the decade.

British politicians were increasingly desperate to find a means to pacify trade unions in the 1970s and curtail the huge number of days lost to strikes and seemingly never-ending wage demands.[78] This was one focal point of the neoliberal critique of the British economy, that trade unions had accumulated too much power, one that was seized upon by Conservative politicians. Nevertheless, owing to the feverishness nature of the era, even Tory economic liberals were very careful around the issue, as seen in the only incremental steps taken in policy documents such as *The Right Approach*[79] and *The Right Approach to the Economy*,[80] although the unpublished *Stepping Stones* project offered more radical proposals.[81]

Economic competition also garnered attention in the 1970s. Adrian Williamson, in *Conservative Economic Policymaking and the Birth of Thatcherism*, has outlined how increasing economic competition became a central—and mainstream—concern for many in the Conservative Party from the 1960s.[82] The issue was primarily linked with enthusiasm for EEC membership, Tories believing that the community would force British industry and business to become more competitive and efficient. The nationalist dimension should also not be ignored. British politicians were clearly concerned about the perceived relative decline of the country's economy and prestige after the war. Historians such as David Edgerton, for example, have framed a state-guided 'national economy' that British governments pursued during the post-war era.[83]

Conservative concern about economic competition also led to more practical domestic policy suggestions. By the 1979 manifesto, the Tory Party made a commitment to reinvigorate the Monopolies and Mergers Commission (MMC) and the OFT, both important in regulating competition and concentration of economic power.[84] This latter approach—using regulators to enforce competition—had echoes of Ordoliberal proposals. The attitudes of prominent Tory economic liberals to competition and monopolies, however, was inconclusive. Margaret Thatcher, Geoffrey Howe and Keith Joseph all had pro-competition inclinations but were never particular proponents of preventing concentration of economic power per se. Keith Joseph's output during the mid-1970s, when he enthusiastically went about promoting economic liberal alternatives to the status quo, did apparently embrace the subject. Joseph famously set up a think-tank in 1974 (in conjunction with Thatcher) called the Centre for Policy Studies (CPS) as a home for his research. Initially, he talked about the social market economy and had actually discussed calling the think-tank the 'Ludwig Erhard Foundation' and Institute for a Social Market Economy, before settling on CPS.[85] Indeed, Joseph was also introduced to the work of Wilhelm Röpke during this period. The 1975 CPS pamphlet "Why Britain Needs a Social Market Economy" (introduced by Joseph) reads like an Ordoliberal manifesto and displayed remarkable similarities with some of the key works of thinkers such as Walter Eucken and Ludwig Erhard written decades earlier; it even explained the approach of social market economy author Alfred Müller-Armack.[86] In discussions of power and the economy, the 1975 pamphlet said:

> Government has a clear responsibility to curtail restrictive practices and the abuse of monopoly power whether perpetrated by companies, trade unions, or professional associations.[87]

This statement would hold some resonance for the Thatcher government itself. Yet Joseph seemed to lose interest in the social market approach and the kind of regulation this implied. Historians have suggested that Joseph used the 'social' prefix as window dressing for the harsher policies he really wanted to implement, such as austere public spending cuts and monetary control.[88] Others have also suggested that competition through bodies such as the MMC and OFT were not priorities for Thatcherites after 1979, including Geoffrey Howe.[89] How the Thatcher government approached economic competition and concentration will be discussed in later chapters, as well as its attitude towards political power.

Many of its policies in these areas were already developed by 1979, or at least showed glimmers of the principles subsequently put into practice when it was in government.

Conclusion

This chapter has defined some of the key themes of market power and framed a number of the ideological approaches to concentration. It has mainly focused on the resurgence of economic liberalism during the mid-20th century because this was subsequently the primary ideological influence on the Thatcher government and, to a lesser extent, its successors. As a result, we have explored a number of the key strands of what was termed neoliberalism, splitting this into three main components: the Ordoliberal, Austrian and Chicago schools. Particular emphasis has been paid to the Ordoliberals, emanating from pre-war Germany, because they put emphasis on preventing economic power concentrating. A number of these insights will recur throughout this book to gauge how so-called neoliberal governments in Britain measure up to the label. Whereas the Austrians took a more radical anti-state approach to economic questions, the Chicago School, under Milton Friedman, was more pragmatic, if less interested in curbing monopolies and cartels than the Ordoliberals. British governments would include some neoliberal principles, particularly from the Ordoliberal and Chicago strands, including inflation control and, to some extent, competition regulation. Despite the focus on ideology, British political economy nevertheless developed during the 20th century, responding to a number of specific events, through the lens of its own particular history and institutions. This would be the case with regulating the economy, which progressed in its own idiosyncratic manner before, during and after Thatcherism.

Notes

1 Conservative Party Manifesto 2019, "Get Brexit Done: Unleash Britain's Potential", December 2019, https://assets-global.website-files.com/5da42e2cae7ebd3f8bde353c/5dda924905da587992a064ba_Conservative%202019%20Manifesto.pdf [accessed 2 January 2020].
2 Labour Party Manifesto 2019, "It's Time for Real Change", December 2019, https://labour.org.uk/wp-content/uploads/2019/11/Real-Change-Labour-Manifesto-2019.pdf [accessed 2 January 2020].
3 Jamie Peck, *Constructions of Neoliberal Reason* (Oxford: Oxford University Press, 2010), xiii.
4 Anne Perkins, "Labour Needs to Rethink Harold Wilson's Legacy. It Still Matters", *The Guardian*, 10 March 2016, www.theguardian.com/commentisfree/2016/mar/10/labour-harold-wilson-legacy-100-years [accessed 2 January 2020].
5 For instance, from David Owen, former Labour foreign secretary, 1977–79, and then part of the 'Gang of Four', who broke away from Labour to form the Social Democratic Party in 1981, *Time to Declare* (London: Penguin, 1992), 158.
6 Dick Leonard, *A Century of Premiers: Salisbury to Blair* (Basingstoke: Palgrave Macmillan, 2005), 322–341.

7 Simon Jenkins, *Thatcher and Sons: A Revolution in Three Acts* (London: Penguin, 2007).

8 Thomas Piketty, *Capital in the Twenty-First Century* (Harvard: Harvard University Press, 2014).

9 For a selection see: *The Economist*, "Market Power: Big, Bad Amazon", 20 October 2014, www.economist.com/free-exchange/2014/10/20/big-bad-amazon [accessed 6 January 2020]; *The Economist*, "Internet Monopolies: Everybody Wants to Rule the World", 27 November 2014, www.economist.com/briefing/2014/11/27/everybody -wants-to-rule-the-world [accessed 6 January 2020]; *The Economist*, "More Money, More Problems: The British Economy Is Becoming More Concentrated and Less Competitive", 26 July 2018, www.economist.com/britain/2018/07/26/the-british-e conomy-is-becoming-more-concentrated-and-less-competitive [accessed 6 January 2020]; *The Economist*, "Like America, Britain Suffers from a Lack of Competition", 26 July 2018, www.economist.com/leaders/2018/07/26/like-america-britain-su ffers-from-a-lack-of-competition [accessed 6 January 2020]; *The Economist*, "An Economic Theory of Everything: The IMF Adds to a Chorus of Concern about Competition", 4 April 2019, www.economist.com/finance-and-economics/2019/04 /03/the-imf-adds-to-a-chorus-of-concern-about-competition [accessed 6 January 2020].

10 International Monetary Fund, "World Economic Outlook: Growth Slowdown, Precarious Recovery", IMF, April 2019, www.imf.org/en/Publications/WEO/Issues/2 019/03/28/world-economic-outlook-april-2019 [accessed 6 January 2020].

11 Torsten Bell and Dan Tomlinson, "Is Everybody Concentrating? Recent Trends in Product and Labour Market Concentration in the UK", Resolution Foundation, July 2018, www.resolutionfoundation.org/app/uploads/2018/07/Is-everybody-con centrating_Recent-trends-in-product-and-labour-market-concentration-in-the-UK .pdf [accessed 6 January 2020].

12 Social Market Foundation, "Press Release: New 'Minister for Competition' Needed after Brexit, Think-Tank Says", 31 July 2018, www.smf.co.uk/press-release-competi tion-not-concentration/ [accessed 6 January 2020].

13 Cas Mudde and Cristobal Rovira Kaltwasser, *Populism: A Very Short Introduction* (Oxford: Oxford University Press, 2017), 6.

14 Office of Fair Trading, "Assessment of Market Power: Understanding Competition Law", 2004, https://assets.publishing.service.gov.uk/government/uploads/system/upl oads/attachment_data/file/284400/oft415.pdf [accessed 7 January 2020], 8–9.

15 Norman Barry, *The New Right* (Beckenham: Croom Helm, 1987), 35–36. Robert Ledger, *Neoliberal Thought and Thatcherism: "A Transition from Here to There?"* (Abingdon: Routledge, 2017), 67.

16 James M. Buchanan, "Rent Seeking and Profit Seeking", eds. J.M. Buchanan, R.D. Tollison and G. Tullock, *Toward a Theory of the Rent-Seeking Society* (College Station: Texas A&M University Press, 1980), 3, 7; Ledger, *Neoliberal Thought*, 25.

17 The New Right was a term popularized from the late 1960s, in response to the New Left movement of that era, to describe the renewed intellectual vigour of conservatives, primarily in the United States and Britain, where the label was most commonly attached to Thatcherite politicians. To generalize, New Right politicians embraced a more socially conservative and economically liberal policy agenda than their predecessors in the post-war period.

18 J.R. Branston, K. Cowling and P.R. Tomlinson, "Profiteering and the Degree of Monopoly in the Great Recession: Recent Evidence from the US and the UK", *Journal of Post Keynesian Economics*, 37:1 (2014), 135–162, 136.

19 Carl Shapiro, "Antitrust in a Time of Populism", *International Journal of Industrial Organization*, 61 (2018), 714–748, 723.

20 UK Government, 1998 Competition Act (1998), www.legislation.gov.uk/ukpga/1998 /41 [accessed 2 February 2020].

21 Office of Fair Trading, "Assessment of Market Power", 8.
22 Peter A. Hall, "Policy Paradigms, Social Learning, and the State: The Case of Economic Policymaking in Britain", *Comparative Politics*, 25:3 (April 1993), 275–296, 279, 290.
23 *The Economist*, "Political Power Follows Economic Power", 3 February 2016, www.e conomist.com/buttonwoods-notebook/2016/02/03/political-power-follows-economic -power [accessed 13 January 2020].
24 Tony Blair, "Labour's Task Is not to Make Itself Feel Better—It's to Win Power", *The Guardian*, 11 January 2020, www.theguardian.com/commentisfree/2020/jan/11/labour -task-not-make-itself-feel-better-its-about-winning [accessed 13 January 2020].
25 Taylor Boas and Jordan Gans-Morse, "Neoliberalism: From New Liberal Philosophy to Anti-Liberal Slogan", *Studies in Comparative International Development*, 44:2 (June 2009), 137.
26 Milton Friedman and Anna Schwartz, *A Monetary History of the United States* (Princeton: Princeton University Press, 2015, first published 1963).
27 Milton Friedman, *Why Government is the Problem* (Stanford: Stanford University Press, 1993).
28 Rachel S. Turner, *Neoliberal Ideology. History, Concepts and Policies* (Edinburgh: Edinburgh University Press, 2008), 219.
29 For instance, Wilhelm Röpke, *The Social Crisis of Our Time* (London: William Hodge & Co, 1950, first published in 1941, translated from the German by Annette and Peter Schiffer Jacobsohn); Wilhelm Röpke, *Two Essays by Wilhelm Röpke: The Problem of Economic Order. Welfare, Freedom and Inflation* (London: University Press of America, 1987, originally published 1951 and 1957); Wilhelm Röpke, *A Humane Economy: The Social Framework of the Free Market* (Chicago: Henry Regnery, 1960, translated by Elizabeth Henderson, originally published 1958).
30 Samuel Gregg, *Wilhelm Röpke's Political Economy* (Cheltenham: Edward Elgar, 2010), 7.
31 Werner Bonefeld, "Adam Smith and Ordoliberalism: On the Political Form of Market Liberty", *Review of International Studies*, 39:2 (July 2012), 233–250, 238.
32 Röpke, *Social Crisis*, 173.
33 Discussed in Mark E. Spicka, *Selling the Economic Miracle: Economic Reconstruction and Politics in West Germany, 1949–1957* (Oxford: Berghahn, 2000), 29; Christian Watrin, "Alfred Müller-Armack—Economic Policy Maker and Sociologist of Religion", ed. Peter Koslowski, *The Theory of Capitalism in the German Economic Tradition* (London: Springer, 2000, 192–220), 208. Müller-Armack traces his thinking on his economic model in Alfred Müller-Armack, *Genealogie der Sozialen Marktwirtschaft* (Genealogy of the Social Market Economy; Stuttgart: Haupt, 1981).
34 Alfred C. Mierzejewski, *Ludwig Erhard. A Biography* (London: University of North Carolina Press, 2004), 62.
35 Gregg, *Wilhelm*, 118.
36 Philip Mirowski and Dieter Plehwe (eds.), *The Road from Mont Pelerin. The Making of the Neoliberal Thought Collective* (Harvard: Harvard University Press, 2009).
37 Daniel Stedman-Jones, *Masters of the Universe. Hayek, Friedman, and the Birth of Neoliberal Politics* (Oxford: Princeton University Press, 2012), 122.
38 Henry C. Simons, *Economic Policy for a Free Society* (Chicago: University of Chicago Press, 1948, first published 1934), 43, 105; Ben Jackson, "At the Origins of Neoliberalism: The Free Economy and the Strong State, 1930–1947", *The Historical Journal*, 53:1 (March 2010), 142; Stedman-Jones, *Masters*, 99.
39 Ben Jackson, "Freedom, the Common Good, and the Rule of Law: Lippmann and Hayek on Economic Planning", *Journal of the History of Ideas*, 73:1 (2012), 47–68; Peter Sloman, *The Liberal Party and the Economy, 1929–1964* (Oxford: Oxford University Press, 2015), 239; Ben Jackson, "Currents of Neo-Liberalism: British Political Ideologies and the New Right, c. 1955–1979", *English Historical Review*, 131 (2016), 823–850, 830.

40 Oliver Marc Hartwich, *Neoliberalism: The Genesis of a Political Swearword* (St Leonards: CIS Occasional Papers, 114, July 2009), 24.

41 Angus Burgin, *The Great Persuasion, Reinventing Free Markets Since the Depression* (London: Harvard University Press, 2012), 94; Alan Ebenstein, *Friedrich Hayek, A Biography* (Basingstoke: Palgrave, 2001), 142.

42 Gregg, *Wilhelm*, 32–42.

43 Hartwich, *Genesis*, 24. See also Philip Plickert, *Wandlungen des Neoliberalismus— Eine Studie zur Entwicklung und Ausstrahlung der "Mont Pelerin Society"* (Stuttgart: De Gruyter Oldenbourg, 2008), 87–106, 105.

44 The Margaret Thatcher Foundation website (hereafter MTF), MTF 117203, Letter from Friedrich Hayek to Arthur Seldon, 13 May 1985, www.margaretthatcher.org/document /117203 [accessed 18 January 2020].

45 Philip Mirowski, "Postface: Defining Neoliberalism", eds. Philip Mirowski and Dieter Plehwe, *The Road from Mont Pelerin. The Making of the Neoliberal Thought Collective* (Harvard: Harvard University Press, 2009), 446; Dieter Plehwe, "Introduction", eds. Philip Mirowski and Dieter Plehwe, *The Road from Mont Pelerin. The Making of the Neoliberal Thought Collective* (Harvard: Harvard University Press, 2009), 8.

46 Dieter Plehwe, Bernhard J.A. Walpen and Gisela Neunhöffer, "Introduction: Reconsidering Neoliberal Hegemony", eds. Dieter Plehwe, Bernhard J.A. Walpen and Gisela Neunhöffer, *Neoliberal Hegemony: A Global Critique* (Abingdon: Routledge, 2007), 2.

47 Jackson, "At the Origins", 132–139, Stedman-Jones, *Masters*, 335.

48 See: Ledger, *Neoliberal Thought*.

49 See Spicka, *Selling the Economic Miracle*, 29.

50 Centre for Policy Studies, "Why Britain Needs a Social Market Economy" (Chichester: Barry Rose, 1975), 1–8, www.cps.org.uk/files/reports/original/111028103106-WhyB ritainneedsaSocialMarketEconomy.pdf; [accessed 1 November 2020] Andrew Denham and Mark Garnett, *Keith Joseph* (Chesham: Acumen, 2001), 241; MTF114757, "Ralph Harris Record of Conversation (visit from Keith Joseph)", 14 March 1974; MTF114760, "Sir Keith Joseph note ('The Erhard Foundation')", 21 March 1974; Parliamentary Debates, John Biffen, House of Commons (hereafter HC Deb), 19 November 1986, vol. 105 cc. 565–666; David Steel, HC Deb, 25 June 1987, vol. 118 cc. 41–145, David Owen, HC Deb, 2 July 1987, vol. 118 cc. 643–734.

51 Stedman-Jones, *Masters*, 125.

52 The concept of antitrust is discussed in Part 2. It is used here as a synonym for actions to break up or prevent monopolies and promote competition.

53 Mark Skousen, *Vienna & Chicago. Friends or Foes? A Tale of Two Schools of Free-Market Economics* (Washington: Capital Press, 2005), 43.

54 Michael Kinsley, "Greenspan Shrugged", *The New York Times*, 14 October 2007, www.nytimes.com/2007/10/14/books/review/Kinsley-t.html [accessed 20 January 2020].

55 Skousen, *Vienna & Chicago*.

56 Ibid., 7–8, 37.

57 Stedman-Jones, *Masters*, 200.

58 Andrew Gamble, *Hayek. The Iron Cage of Liberty* (Cambridge: Polity Press, 1996), 72–73.

59 Stedman-Jones, *Masters*, 125.

60 Skousen, *Vienna & Chicago*, 83.

61 Friedman's 1951 essay, "Neoliberalism and Its Prospects", *Farmand* (February 1951, 89–93), stated that government should preserve competition.

62 Milton Friedman, *Capitalism and Freedom* (Chicago: University of Chicago Press, 1962), 121–123; Stedman-Jones, *Masters*, 96–98.

63 Skousen, *Vienna & Chicago*, 214.
64 Jackson, "Currents", 839–840.
65 For instance, Andrew Gamble, *The Free Economy and the Strong State. The Politics of Thatcherism* (Basingstoke: Palgrave Macmillan, 1994); Thomas Biebricher, *The Political Theory of Neoliberalism* (Stanford: Stanford University Press, 2019).
66 Aisha Gani, "Clause IV: A Brief History", *The Guardian*, 9 August 2015, www.thegua rdian.com/politics/2015/aug/09/clause-iv-of-labour-party-constitution-what-is-all-the -fuss-about-reinstating-it [accessed 23 January 2020].
67 F.A. Hayek, *The Road to Serfdom* (London: Routledge, 2007, originally published 1944).
68 F.A. Hayek, *Social Justice, Socialism & Democracy. Three Australian Lectures by F.A. Hayek* (Turramurra: Centre for Independent Studies, 1979), 39–45.
69 Bruno Molitor, "Schwäche der Demokratie" ("The Weakness of Democracy"), *ORDO. Jahrbuch für die Ordnung von Wirtschaft und Gesellschaft* (The Ordo Yearbook of Economic and Social Order; Stuttgart: Gustav Fischer Verlag, Band 34, 1983, 17–38), 38.
70 Astrid Ringe, "Background to Neddy: Economic Planning in the 1960s", *Contemporary British History*, 12:1 (1998), 82–98.
71 Peter Dorey, *British Conservatism and Trade Unionism, 1945–1964* (Farnham: Ashgate, 2009).
72 Ringe, "Background to Neddy".
73 Matthias Matthijs, *Ideas and Economic Crises in Britain from Attlee to Blair (1945–2005)* (Abingdon: Routledge, 2011), 114.
74 Martin Holmes, *The First Thatcher Government, 1979–83* (Brighton: Wheatsheaf, 1985), 34, 203.
75 Max Roser, "Economic Growth", *Our World in Data*, 2020, https://ourworldinda ta.org/economic-growth [accessed 28 January 2020]. GDP per capita (adjusted for inflation in 2013 prices) was £7,300 in 1950, £9,800 in 1960, £12,500 in 1970 and £15,500 in 1979.
76 Max Roser and Esteban Ortiz-Ospina, "Income Inequality", *Our World in Data*, 2020, https://ourworldindata.org/income-inequality [accessed 28 January 2020].
77 Despite steady growth in Britain during the 1950s and 1960s, it was outpaced by France and West Germany (which had been in ruins until the late 1940s) and the European Economic Community in aggregate, over this period.
78 Days lost through strikes increased from 2.28 million days in 1964, to 4.69 million in 1968, to a peak of 23.91 million during 1972. Figures taken from Office of National Statistics, "The History of Strikes in the UK", 21 September 2015, www.ons.gov.uk/ employmentandlabourmarket/peopleinwork/employmentandemployeetypes/articles/ thehistoryofstrikesintheuk/2015-09-21 [accessed 20 January 2020].
79 MTF 109439, *The Right Approach* (London: Conservative Central Office, 1976), 21.
80 MTF 110203, *The Right Approach to the Economy* (London: Conservative Central Office, 1977), 7.
81 One of the reasons *Stepping Stones* was not published was that it was considered too radical and would deter voters from voting for the party. For full report see: MTF 111771, "'Stepping Stones' Report (final text)", 14 November 1977; The Hoskyns' Papers (Cambridge: Churchill Archives, hereafter HOSK), HOSK 1/21, "Second Draft of Note by Hoskyns to Keith Joseph Summarising the 'Assignment You Would Like Me to Undertake'", 14 July 1977.
82 Adrian Williamson, *Conservative Economic Policymaking and the Birth of Thatcherism, 1964–1979* (Basingstoke: Palgrave Macmillan, 2015), 21.
83 David Edgerton, *The Rise and Fall of the British Nation: A Twentieth-Century History* (London: Allen Lane, 2018).
84 The Conservative Party, 1979 General Election Manifesto, 1979, www.conservativ emanifesto.com/1979/1979-conservative-manifesto.shtml [accessed 7 August 2017].

85 Denham and Garnett, *Keith Joseph*, 241; MTF114757, "Ralph Harris Record of Conversation (visit from Keith Joseph)", 14 March 1974, MTF114760, "Sir Keith Joseph Note ("The Erhard Foundation")", 21 March 1974.
86 Centre for Policy Studies, "Social Market Economy", 1–8.
87 Ibid.
88 Andrew Denham, *Think-Tanks of the New Right* (Aldershot: Dartmouth, 1996), 42.
89 Jackson, "Currents", 842; Williamson, *Conservative*, 140, 155.

2 History and development of competition policy in Britain

The previous chapter looked at some of the ideological approaches to concentration of power, particularly the thinking of economic liberals. This chapter will set out the major roles and interpretations of the role of government towards power concentration, particularly regulation, which played an important role in the British economy between 1979 and 2007. For Britain, that has meant a regulatory approach that includes the Monopolies and Mergers Commission (MMC), the Office of Fair Trading (OFT) and also the European Commission's Competition Directorate. The 1998 Competition Act was one of the key pieces of legislation in this area during the era and, interestingly, was designed and implemented by Tony Blair's nominally centre-left Labour government. To conceptualise the modern British approach, however, we will also take a brief look at how British governments regulated competition before Thatcherism and the neoliberal period. The influence of the United States is noteworthy here, in particular the development of its antitrust policies and laws, as well as, to a lesser extent, the approaches taken by contemporaries such as Germany and at the European level.

British anti-competitive practices pre-20th century

The concept that the government should play some role in regulating economic competition, cartels and monopolies in the UK is relatively novel and did not see significant development until after the Second World War. Nevertheless, some principles of competition emerged in a number of different ways, even before the 20th century.

Scottish economist and philosopher Adam Smith identified vested interests as harmful to free markets. Smith warned against monopolies in markets, stating in his major economic work *The Wealth of Nations*, published in 1776, how they were likely to maintain higher prices and mean markets were undersupplied.[1] The enlightenment thinker's best-known uttering on competition was more linked to the concept of 'restraint of trade', or collusion of producers to block new market entrants and to prevent better information in a market.

People of the same trade seldom meet together, even for merriment and diversion, but the conversation ends in a conspiracy against the public, or in some contrivance to raise prices.[2]

In this way, Smith outlined an enduring description of cartel formation and how the process often leads to higher prices for consumers and a worse deal for the general public. Although neoliberals would debate Smith's heritage, some arguing he was the original free market proponent, while others took a more nuanced approach highlighting his social agenda, in the late 20th century policy-makers appeared to have embraced his notion that intervention in a market should primarily depend on consumer welfare.

Smith continued on the same point, "But though the law cannot hinder people of the same trade from sometimes assembling together, it ought to do nothing to facilitate such assemblies, much less to render them necessary".[3] Although Smith was not envisaging the kind of antitrust arrangements that would emerge in the United States at the end of the following century, he was wary of the restrictive practices of producers, which could also impede economic competition. In Britain, this concern was known as 'restraint of trade'. Despite trade being relatively localised until the industrial revolution, a number of issues existed between business owners and producers. Some attempted to exclude competitors either by location, for a certain amount of time or in the breadth of business activity. Often, these kinds of arrangement were guaranteed by contracts and 'non-compete' agreements. From the 15th century, this trend was accompanied by the rise of guilds.[4] Groups formed that acted as gatekeepers for certain professions and trades, mandating apprenticeships or training periods, entrance exams and how and where trading could be conducted. As historian William Letwin has outlined:

The whole guild system, therefore, made it nearly impossible for a tradesman to earn his living if he did not practice his own trade in his own town, and this was the main reason why, as long as the guilds maintained their power, contracts in restraint of trade were held void.[5]

The guild system survived into the 19th century, but its principles endured in the UK's numerous professional bodies, later derided by Conservative politicians during the Thatcher government and beyond.[6] Therefore, we can see some of the attempts by producers to reduce competition in Britain before central government attempted any significant regulation. These practices would also be the focus of the 1890 Sherman Act in the United States.

Another anti-competitive trend that developed in the UK—although not exclusively—as its empire expanded, was that of the charter. The 18th and 19th centuries are often considered as the peak of British imperialism. Subsequently, economic liberals have portrayed British trade in this period as being uniquely laissez-faire and free market in its approach. Indeed, key neoliberal thinkers such as Friedrich Hayek critiqued, but also saw themselves as in the spirit of, 'Manchester Liberalism',[7] to denote the mid-19th-century British free market approach.[8] Similarly, Margaret Thatcher invoked Victorian-era Liberal Prime Minister William Gladstone in conjunction with some of her government's policies in the 1980s.[9] Usually forgotten in these stories are the anti-competitive practices, such as charters, that amounted to powerful monopolies. Along with other European monarchies, Britain granted royal charters first to landholders, then to private firms. The charters made some kind of provision for exclusive rights over shipping lanes or markets; the best-known of these in the British context was the British East India Company. Some royal charters expired, allowing competitors to enter a market, whereas others continued.

The British East India Company was a monopoly in the front seat of the empire's expansion. It restrained trade in the colonies themselves to bolster the British economic network—for instance, in the cotton trade. When the company was threatened, it was supported by military intervention from the British government, which essentially 'nationalised' the company to formalise London's control over its activities. Therefore, to see the British economy as a beacon of free markets during its imperial period is both too simplistic and to ignore the significant role played by the British government in creating and sustaining monopolies. This can be interpreted as part of the 'national economy' approach, where economic decisions were subordinated to the national interest. We can also see how a number of anti-competitive practices had emerged by the end of the 19th century, some of which were encouraged by the British government. Taking this into consideration, it is perhaps unsurprising Britain was not at the forefront of promoting competitive practices in its version of capitalism. Indeed, the first explicit piece of legislation that aimed to promote competition and impede protectionism would come from the United States in 1890, with the Sherman Act.

1890 Sherman Act and US antitrust

One of the capitalist world's first significant pieces of legislation to target anti-competitive practices was the Sherman Act. Although this was designed and enacted in the United States it exerted an important impact outside of the country, including in Britain. Antitrust policy, as it became known, spurred similar, although not identical, moves in Britain and Europe. In addition, the Sherman Act and its successors sought to clamp down on business behaviour that had long been practised in Britain.

The Sherman Act, named after US Senator John Sherman, aimed to curtail some business methods, including the kinds of anti-competitive contract we have already looked at in this chapter. The Act set out that:

> Every contract, combination in the form of trust or otherwise, or conspiracy, in restraint of trade or commerce among the several States, or with foreign nations, is declared to be illegal.[10]

The legislation was implemented during the US's so-called 'Gilded Age', where a number of US businesses made huge gains, amid widespread industrialisation and an economic boom. The wealthiest tycoons—steel magnate Andrew Carnegie, oil man John D. Rockefeller (Standard Oil), bankers Andrew W. Mellon and J.P. Morgan and railroad investor Cornelius Vanderbilt—controlled huge monopolies. When sentiment towards them turned sour—owing to corrupt business practices and efforts to impede rivals—these figures were derided as 'robber barons'. Typically, they built 'trusts' that were essentially cartels or monopolies. The power of a trust usually compelled traders to enter into agreements on preferential terms with it, a situation resented by many. Indeed, the end of the 19th century and beginning of the 20th century in the United States saw a period of rising populism, a trend not unconnected with the actions of trusts.[11]

In the early years after its enactment, however, the Sherman Act had little impact on its supposed targets: big corporations. Instead, the Act was used to reduce the power of trade unions, another group that was criticised for accumulating power and distorting the free market, but could hardly be considered as harmful to competition as the trusts. It took a Republican Party politician, Theodore "Teddy" Roosevelt, to really direct the Sherman Act against over-mighty businesses. In office between 1901 and 1909, Teddy Roosevelt had a reputation as an anticorruption crusader with a populist streak. Although he cultivated a status as a 'trust-buster', Roosevelt broke up trusts, in the case of the rail monopoly of Northern Securities Company, but mainly regulated them, as in the case of Standard Oil.[12] Although some historians have debated the extent of his antimonopoly approach, Roosevelt was more enthusiastic in his interpretation of the Sherman Act than his predecessors and brought 44 antitrust cases when he was in office.[13] A landmark case came in 1904 when the US Supreme Court allowed the government to use the Act in *Northern Security Co. vs. US* as a means of forcing the break-up of a monopoly.

The 1912 US presidential election, unusually, turned into one about monopolies and regulation.[14] This demonstrated the strong feeling about concentration of economic power, and more specifically monopolies, in the US at the time. Teddy Roosevelt had stepped down after two terms but returned as the candidate for the Progressive Party in 1912, with a more populist message. Roosevelt actually beat the Republican incumbent, William Howard Taft, into third place, although he ultimately lost to Democrat Woodrow Wilson. Antitrust was a key theme in the campaign, and three-quarters of the popular vote was cast for anti-monopoly candidates. The approach to antitrust mirrored the debates that emerged in subsequent decades. Woodrow Wilson advocated breaking monopolies up, Roosevelt wanted to regulate them, while a socialist candidate, fourth-placed Eugene V. Debs, backed outright nationalisation.

Although Wilson won the election, it was Teddy Roosevelt's regulatory approach that eventually triumphed. Over the course of the 1914 Clayton Antitrust Act, which legislated against certain mergers and acquisitions, price discrimination and remedial measures, and the establishment of a regulator (the Federal Trade Commission (FTC)), both passed by Wilson's administration, antitrust regulation accrued a number of tools that targeted anti-competitive behaviour rather than monopolies per se.[15] In fact, the process took another two decades, under the auspices of Roosevelt's (distant) relation, President Franklin Delano Roosevelt (FDR) in the 1930s, against the opposition of a conservative Supreme Court.[16] Opponents of these moves complained about the ever larger scope of the federal government to regulate business and intervene in markets, a critique that would mushroom in the 1960s, led by the likes of Milton Friedman.

Pre-1945 antitrust in Britain

The lineage of antitrust regulation shows both convergence and deviation throughout the 20th century. The idea existed in Britain of 'natural monopolies'— for instance, the railways—which generally attracted little demand for regulation. British policymakers, however, did come round to potential problems with monopolies in competitive markets at the start of the 20th century. A 1909 Royal Commission on shipping considered the American approach to competition:

> a more drastic, and probably more effective and simpler, remedy would be legislation on the lines of the Sherman Act of the United States of America prohibiting combinations or associations ... which had for their object the establishment of a monopoly in restraint of trade.[17]

Nevertheless, British governments were less enthusiastic about introducing their version of the Sherman and Clayton Acts or setting up a body like the FTC. British capitalism did develop in a different fashion to that in the US, with a less pronounced shift to managerialism and corporate consolidation during the 1920s. The exception were the Profiteering Acts, described by historian of US and UK antitrust policy Tony Freyer as Britain's "brief experiment" with the concept in the early part of the century.[18] The 1919 Profiteering Act was an attempt to curb profits gained from restrictive behaviour and regulate these practices under the Board of Trade.[19] However, this was essentially shelved in the early 1920s as Britain entered a new phase of concentration, rising mergers and conglomeration. This small move in support of competition was reversed in the interwar period, coinciding with the establishment of the pro-business lobby group the Federation of British Industries (FBI) in 1916, which generally considered antitrust unnecessary.[20] This was reinforced by the 1929 Report of the Balfour Committee on Trade and Industry, which saw no immediate need for legislation in this area.[21]

British economic policy lurched into crisis mode after the 1929 Wall Street Crash. Neither competition nor concentration of economic power was near the top of the agenda during the 1930s. The situation in the United States was somewhat different, as we have noted, and FDR entrenched several antitrust measures during the 1930s. In Britain, it was not until after the Second World War that competition and monopolies issues were seriously broached.

1945–79: post-war 'consensus' on regulation

As we have seen, the concept of antitrust was more developed in the United States, compared with Britain, in the decades before the Second World War. The most prominent economic liberal thinkers in terms of economic concentration were based in Germany and the United States during this period. Subsequently, a number of British politicians took interest in the Ordoliberal approach, particularly the work of Wilhelm Röpke, although these were predominantly in the Liberal Party, which reached a low point in terms of representation in the middle of the 20th century.[22] Röpke developed links with a number of British journals and magazines during the 1940s and 1950s, which translated and syndicated his work,[23] as he attempted to promulgate his core ideas: free trade, stable monetary conditions, preventing cartels and monopolies, and avoiding 'proletarianisation'.[24] Nevertheless, the Ordoliberal approach was very much a fringe interest in Britain in the post-war period. From the 1945–51 Labour government led by Clement Attlee onwards, Britain apparently moved into a period of 'consensus' regarding a number of key economic and political questions.

The notion of a post-war British 'consensus' has animated some commentators and, in a more enduring fashion, historians. Although some essentially bought into the caricature of 'Butskellism', as set out by *The Economist* in 1954[25]—a broadly accepted Keynesian economic policy committed to full employment and heavy intervention in markets—others rejected the notion, or thought a consensus was more prevalent in foreign policy—for instance, Cold War strategy and decolonisation. For those who saw something in the concept, the consensus then morphed into a cross-party policy of corporatism by the early 1960s, as discussed in the previous chapter.[26] Although not one of the areas usually included in the consensus debates, competition policy and approaches to market power did follow a similar trajectory to other areas; broadly speaking, that included legislation in the 1940s and 1950s, followed by a deepening of the approach in the 1960s and early 1970s.

The Attlee government is not remembered for its attempts to tackle concentration of economic power. In fact, it is more noted for its centralising approach and for broad-ranging nationalisation, whether in industry, utilities or the National Health Service. Yet, it was Labour that introduced Britain's first significant law—with enforcement mechanisms—on economic concentration: the 1948 Monopolies and Restrictive Practices Act, which reversed the policy of the interwar years.[27] The Labour government was, in effect, responding to a 1944 White Paper on employment[28] that had identified monopolies and restrictive practices as leading to higher prices and reduced output.[29] A 1943 memorandum, titled "Control of Monopoly", written by future Labour leader Hugh Gaitskell and economist George Cyril Allen also laid some of the groundwork for a monopolies bill and competition policy.[30] The 1948 Act established a Monopolies and Restrictive Practices Commission, which would investigate markets upon reference from the Board of Trade. Criteria included more than one-third market share[31] being controlled by a particular firm or several firms acting in concert, or as a cartel.[32] The commission would then investigate whether the situation was in the 'public interest'.

Introducing the 1948 Act in the House of Commons, President of the Board of Trade Harold Wilson referenced the importance of the 1944 White Paper and the rationale for legislating, setting out the trend towards concentration: "during the past half-century monopoly or monopolistic conditions have taken hold of an important section of British industry"; the country "cannot afford the restrictive practices that grew up on both sides of industry between the two wars".[33] Wilson went on to say there was a need for a new body that would investigate "all the facts to see whether this power to do harm is, in fact, being used in an antisocial way and, where it is, of taking effective and appropriate steps to curb any of these anti-social practices".[34]

Although historians have suggested that the legislation was not really used in the aftermath of the Act, its core pillars set the tone for post-war competition policy.[35] Indeed, historian of British antitrust policy Helen Mercer identified this first piece of legislation as crucial for the future direction of competition policy in Britain, as well as how Labour took a consensual approach to the topic, one "with which the Conservative Party and the FBI could concur and to which the United States could give (qualified) approval".[36] Subsequent legislation by both Labour and the Conservatives suggests that this was one policy area where a tacit consensus existed after 1945.

The Conservatives returned to office after winning the 1951 general election, beginning a 13-year stretch in government under the leadership of Winston Churchill, Anthony Eden, Harold Macmillan and Alec Douglas Home. It was this period, perhaps more than any other in the post-war decades, that solidified the consensus concept. Instead of scrapping Labour's radical 1945–51 programme, the Conservatives, with exceptions such as attempts to 'denationalise' the steel industry, deepened it in some areas. Competition policy was an example of the trend. In 1956, the Eden government passed the Restrictive Trade Practices Act, under President of the Board of Trade Peter Thorneycroft, in an attempt to give more enforcement power to the 1948 Act. A Restrictive Practices Court was established to which cases could be referred. Indeed, the 1956 changes did bring a considerable number of price-fixing cases in front of the court.[37]

1960s and 1970s: high corporatism

As noted in the previous chapter, the 1960s and 1970s were the peak years of corporatism in Britain, characterised by coordinating bodies such as the National Economic Development Council as well as prices and incomes policies. Successive governments also added to the competition legislation started in 1948. Further laws included the 1964 Resale Price Act, 1965 Monopolies and Mergers Act and 1973 Fair Trading Act. The frequency of the legislation suggests that the competition regime was proving ineffective. Indeed, some thought concentration was becoming more of a problem, despite the laws, and that monopolies or mergers were not being prevented by existing legislation. On the other hand, economic liberals[38] believed that free markets were being strangled, through state intervention, to such an extent that competition legislation was somewhat moot.[39] For liberals, Britain needed wide-ranging deregulation, not more controls. Some Conservative politicians, meanwhile, thought that the British economy was in such dire need of competition during these decades that the only solution was membership of the European Economic Community (EEC).[40]

The Conservatives, during the final months of the Alec Douglas Home government, passed the Resale Price Act, which abolished minimal pricing and shifted the balance of power between manufacturers and retailers to the latter.[41] Retail price maintenance (RPM) was deemed a restrictive practice by the government. President of the Board of Trade Edward Heath described RPM as "price-fixing" and said that, "all competition is ruled out".[42] Heath explained that the "object of this policy is to promote more competition throughout the economy".[43] Heath would soon to be returned to opposition after the October 1964 election, subsequently becoming leader of the Conservative Party and initiating a more managerial approach to policy.[44] Labour, however, would add to competition legislation shortly after taking office, with the 1965 Monopolies and Mergers Act. As the name suggests, the 1965 Act brought the issue of prospective and completed mergers, as well as monopolies, under the authority of the commission.[45]

Labour's president of the Board of Trade, Douglas Jay, attempted to differentiate the Wilson government's approach from its predecessor's, claiming, "13 years government by the party opposite have left so many things undone". As we have seen, in the sphere of competition policy that was perhaps an exaggeration; Jay went on to say that the 1940s approach to the issue had been "bipartisan".[46] Jay painted the bill as an attempt to modernise British industry, saying—perhaps surprisingly for a Labour politician during this era—that, "competition is essential as one safeguard of the efficiency and progressiveness of … [the] private sector".[47] He identified a problem of enforcement, saying that the "watchdogs [MMC and Restrictive Practices Court] have barked, or prepared to bark, but meanwhile the monopolies have gone marching on", the watchdogs waiting too long to act and being too "timid" regarding mergers.[48] The 1965 Act, therefore, attempted to "put an end to all this irresolution and impotence" by expanding the powers of the commission and broadening its remit to mergers.[49] Crucially, however, referrals, or references, to the new MMC would still be at the discretion of the president of the Board of Trade.

The dual system of regulation—one component examining mergers and monopolies and the other restrictive practices—would continue until Edward Heath's government, which consolidated and reformed the arrangement in the 1973 Fair Trading Act. Setting up an OFT after repackaging the Board of Trade as the Department of Trade and Industry, the moves came as part of Heath's nominally more pro-market, pro-competition approach, derided by Harold Wilson as "Selsdon Man" after the hotel in South London where the principles of the 1970 Tory manifesto were developed. The post-1973 compact was the legislative and regulatory model broadly adopted by the Thatcher government in 1979.

The 1973 Fair Trading Act was indicative of its era. In some ways, it was again building upon previous legislation to improve the functioning of monopolies and mergers policy, as well as restrictive practices regulation. In this respect, it was a continuation of the post-war consensus. Indeed, the Heath government may have been lambasted as Selsdon Man, but, when trouble came, it appeared to quickly revert to Keynesian deficit spending to pacify public opinion and ensure full employment. The 'U-turns' of the 1970–74 government were loyally pursued by the likes of Keith Joseph and Margaret Thatcher, latterly seen as neoliberal radicals. In other ways, we can begin to see the breaking down of the consensus and how liberal-minded politicians challenged the status quo. The 1973 bill was introduced by Conservative Minister for Trade and Consumer Affairs Geoffrey Howe. A mild-mannered but convinced economic liberal, Howe would be a key Thatcherite policymaker after 1979. His statements in the House of Commons during the passage of the fair trading legislation also reveal a more pro-competitive philosophy.

Howe said, upon the second reading of the legislation, that the Bill had two "complementary" purposes, "first, the promotion of increased economic efficiency and, secondly, the protection of the consumer against unfair trading practices".[50] He went on to say this was:

[f]ounded on the Government's firm belief that competition provides a means of diffusing power and responsibility throughout the community and of continually widening the area of freedom and opportunity. Competition provides spurs to efficiency and incentives to seek out and supply the varied wants of the consumer and methods of sharing the benefits of technical progress in lower prices and higher incomes. Finally, it offers the means of discovering what to produce and where and how to produce it. It is on that basis that the Bill recognises and in no way impairs the importance of the role played by the army of traders, entrepreneurs and retailers in our market economy.[51]

With this statement, we can see a harbinger of the principles that would be important components of Thatcherism. Howe put the emphasis on the economic case for competition, market mechanisms and even the idea that capitalism can spread freedom and power, two watchwords of the Thatcher government's approach. Moving on, Howe invoked Adam Smith by noting that competition was not an "automatic panacea" because it

may be used to concentrate power, to limit [further] competition, and may be used in ways contrary to the public interest. It thus requires—in the interests of the community as a whole, within a properly designed framework of law—a competition policy.

Then, focusing on the rights of customers within a market, as well as the role information plays in a market economy, Howe set out that, "the consumer should be adequately and accurately informed and adequately protected against unfair or misleading marketing techniques, and adequately protected, finally, against abuse of market power, monopoly or aspects of imperfect competition".[52] Taken as a whole, we can see a shift, at least rhetorically, in the 1970s where Conservatives predating Thatcherism sought to modify competition policy in a more pro-market fashion than other post-war governments. To summarise, Howe's statements concerning the 1973 Act fit comfortably with an Ordoliberal approach.

Despite Howe's rhetoric on the 1973 Act, however, analysis of the reform suggests its impact was somewhat muted. The objective of the law was to investigate monopolies and markets where there had been market failure, in cases where competition was not present and that implicitly required state intervention or regulation.[53] In their history of UK competition law, Angus MacCulloch and Barry J. Rodger state that the 1973 Act failed to provide any deterrent effect or effective sanctions, and that the new regulatory regime simply required consideration of the 'public interest'.[54] Some of the details of antitrust regulation did change. The market share threshold that could be investigated was reduced to a quarter, from a third.[55] The new OFT was also given the power to make references to the MMC.[56] The list of matters that might affect the public interest was also increased.[57]

In summary, the suite of legislation between 1948 and 1973 developed a specifically British version of competition policy, built around a monopolies (and later mergers) commission working alongside a restrictive practices body. In theory, the regulators could intervene significantly in markets to promote competition. The reality, however, was that this was rarely the case—concentration increasing over this period—because domestic economic competition was seldom a priority for British post-war governments, and the legislation gave discretion to politicians, rather than the Ordoliberal model of constitutionally mandated dispersion of power. Yet, we cannot solely look at antitrust in terms of domestic policy. Changes in the global economy and trends in the EEC, which Britain would join in 1973, would also prove important.

International trends pre-Thatcherism

After the 1973 Fair Trading Act, a British government would not pass another major piece of competition legislation for 25 years, until the 1998 Competition Act. This may be owing to a number of factors, including the Thatcher government's focus on liberalisation and regulation, rather than setting more parameters for markets. Another important development was the UK's accession to the EEC in 1973, therefore bringing the country into a supranational competition authority. At the same time, the growing proportion of global trade in comparison with trade simply within a country—that is to say, accelerating globalisation—further changed antitrust considerations.

Britain was late to the process of European integration, which had started in the early 1950s with the formation of the European Coal and Steel Community, followed by the 1957 Treaty of Rome that paved the way for the EEC. It was only in the 1960s that Britain, under the leadership of first Harold Macmillan and then Harold Wilson, unsuccessfully attempted to join the EEC. By this point, however, Britain had missed its opportunity to shape the early direction of the bloc. The project's institutions would develop in idiosyncratic ways, reflecting the interests of the founding members. The EEC's Competition Directorate would be the best example of direct German influence on the bloc's foundational approach. Some accounts have suggested that Ordoliberal politicians were particularly keen to leave their imprint on the competition body because domestic policy was proving difficult to navigate.[58] Indeed, prominent Ordoliberals such as Ludwig Erhard and Alfred Müller-Armack were active in promoting their ideas regarding cartels and concentration of power in the Spaak Report during the pre-Treaty of Rome period, as well as the Competition Directorate's early years, including Germany's appointments to Brussels.[59] Others have argued that, rather than a full-blooded Ordoliberal competition policy, German influence was primarily seen in the rule of law issues at the European level.[60] Nevertheless, the argument that German Ordoliberalism is in fact imbedded in the 'European project', including the single currency, as well as competition policy, is one that has persisted.[61]

The EEC's Competition Directorate was an ambitious innovation by the bloc's founders. After all, an effective country-based antitrust regime barely existed at this time, let alone one to police monopolies and restrictive practices across the six-country trade area. Perhaps as a result, the scope of the regulator was, to some extent, limited. The directorate was subdivided into four parts. Two would examine state action, one looking at state aid and the other at the harmonisation of legislation. Two units would monitor the behaviour of the private sector, one for cartels and one for monopolies.[62] It wouldn't be until the 1980s and 1990s, however, alongside the Single European Act, that the Competition Directorate's policy matured.[63]

Britain joined the EEC in 1973, the start of what would be a periodically troubled relationship with 'Europe'. As we have already noted, some Conservatives saw one of the benefits as tougher competition within the free trade area as a means of reforming the country's economy. The relative performance of the British economy and the competitiveness of British firms, both widely believed to have been disappointing for much of the post-war period, were important arguments made in favour of joining the 'Common Market'.[64] Britain would encounter challenges in equalising its laws with EEC ones; in competition policy, firms now had, at least in theory, two regulators to satisfy. Nevertheless, the 1970s and early 1980s have been described by historians of European antitrust policy as a period where regulators were more lenient towards concentration. European regulators, for a time, were relaxed towards cartels because they were believed to satisfy social objectives.[65] It would be the Single European Act that would breathe new life into the Competition Directorate in regulating the EEC's, then the European Union's (EU), single market.[66] In the meantime, changes in the global economy were also shifting the calculus for British and EEC antitrust regulators.

Globalisation

The crucial development in most countries' economies in the past half century has been the march of globalisation. Although there are multiple definitions of this trend, perhaps the simplest is that this period has seen a rise in global trade as a proportion of the total—that is to say, increased trade between countries compared with within countries. This has been supercharged by advances in technology and caused greater interdependence between the various components of the world economy. As we will see in later chapters, an increasingly globalised economy has broadly accompanied growing corporate concentration and the advent of multinational or transnational companies.[67] This, in turn, has presented new challenges for antitrust regulators. If firms operate across several jurisdictions, is it appropriate or possible to regulate their actions within one state? Many countries have concluded that the answer to that question is no and are keener to attract foreign direct investment. This has not necessarily led to a more laissez-faire approach by British regulators, despite 11 years of Thatcherism. A clearer shift that seemed to offer a break with antitrust orthodoxy took place in the United States from the 1960s.

As we have seen, the United States was at the forefront of antitrust action at the turn of the 20th century, which was maintained, to different extents, for several decades. After Chicago School economists started to criticise the core principles of the antitrust regime in the 1950s, a shift in establishment, particularly conservative attitudes, gradually occurred. One of the best-known critics of antitrust was Robert Bork. Studying at the University of Chicago just as Friedman and Stigler moved into influential positions, Bork became a lawyer in the 1950s, with links to the Republican Party. In fact, Bork was to serve as Solicitor General under Presidents Richard Nixon and Gerald Ford and was nominated to the Supreme Court by Ronald Reagan, unsuccessfully, in 1987. With such conservative credentials, it was unsurprising that Bork was an opponent of intervention in the economy. His best-known scholarly work refuted antitrust, in articles in the 1960s and, in particular, in his 1978 book *The Antitrust Paradox*.

Bork's central theme was that government and regulators should not attempt to interfere in markets, using a neoliberal principle that intervention raises prices.[68] He stated time and again that the Sherman Act was aimed at consumer welfare and not at enforcing competition between firms.[69] Bork's view of economic competition was that markets "penalize" those that are not efficient.[70] The conclusions of Bork's analysis were that efficiency and concentration are, therefore, complementary and not in and of themselves worthy of antitrust action. Vertical mergers may be tolerated in this line of thinking. *The Antitrust Paradox*, apart from its wider influence on competition policy, has been cited in several high-profile US court cases.[71] Nevertheless, Bork's argument about antitrust, its focus on consumer welfare and the essence of the Sherman and Clayton Acts have all been disputed.[72]

A number of historians have outlined how Bork and another judge and economist, Richard Posner, were at the vanguard of a shift in thinking on antitrust during the 1970s and 1980s, inspired by the Chicago School, exerting a potent impact on real-world Supreme Court decisions.[73] Perhaps his unusual position as an economic and legal academic, establishment judge and political figure allowed Bork to achieve influence in this field. Certainly, the US approach to antitrust changed during the neoliberal era. Although this resonated in other countries, competition policy would evolve in a different manner in Britain and other European countries, as well as at the EEC and EU level.

1979: Margaret Thatcher comes to power

A fateful year in post-war British history, 1979 saw the Conservative government led by Margaret Thatcher apparently make a sharp break from the consensus that had dominated the previous 35 years. Critics have called this the beginning of Britain's neoliberal era—although the 1976 IMF loan is sometimes cited as its key precursor—from which the country has not yet significantly departed.[74] It should be noted that some of the themes explored in this book were important in the 1979 election campaign itself. First, distribution of political power across Britain's regions and nations. The issue that triggered a vote of confidence in Jim Callaghan's government was ostensibly the withdrawal of support by Scottish nationalists following an unsuccessful devolution referendum.[75] Second was the power of trade unions. Britain had experienced a serious of crippling strikes during the 1970s, notably during the Heath government's battle with the mining unions. This was eclipsed when unions went into revolt against the Labour government's pay restrictions, the 5% increases of the 'social contract' period, when soaring inflation meant most workers' real wages were declining. What followed burned itself into Britain's consciousness: the strikes of the 1978–79 'Winter of Discontent'. Therefore, for many British voters in the 1979 election, the power that needed to be broken was, in fact, organised labour. If so, Margaret Thatcher's government skilfully and comprehensively tamed union power during its decade in office. Devolution was never on the Conservative's agenda during the 1980s, and, as this book will demonstrate, political power was centralised for a variety of reasons. Nevertheless, concentration of economic power did feature in Thatcherism's early phase, including in the 1979 manifesto.

What is striking about the competition policy of the Thatcher and Major governments was that no significant piece of legislation was passed on the subject. This did not mean, however, that competition did not feature in Conservative rhetoric. The 1979 Conservative manifesto promised to enact an "Enabling Powers Bill" to end statutory monopolies, which became the 1980 Competition Act.[76] During and leading up to the election, Conservative politicians continued the policy proposals that had gained ground in the party over the previous two decades. The Conservatives sought to strengthen policy towards monopolies and 'reinvigorate' the OFT.[77] The manifesto outlined the party's approach:

> Profits are the foundation of a free enterprise economy. In Britain profits are still dangerously low. Price controls can prevent them from reaching a level adequate for the investment we need. In order to ensure effective competition and fair pricing policies, we will review the working of the Monopolies Commission, the Office of Fair Trading and the Price Commission, with the legislation which governs their activities.[78]

There would not be far-reaching competition legislation or regulation during this period, let alone anything that resembled the kind of Ordoliberal approach suggested by Geoffrey Howe in 1973. Although some Conservatives took an interest in the social market economy model, Thatcher was suspicious of a specifically

'German' approach.[79] Nevertheless, the incoming government was, to a certain extent, acting within a framework established by the previous Labour administration. The Liesner Commission had been set up in 1978, chaired by government official Hans Liesner, who expressed some concern over concentration and also mergers.[80] Liesner's proposals led to both parties committing to broadening 'public interest' standards.[81]

The Thatcher government passed the Competition Act in 1980. It sought to widen the scope of anti-competitive practices, which would be investigated in the first instance by the OFT before a referral to the MMC. Introduced by Secretary of State for Trade, John Nott, the bill's objectives were outlined as follows:

> First, it strengthens the power of the Director General of Fair Trading and the Monopolies and Mergers Commission to investigate practices which restrict or limit competition in both the public and private sectors. Secondly, it gives a new power to the Secretary of State to refer nationalised industries and other public undertakings to the Monopolies and Mergers Commission for an investigation into their efficiency and costs and into any possible abuse by these public sector bodies of their monopoly power which might work adversely for the consumers ... Thirdly, the Bill abolishes the Price Commission.[82]

The statement gives us an insight into some of the government's underlying priorities. Although the actual anti-monopoly elements of the legislation were relatively minor, the law takes aim at practices in the public sector, not only the private sector. Perhaps most importantly, by abolishing the Price Commission, which had set prices as part of corporatist prices and incomes policies, the Thatcher government took a step to liberalising a crucial pillar of the market economy, the price mechanism.

Subsequently, Secretary of State for Trade and Industry Norman Tebbit would introduce new rules in 1984 around antitrust regulation. The 'Tebbit Guidelines' moved the focus of competition policy to overseeing 'horizontal' mergers whereby firms buy competitors.[83] Vertical mergers are when firms buy others within the supply chain or that provide the buyer with services. The guidelines outlined the continuing 'public interest' element of competition policy. Economic historians, however, have suggested that the approach changed during the period to reflect the "underlying shift in the political environment towards market-based economics that accompanied the election of Mrs Thatcher's governments" and to "redirect attention in an increasingly economics-oriented direction."[84]

Yet the Thatcher government's real contribution towards competition in the UK was its deregulation of markets. Thatcherism was characterised by supply-side reforms, policies to encourage private enterprise, accumulate capital, promote ownership and stimulate economic activity. Thatcherite policies ranged from business incentivisation such as the enterprise zones initiative, actually a favourite policy of Geoffrey Howe and implemented in part by Michael Heseltine, and liberalisation of the financial services sector, which will be examined later in this book.[85] One of the key reforms of the Thatcher era, also examined in this study, was privatisation. State-owned utilities and companies were sold off into the private sector, and, more characteristically of the 1983–87 and 1987–90 governments, monopolies such as in energy, telecommunications and water were broken up and opened to competition. The outcomes of these policies, in terms of dispersing economic power, were mixed, as we shall see. One area where the Thatcher government clearly succeeded in shifting economic and political power was its trade unions policy. Over the course of the 1980s, the number of strike days fell, and, through a series of high-profile disputes, including the 1984–85 coal mining and the 1986–87 print union strikes, the place of unions in public life, and their influence on government decision-making, diminished.[86] The Thatcher government's broader programme, including high interest rates to squeeze inflation in the first term and a turn away from supporting heavy industry, also accelerated this trend by reducing the number of traditionally unionised jobs and, therefore, union members.

1990s: John Major and competition

John Major came to office with the objective of, if not reversing Thatcherism, then softening—at least in terms of presentation—the policies of his predecessor. Major's first Secretary of State for Trade and Industry, however, was the Thatcherite Peter Lilley, who introduced some non-competition factors into decisions on mergers. The 'Lilley Doctrine' increased referrals when potential mergers included a foreign company, adding a national interest element into antitrust policy.[87] Lilley was a notable Eurosceptic politician, in an era where this sentiment was growing within the Conservative Party—particularly after Margaret Thatcher's 1988 Bruges Speech that railed against a more integrated European Community—and it was in Brussels where the most significant changes were happening in competition policy.

The 1991 Maastricht Treaty paved the way for the European Union, which led to deeper integration between member states, including a single currency, but also a greater role for the Competition Directorate. Although there were not significant changes to competition regulation in the Maastricht Treaty, the development of a single market and greater intra-EU trade increased the likelihood that cases would come under the purview of the supranational watchdog. At the same time, many member states were strengthening their own national competition regimes, and, therefore, the EU Competition Directorate continued to restrict its investigations to cases with cross-border consequences.[88] Meanwhile, accelerating globalisation meant EU mergers and monopolies cases could have international implications. The 1990s and 2000s saw the start of rulings from the EU Competition Directorate that impacted upon business decisions outside the bloc—for instance, the 2001 ruling that successfully blocked the merger between General Electric and Honeywell, which had already been approved by US regulators.[89]

The head of Britain's MMC from 1988 to 1993, Sidney Lipworth, thought that the Brussels watchdog was not interested in most merger cases.[90] Interestingly,

Lipworth had previously supported a European-level cartel office modelled on its German, Ordoliberal-inspired equivalent, the *Bundeskartellamt*.[91] Nevertheless, the Major government did not pass any significant legislation during the 1990s. New Labour, meanwhile, would introduce a new competition law shortly after taking office.

1997: New Labour

Much has been made of New Labour's pro-market, even neoliberal, leanings. Yet, having stormed to electoral victory in May 1997, the Blair government broke from Thatcherite orthodoxy by passing a significant piece of competition legislation the following year. New Labour was self-consciously more economically liberal than previous Labour governments. It retained cordial relations with the booming City of London and supported 'light touch regulation' while riding the gains of increased global trade and a technological revolution.[92] Whereas some critics chastised the Blair government for pursuing a neoliberal strategy, others, such as Carstensen and Matthijs, have outlined how New Labour moderated neoliberalism by aligning some of its practices with social democratic goals.[93] The introduction of a national minimum wage and increasing access to higher education, albeit within a framework of rising tuition fees, are two examples of this strategy. Blair himself framed his approach as 'Third Way' social democracy, which was shared by other centre-left leaders of the era such as Bill Clinton and Gerhard Schröder.[94] We can observe some of this approach in New Labour's competition legislation.

The 1998 Competition Act and the 2002 Enterprise Act were the key planks of Labour's competition policy. Taken together they formed a "rounded scheme of law" to align UK competition policy as closely as possible with EU regulation.[95] The 1998 law sought to bring together existing competition legislation and update it, creating a new body, the Competition Commission (to replace the MMC), and to toughen the penalties for restrictive practices and abuse of a dominant market position. The 2002 Enterprise Act increased the penalties for cartels and also introduced a more objective measure to determine competition and whether certain markets or firms required investigation. The legislation appeared to create a more credible competition regime by reducing, although not eliminating, ministerial discretion.

Antitrust regulation

By the end of the 20th century, antitrust bodies had developed an array of approaches for promoting competition and preventing concentration. As we have seen, regulators may have a particular focus on horizontal or vertical integration. To prevent this leading to concentration, regulators may block a merger or force firms to divest or restructure other parts of their business.[96] A high-profile instance of the latter, in the American context, was the break-up of telecommunication monopoly AT&T, a process that started in 1974, invoking the Sherman Act, and was completed during the Reagan era.[97] Stephen Davies and Bruce Lyons examined the different approaches of EU regulators, stating how, although divestiture was the preferred remedy, 'behavioural remedies' such as price controls could be more satisfactory for consumers.[98] Another action antitrust regulators have taken is fining businesses for anti-competitive behaviour, as we have seen in recent years in a number of high-profile cases against giant tech firms.

Competition regulators also monitor patents and intellectual property. Some firms may attempt to misuse material still under patent, while others attempt to alter the terms of a patent to prolong its life. The latter usually means higher prices and less consumer choice. The case for antitrust intervention, however, is not always made solely on behalf of consumers. Nicholas Crafts, for instance, has shown that increasing concentration also impedes productivity, and that EEC membership had the impact of reviving the UK economy: "the UK benefited greatly from strengthening competition in product markets by abandoning protectionism, de-regulating and, eventually, strengthening competition policy".[99] This analysis demonstrates that antitrust policy and attitudes to concentration can potentially be multifaceted.

Public faith in the troika of politics, regulation and business has been undermined in recent years, and we have increasingly seen that conflicts of interests potentially inhibit markets by the 'revolving door' phenomenon. This had led some, even publications such as *The Economist*, to talk about the concept of 'regulatory capture'.[100] How effective the regulatory system has proved since 1979 and its attendant impact on public perceptions of governance is one of the core themes of this book. Nevertheless, and related to the last point, the trend towards globalisation has fundamentally altered the power relationships between companies and the state, making effective competition enforcement increasingly challenging. The subsequent chapters will look at this process in a number of case studies, including the deregulation of the finance and energy sectors.

Conclusion

This chapter has outlined the key historical trends of the UK's approach to concentration and regulation. British competition policy was a relatively minor concern before 1945, with some, albeit limited, influence from the United States' antitrust approach. It was not until the post-war Labour government under Prime Minister Clement Attlee that a formalised system emerged. Developing in an idiosyncratic manner, partly reflecting British economic history—for instance, on restraint of trade issues—competition policy included some liberal economic elements in wanting to limit monopolies and concentration. A certain degree of consensus arose during the 1945–79 period through a number of pieces of legislation on monopolies and mergers, fair trading and the regulatory bodies set up to monitor business practices. The Thatcher government inherited a system regulated by the OFT and the MMC. The crucial component in the British approach, however, was the referral mechanism. The Secretary of State for Trade (the title changed over the decades) was required to refer individual cases for investigation, which provided enough political discretion for cases to be waived in a number of high-profile instances. Although an example of pragmatism in British policymaking, for effective antitrust policy the referral caveat proved a significant flaw.

Margaret Thatcher's governments passed little in terms of formal antitrust policy but still had a dramatic impact on UK market competition through supply-side deregulation and liberalisation. Nevertheless, more open markets appeared to allow concentration without sufficient regulation. Alongside a globalising world economy, Thatcherism would leave a legacy of market power. Thatcher's successor, John Major, was also reluctant to legislate on competition, despite the UK being required to catch up with EU integration by the mid-1990s. Despite being one of the most market-orientated economies in the EU, Britain lagged behind in antitrust policy. The Major government would see significant coordination between business, regulators and the state, personified by the policies of Michael Heseltine, an unusually enthusiastic interventionist Tory, during the 1990s. The most significant piece of competition legislation passed during the entire 1979–2007 period, and arguably the most pro-market and pro-competition, was the Blair government's 1998 Competition Act, which introduced an overhaul of antitrust policy in the UK and fully aligned the British system with the approach of the EU Competition Directorate. The reforms were indicative of New Labour's social democratic approach, which contained echoes of the social market economy pioneered in post-war Germany and inspired by Ordoliberal thinkers and politicians. Yet, as subsequent chapters will show, antitrust legislation and regulators would only have limited impact on preventing concentration in the British economy.

Notes

1 Adam Smith, *The Wealth of Nations Books I–III* (London: Penguin, 1986, originally published in 1776), 164.
2 Adam Smith, *The Wealth of Nations, Book IV* (London: Penguin, 1986, originally published in 1776) 145.
3 Ibid.
4 William L. Letwin, "The English Common Law Concerning Monopolies", ed. Richard A. Epstein, *Contract - Freedom and Restraint: Liberty, Property, and the Law* (Abingdon: Routledge, 2000, 93–124), 113.
5 Letwin, "The English Common Law", 113.
6 Ken Clarke identified entrenched 'Spanish practices' of traditional professions on several occasions. For instance: Ken Clarke House of Commons Debates (hereafter HC Deb), (28 October 1987) vol. 121, col. 283.
7 Bruce Caldwell, *Hayek's Challenge: An Intellectual Biography of F.A. Hayek* (Chicago: Chicago University Press, 2005), 84.
8 Manchester Liberalism might best be summarised as the "nineteenth century belief that the market should be seen as a self-regulating mechanism and that the state's role was to remove itself as far as possible from intervening in it or regulating it". Quoted in Ben Jackson, "At the Origins of Neoliberalism: The Free Economy and the Strong State, 1930–1947", *The Historical Journal*, 53:1 (March 2010), 132–139, 134.
9 Margaret Thatcher said in her conference speech that, "I would not mind betting that if Mr. Gladstone were alive today he would apply to join the Conservative Party". Margaret Thatcher Foundation (hereafter MTF), MTF 105454, "Speech to Conservative Party Conference", 14 October 1983.

10 "Transcript of Sherman Anti-Trust Act (1890)", Our Documents, www.ourdocu-ments.gov/doc.php?flash=false&doc=51&page=transcript [accessed 5 February 2020].

11 Perhaps best seen in the populist support for Democrat presidential nominee in 1896, 1900 and 1908, William Jennings Bryan. Indeed, the Populist Party was the third force in American politics during the 1890s.

12 Daniel Ruddy, *Theodore the Great: Conservative Crusader* (Washington: Regnery History, 2016).

13 Frank Bealey, *Power in Business and the State: An Historical Analysis of Its Concentration* (Abingdon: Routledge, 2001), 52.

14 Talking Politics, "Monopoly and Muckraking", 29 December 2019, www.talkingpoli ticspodcast.com/blog/2019/211-monopoly-and-muckraking [accessed 4 January 2020].

15 Tony Freyer, *Regulating Big Business: Antitrust in Great Britain and America; 1880–1990* (Cambridge: Cambridge University Press, 1992), 111.

16 Talking Politics, "Monopoly and Muckraking", 29 December 2019, www.talkingpoli ticspodcast.com/blog/2019/211-monopoly-and-muckraking [accessed 4 January 2020].

17 Freyer, *Regulating*, 108. Quoting: Arthur Cohen, Sir Alfred Edmund Bateman, Sir David Miller Barbour, "Report of the Royal Commission on Shipping Rings" (H.M. Stationery Office, 1909), 117–118.

18 Ibid., 4.

19 Ibid., 160.

20 Ibid., 4, 162, 172.

21 The report said that, "regarding abuses connected with trusts and combinations … the case for immediate legislation … cannot be said to be an urgent one", 6–7. Records of the Cabinet Office (hereafter CAB), London: Public Record Office, CAB 24/203/1, Philip Cunliffe-Lister, "Committee on Industry and Trade", 27 March 1929. Helen Mercer, *Constructing a Competitive Order: The Hidden History of British Antitrust Policies* (Cambridge: Cambridge University Press, 1995), 48.

22 Peter Sloman, *The Liberal Party and the Economy, 1929–1964* (Oxford: Oxford University Press, 2015), p. 11, 18, 223.

23 The Papers of Wilhelm Röpke, Institut für Wirtschaftspolitik an der Universität Köln, letter from Liberal activist, author and editor of *The Free Trader*, Deryck Abel to Röpke, 16 January 1946; letter from Abel, to Röpke, 10 April 1946; corre-spondence between Röpke and Veronica Wedgwood, deputy editor of *Time & Tide*, 20 September 1949; Wilhelm Röpke, "The Proletarianized Society I", *Time & Tide*, 30:40 (1 October 1949), 973–974; Wilhelm Röpke, "The Proletarianized Society II", *Time & Tide*, 30:41 (8 October 1949), 998–999.

24 Werner Bonefeld, "Adam Smith and Ordoliberalism: On the Political Form of Market Liberty", *Review of International Studies*, 39:2 (July 2012), 233–250, 238; Taylor Boas and Jordan Gans-Morse, "Neoliberalism: From New Liberal Philosophy to Anti-Liberal Slogan", *Studies in Comparative International Development*, 44:2 (June 2009), 146; Samuel Gregg, *Wilhelm Röpke's Political Economy* (Cheltenham: Edward Elgar, 2010), 77; Manfried E. Streit and Michael Wohlgemuth, "The Market Economy and the State. Hayekian and Ordoliberal Conceptions", ed. Peter Koslowski, *The Theory of Capitalism in the German Economic Tradition* (London: Springer, 2000, 224–260), 231.

25 *The Economist*, "Mr Butskell's Dilemma", 13 February 1954.

26 Keith Middlemas, *Power, Competition and the State. Volume I. Britain in Search of Balance 1940–61* (Basingstoke: Macmillan, 1986), 1, 342.

27 Freyer, *Regulating*, 4.

28 MTF 110368, "1944 Employment White Paper", 19.

29 Nicholas Woodward, *The Management of the British Economy, 1945–2001* (Manchester: Manchester University Press, 2004), 45.

30 Stephen Wilks, *In the Public Interest: Competition Policy and the Monopolies and Mergers Commission* (Manchester: Manchester University Press, 1999), 134; Records of the Board of Trade (hereafter BT), London: Public Record Office, BT 64/318, Post War Reconstruction. Policy towards Industrial Organisations and Control of Monopolies, "Memorandum by G.C. Allen and H. Gaitskell, 'The Control of Monopoly'", 17 July 1943, 1.

31 Harold Wilson, during the second reading of the 1948 Act, explained the thinking behind the one-third threshold: "This proportion of one-third was chosen as the lower limit on what could in future constitute control of the market. In fact, a very high proportion of the cases we should wish to submit involve a much greater control of the market than one-third. All the cases I have myself examined, for instance, cover more than 50 per cent., generally a very much higher proportion than that. But we rejected the figure of 50 per cent. Since some trade association or monopolist could then have attempted to prove themselves outside the scope of the Act by producing figures showing that they covered not more than 49 per cent." HC Deb (22 April 1948) vol. 449, col. 2032–2033.

32 Woodward, *Management*, 45.

33 Harold Wilson, HC Deb (22 April 1948) vol. 449, col. 2018–2019.

34 Harold Wilson, HC Deb (22 April 1948) vol. 449, col. 2019.

35 Woodward, *Management*, 45.

36 Mercer, *Constructing*, 83.

37 Jeremy Lever, "The Development of British Competition Law: A Complete Overhaul and Harmonization" (WZB Discussion Paper, No. FS IV 99-4, Wissenschaftszentrum Berlin für Sozialforschung, 1999), www.econstor.eu/bitstream/10419/51159/1/30115 2780.pdf [accessed 11 February 2020].

38 The work of economic liberal Samuel Brittan was particularly influential during this period. Roger Middleton, "Brittan on Britain: 'The Economic Contradictions of Democracy' Redux", *The Historical Journal*, 54:4 (December 2011), 1141–1168.

39 For instance, Margaret Thatcher later wrote that her toleration of economic policy during this period was "wrong. State intervention in the economy is not ultimately an answer to over-mighty vested interests: for it soon comes to collude with them." Margaret Thatcher, *The Path to Power* (London: Harper Collins, 1995), 220.

40 Adrian Williamson, *Conservative Economic Policymaking and the Birth of Thatcherism, 1964–1979* (Basingstoke: Palgrave Macmillan, 2015), 24.

41 Helen Mercer, "The Abolition of Resale Price Maintenance in Britain in 1964: A Turning Point for British Manufacturers?", London School of Economics (Working Papers in Economic History 39/98, 1998).

42 Edward Heath, HC Deb (10 March 1964), Vol. 691, col. 258.

43 Edward Heath, HC Deb (10 March 1964), Vol. 691, col. 255.

44 Tim Bale, *The Conservatives Since 1945* (Oxford: Oxford University Press, 2012), 130–135, 138.

45 Lever, "British Competition Law", 5–7.

46 Douglas Jay, HC Deb (29 March 1965), vol. 709, col. 1207.

47 Ibid.

48 Douglas Jay, HC Deb (29 March 1965), vol. 709, col. 1208.

49 Douglas Jay, HC Deb (29 March 1965), vol. 709, col. 1209.

50 Sir Geoffrey Howe, HC Deb (13 December 1972), vol. 848, col. 453.

51 Ibid.

52 Sir Geoffrey Howe, HC Deb (13 December 1972), vol. 848, col. 453–454.

53 Angus MacCulloch and Barry J. Rodger, *Competition Law and Policy in the EU and UK* (Abingdon: Routledge, 1999), 128.

54 Ibid.
55 Lever, "British Competition Law", 6.
56 Ibid., 7.
57 Ibid., 9.
58 Tim Büthe, "The Politics of Competition and Institutional Change in European Union: The First Fifty Years", eds. Sophie Meunier and Kathleen R. McNamara, *Making History: European Integration and Institutional Change at Fifty* (Oxford: Oxford University Press, 2007, 175–194), 182; Michelle Cini and Lee McGowan, *Competition Policy in the European Union* (Basingstoke: Macmillan, 1998), 8–9.
59 Sigfrido M. Ramirez and Sebastian van de Scheur, "The Evolution of the Law on Articles 85 and 86 EEC [Articles 101 and 102 TFEU]: Ordoliberalism and Its Keynesian Challenge", eds. Kiran Klaus Patel and Heike Schweitzer, *The Historical Foundations of EU Competition Law* (Oxford: Oxford University Press, 2013, 19–53), 19, 23.
60 Kiran Klaus Patel and Heike Schweitzer, "Introduction", eds. Kiran Klaus Patel and Heike Schweitzer, *The Historical Foundations of EU Competition Law* (Oxford: Oxford University Press, 2013, 1–18), 10.
61 Pierre Dardot and Christian Laval, *The New Way of the World: On Neo-Liberal Society* (translated by Gregory Elliott, London: Verso, 2013), 194.
62 Ramirez and Van de Scheur, "Evolution", 25.
63 Neil Rollings and Laurent Warlouzet, "Business History and European Integration: How EEC Competition Policy Affected Companies' Strategies", *Business History* (11 July, 2018), www.tandfonline.com/doi/abs/10.1080/00076791.2018.1488966 [accessed 18 February 2020].
64 Nauro F. Campos and Fabrizio Coricelli, "How Does European Integration Work? Lessons from Revisiting the British Relative Economic Decline", eds. Nauro F. Campos and Fabrizio Coricelli, *The Economics of UK–EU Relations: From the Treaty of Rome to the Vote for Brexit* (Basingstoke: Palgrave Macmillan, 2017, 47–78), 71. For another account of Britain's economic crisis in the 1970s, see Kathleen Burk and Alec Cairncross, *Goodbye Great Britain* (London: Yale University Press, 1992), 212–213.
65 Ramirez and Van de Scheur, "Evolution", 52–53.
66 Umut Aydina and Kenneth P. Thomas, "The Challenges and Trajectories of EU Competition Policy in the Twenty-First Century", *Journal of European Integration*, 34:6 (2012), 531–547, 532.
67 Keith Cowling and Philip R. Tomlinson, "Globalisation and Corporate Power", *Contributions to Political Economy*, 24:1 (2005), 33–54, 35–36.
68 Bork cited leading member of the Second Chicago School, Aaron Director. He also interviewed Friedrich Hayek in 1978, and part of the interview was transcribed into the *Hayek on Hayek* collection. See: Freyer, *Regulating*, 278; Friedrich Hayek, *Hayek on Hayek: An Autobiographical Dialogue*, eds. Leif Wenar and Stephen Kresge (Chicago: University of Chicago, 1994).
69 Robert Bork, *The Antitrust Paradox* (New York: Free Press, 1978).
70 Bork quoted in Freyer, *Regulating*, 278.
71 One article in 2014 stated that Bork's "consumer welfare prescription" had been quoted in 29 US federal antitrust decisions. See: Daniel A. Crane, "The Tempting of Antitrust: Robert Bork and the Goals of Antitrust Policy", *Antitrust Law Journal*, 79:3 (2014), 835–53, 847.
72 Stephen Martin "Dispersion of Power as an Economic Goal of Antitrust Policy", ed. Manuela Mosca, *Power in Economic Thought. Palgrave Studies in the History of Economic Thought* (Palgrave Macmillan, 2018, 251–290), 283–284.
73 George L. Priest, "Bork's Strategy and the Influence of the Chicago School on Modern Antitrust Law", *The Journal of Law & Economics*, 57:3 (2014), 1–17;

Patrice Bougette, Marc Deschamps and Frédéric Marty, "When Economics Met Antitrust: The Second Chicago School and the Economization of Antitrust Law", *Enterprise & Society*, 16:2 (June 2015), 313–353; Louis Kaplow, "Antitrust, Law & Economics, and the Courts", *Law and Contemporary Problems*, 50: 4 (Autumn 1987), 181–216).

74   Daniel Stedman-Jones, *Masters of the Universe. Hayek, Friedman, and the Birth of Neoliberal Politics* (Oxford: Princeton University Press, 2012), 5, 257; Andre Gunner Frank, "No End to History! History to No End?", *Social Justice*, 17:4 (42) (Winter 1990), 17.

75   The Scottish Devolution referendum was held on 1 March 1979, and, although 'Yes' won 51.62% of the vote, the minimal threshold requirements were not met, which was 40% of the electorate voting in favour. The turnout of the referendum was 64%, which meant only 32.9% of the electorate voted yes.

76   Williamson, *Conservative Economic Policymaking*, 140.

77   Ibid., 155.

78   MTF 110858, "Conservative General Election Manifesto 1979".

79   Sir Geoffrey Howe, HC Deb (10 November 1977), vol. 938, col. 874–997; Andrew Denham and Mark Garnett, *Keith Joseph* (Chesham: Acumen, 2001), 240.

80   Freyer, *Regulating*, 313.

81   Ibid., 313.

82   John Nott, HC Deb (23 October 1979), vol. 972, col. 222.

83   Freyer, *Regulating*, 310.

84   Andrew Scott, "The Evolution of Competition Law and Policy in the United Kingdom", LSE Working Papers 9/2009, 13, http://eprints.lse.ac.uk/24564/1/WP S2009-09_Scott.pdf [accessed 25 February 2020].

85   See: Robert Ledger, *Neoliberal Thought and Thatcherism: "A Transition from Here to There?"* (Abingdon: Routledge, 2017), 64–75.

86   Carole Thornley and Dan Coffey, *Globalization and Varieties of Capitalism: New Labour, Economic Policy and the Abject State* (Basingstoke: Palgrave Macmillan, 2009), 12.

87   Scott, "Evolution of Competition Law", 12.

88   Freyer, *Regulating*, 315.

89   Erin E. Holland, "Using Merger Review to Cure Prior Conduct: The European Commission's GE/Honeywell Decision", *Columbia Law Review*, 103:1 (2003, 74–110), 74–75.

90   Freyer, *Regulating*, 315.

91   Kenneth A. Armstrong and Simon J. Bulmer, *The Governance of the Single European Market* (Manchester: Manchester University Press, 1998), 103.

92   For one of the many mentions of light-touch regulation, see Gordon Brown, "Mansion House Speech", 22 June 2006, *The Guardian*, www.theguardian.com/business/2006/jun/22/politics.economicpolicy [accessed 27 February 2020].

93   Martin B. Carstensen and Matthias Matthijs, "Of Paradigms and Power: British Economic Policy Making Since Thatcher", *Governance*, 31:3 (July 2018), 431–447.

94   Hanco Jürgens, "The Short History and Long Legacy of the Third Way: Social Democracy and Moderation at the End of the Twentieth Century", eds. Ido de Haan and Matthijs Lok, *The Politics of Moderation in Modern European History* (Basingstoke: Macmillan, 2019, 205–221), 207.

95   Scott, "Evolution of Competition Law", 2, 17.

96   Stephen Davies and Bruce Lyons, *Mergers and Merger Remedies in the EU: Assessing the Consequences for Competition* (Cheltenham: Edward Elgar, 2007), 243.

97   W. Kip Viscusi, Joseph E. Harrington Jr. and John M. Vernon, *Economics of Regulation and Antitrust* (Cambridge: MIT Press, 2005), 550.

98 Davies and Lyons, *Mergers*, 247.
99 Nicholas Crafts, "Creating Competitive Advantage: Policy Lessons from History", University of Warwick Working Papers, No. 91 (2012), 14, http://wrap.warwick.ac .uk/57857/ [accessed 27 July 2020].
100 *The Economist*, "The Sweet Hereafter: Cheer Up, Sacked MPs. A Big Payday Awaits", 12 December 2019.

3 Structural shifts in the British economy

The period between 1979 and 2007 was a remarkable era of change in British political economy, not least for the longevity in office of the three prime ministers—Margaret Thatcher (1979–90), John Major (1990–97) and Tony Blair (1997–2007)—but also because of the fundamental shifts that took place in the economy itself. This chapter will look at a number of examples to demonstrate how power and concentration shifted within this period. First, the broad changes in ownership that took place in Britain will be examined, in particular the movement of state-owned utilities and companies into the private sector. Despite this usually being described as an act of liberalisation, the results often did not mean a dispersal of power. Second, we shall look at the rise of the financial services sector as the lynchpin of the British economy and political attitudes to this example of concentration of power. Third, the approach to media and broadcasting will be examined, as an area that has often drawn much attention. The 1979–2007 period was unique in so far as it coincided with rapid changes in the scope of the media, accompanied by a technological revolution. Fourth, we shall look at the role that globalisation played in the broader picture of the British economy. With policies such as the removal of exchange controls in 1979 and Big Bang in 1986, Britain helped bring about a more globalised world economy. Yet, it was also forced to come to terms with forces increasingly beyond the control of politicians in London. The narrative of this era is partly one of how Britain attempted to adapt to this transformation. Increasing market power and concentration of power more generally are pieces of this story. Although we see a broad increase in economic concentration, the pattern is by no means linear.

Ownership shifts

Margaret Thatcher commented in 1980:

> We've had a tremendous amount of nationalisation. That's created a large number of monopolies in this country ... I think monopoly is bad, and I think socialism did Britain a great dis-service, having so many nationalised industries ... As you know we're trying to do something about some of the nationalised industries.[1]

When Thatcher took office in May 1979, the British economy was dominated by state-owned enterprises and utilities. This followed decades of nationalisation, referred to disparagingly by Conservative politician and committed economic liberal Keith Joseph as the "ratchet effect" of socialism,[2] but more positively by those on the left as the "commanding heights" of the economy.[3] With the exception of two attempts by Conservative governments, in the 1950s and 1970s, to reverse this trend, an increasing number of companies were state-owned by 1979.[4] Government was ultimately responsible for a long list of concerns, albeit through the at arms-length public corporation model pioneered by the Labour deputy prime minister in the Attlee government, Herbert Morrison. Whether in heavy industry (such as British Steel), energy (for instance, British Gas and the British Electricity Authority), telecoms (British Telecom), media and broadcasting (the British Broadcasting Corporation (BBC)), car manufacturing (British Leyland) or transport (British Airways and British Rail), a state-owned monopoly existed in many markets. For several of these companies, their ownership structure would fundamentally change over the 1979–2007 period, with many being broken up and sold partly or wholly into the private sector, decoupling them from the state, at least in theory.

The Thatcher government made significant changes to ownership within the British economy. The most notable trends were privatisation, which reduced the power of state-owned enterprises, and, as a result, reducing the potency of the largest trades unions. The latter issue was at the top of the government's agenda, but it initially moved cautiously. The demands of steel workers and coal miners were satisfied in the first term,[5] and it was not until 1984 that the government decided to confront a strike by the National Union of Mineworkers (NUM).[6] Margaret Thatcher and her ministers, including Keith Joseph, were also strategic towards industry. Joseph continued to subsidise British Leyland in the first term, despite the company making huge losses and seeming to represent everything Thatcherites despised about the British economy: trade union militancy, low productivity, lack of innovation and inefficiency.

Yet, over the course of the Thatcher era, change occurred in all these areas. Several rounds of legislation gradually whittled away trade union privileges, as well as the set-piece confrontations with the NUM and, later, the printing unions over the Murdoch newspapers' move from Fleet Street to Wapping.[7] The battle against inflation and associated high interest rates caused sterling to rise, reducing exports of many industrial and manufactured goods and accelerating the move towards a non-unionised service-based economy. Companies such as British Leyland were put under tougher management, which improved their performance. Nigel Lawson, Chancellor between 1983 and 1989, said this meant "financial disciplines" were "imposed and taken seriously", "preparing State enterprises for privatization, and the prospect of privatization" before splitting them up and adding them to the privatisation programme.[8]

Privatisation was a policy pioneered by the Thatcher government; the trend previously had been to transfer companies into the state sector rather than vice versa. Although the first government, 1979–83, moved relatively cautiously with what was initially described as 'denationalisation'—indeed, the policy was not mentioned in any great detail in the 1979 manifesto—the process gathered momentum as ministers grew in confidence. The early privatisations included companies such as Amersham International, as well as others such as Britoil, Enterprise Oil and National Freight.[9] The government received little public resistance to selling off the state-owned portions of these companies to private investors. The shares themselves were heavily oversubscribed and raised considerable amounts for the Treasury. Amersham International, for instance, raised £65 million.[10] That the government appeared to have developed a popular policy that swelled the Treasury's coffers and reduced state subsidisation and the often-problematic management of these state-owned firms emboldened it for bigger flotations.

The Conservative Party's 1983 election manifesto was more explicit about its privatisation programme. As well as setting out, as mentioned above, how it would bring more discipline to bear on state-owned enterprises that could not be privatised, which would be "given top-quality management and required to work to clear guidelines", the document made an accurate description of what would be enacted:

> We shall transfer more state-owned businesses to independent ownership. Our aim is that British Telecom—where we will sell 51 per cent of the shares to the private sector—Rolls Royce, British Airways and substantial parts of British Steel, of British Shipbuilders and of British Leyland, and as many as possible of Britain's airports, shall become private sector companies. We also aim to introduce substantial private capital into the National Bus Company. As before, we will offer shares to all those who work in them.[11]

Nevertheless, the manifesto also mentioned what would be one of the key criticisms of the privatisation programme, that it was not necessarily promoting competition and free markets:

> Merely to replace state monopolies by private ones would be to waste an historic opportunity. So we will take steps to ensure that these new firms do not exploit their powerful positions to the detriment of consumers or their competitors.[12]

This would be the one of the important ways to determine if power was being distributed more widely or concentrated further. It should also be pointed out here how interpretations can differ about state and private ownership. For many on the left, nationalisation means that every citizen has a stake in a state-owned enterprise, and that government owns a firm on behalf of 'the people'. Indeed, Nikolaos Zahariadis has argued that globalisation increases the necessity of state-owned enterprises because they are more responsive to democratic pressures and have a longer-term view.[13] Economic liberals, on the other hand, believe that individual ownership is a more authentic way to distribute power. Clearly, the Thatcher years took the second viewpoint. Nevertheless, a number of issues emerged to question how far the benefits of privatisation were actually being spread. The sales of the first term were, generally speaking, of smaller companies being transferred into competitive markets. These markets would function more efficiently, as state-owned firms were no longer operating or receiving subsidies. A more competitive market had the potential to disperse power and benefit the end users—that is to say, consumers—with lower prices and better-quality products and services.

The competition argument would be much harder to make as the Conservatives privatised state monopolies in telecoms (1984), gas (1986), water (1989) and electricity (1990), where there were no obvious rivals to challenge the monopoly's domination. Yet criticism soon took aim at the British Telecom and British Gas flotations, that a state monopoly had simply been moved into the private sector, where it continued as a monopoly without competition. Critics believed the regulators put in place, Ofcom in the case of telecoms and Ofgas for gas, were ineffective and quickly became 'captured' by their respective industries.[14] Subsequent studies were ambivalent as to whether the process had reduced prices or improved customer satisfaction in these markets.[15] As a result, the sales of the third Thatcher term were more concerned with promoting competition through effective regulation.[16] In particular, the privatisation of the British Electricity Authority in 1990 was more complex than earlier sales, and the supply of energy, rather than generation, has developed into a competitive market, although the extent of this is the subject of some debate.[17]

The 1980s offered a dramatic shift in government policy towards ownership. But what impact did this have on concentration of power? Unsurprisingly, leading Thatcherite ministers thought the changes were highly significant and liberalising. Privatisation was part of what became known as 'popular capitalism',[18] the Conservative agenda of spreading ownership and, as Geoffrey Howe noted, creating a cohort of Britons with a "vested interest" in the party's success.[19] Over the course of the 1980s, share ownership by the public is estimated to have increased by 7%, while other popular capitalism policies such as Right to Buy led to over a million of these homes being bought by their occupiers.[20] Although owner-occupancy in housing certainly increased over this period, critics have been sceptical as to whether privatisation generated a significant number of shareholders interested in long-term investments. The accusation that investors, including many members of the public, simply made short-term gains out of privatisation was refuted by Nigel Lawson in his memoirs.[21]

Privatisation not only became orthodoxy for British governments during the 1980s and 1990s, but bordered on dogma. Development economist Jeffrey Sachs, who worked on the IMF reform package at the end of the Cold War to help Poland make the transition to a market economy, thought that British officials were preoccupied with privatisation.[22] That could also be levelled at the Major government. Having ousted an increasingly unpopular Margaret Thatcher in October 1990, the Conservatives manoeuvred to install the relatively inexperienced John Major as prime minister. Partly as a result, partly that, after a decade in power, the Tories were running out of steam, partly because the 'enemies' of the pre-Thatcher era—trade unions, communism, chronic inflation (although this was surging in 1990) and corporatism—had been defeated,[23] as well as because of external factors such as German unification and its subsequent impact on the European Exchange Rate Mechanism (ERM; which Thatcher had reluctantly joined in September 1990 under pressure from Major, who was then Chancellor of the Exchequer), the Conservatives went to war with each other in the 1990s. Major simultaneously wanted to be a reliable partner at 'the heart of Europe', lead a more moderate government focused on conservative values, such as his 'Back to Basics' campaign, present a more technocratic approach to improve policy outcomes to the general public (the 'Citizens Charter') and demonstrate enough Thatcherite zeal to satisfy right wingers and economic liberals. The latter issue led the Major government to try and extend the privatisation programme. By the 1990s, however, the obvious candidates for sale had mostly been moved into the private sector, leaving only state-owned enterprises that Thatcher herself feared to privatise.[24] These included the coal industry in 1994 and, even more notoriously, British Rail between 1993 and 1996.[25]

The structure of a privatised rail industry was not immediately obvious, train companies being restricted by infrastructure—that is to say, rail capacity. Ultimately, the Major government chose to split the industry into companies that would operate as franchises for a period of 7 years, on track infrastructure operated by a separate company. The roll-out of the new arrangements was chaotic, prices rose, service was often poor, and loss-making lines had to be subsidised, ironically, by the taxpayer. As one history of Major's time in office sets out, "For a significant body of opinion, this was a privatisation too far."[26] The spotlight also fell on the dividends paid to shareholders while conditions for rail users apparently remained dire.[27] The situation worsened with a series of fatal accidents, stretching into the New Labour period, such as at Ladbroke Grove in 1999, Hatfield in 2000 and Potters Bar in 2002. The Blair government made one of its only decisions to reverse privatisation when it took the infrastructure company, Railtrack, back into public ownership in 2002, renaming it Network Rail.

Although privatisation throughout the 1979–2007 period attracted much criticism, compared with other utilities and companies, the railways have perhaps received the greatest level of opprobrium. One editorial by *The Guardian* newspaper (admittedly already unsympathetic to the scheme), after New Labour had left office, summarised the complaints against rail privatisation succinctly:

> the public suffer from often late, expensive and frequently overcrowded train services. While the cack-handed rollout of infrastructure improvements has led to cancellations and delays on the network, commuters saw ticket prices rise at twice the rate of their wages between 2010 and 2016.[28]

The concept of competition on the railways is plainly problematic, and continuing state subsidisation and intervention make a mockery of the pretence that this is a free market. Nevertheless, the system does have its supporters, who point to investment that has been a result of private ownership and the franchise system.[29] Station upgrades, for instance, are sometimes cited as a result of the process.[30]

However, whereas, with other privatised schemes, reform of a system or a market is often proposed, discussions about rail have most quickly moved to proposals for 'renationalisation'. A number of rail companies have periodically been taken back into state hands during the privatisation period. Indeed, if one of the policies of the Labour Party leader between 2015 and 2020, Jeremy Corbyn, had greatest support, it was returning the rail companies to state ownership.

In summary, changing the ownership of British industry and companies proved to be one of Thatcherism's most far-reaching, and novel, policies. Under Thatcher's successor, John Major, the idea was extended to areas that have provoked more disquiet, most notably the privatisation of British Rail. Moreover, what was significant about Tony Blair's New Labour government was that it showed little interest in reversing any of the privatisations, with the partial exception of the rail infrastructure company Railtrack. What can a change in ownership of British industry during this period, however, tell us about concentration of economic power? This question is less straightforward than some of the others that will be discussed in this book, although some of the privatised markets have quantitative measurements of monopoly and market power that will be considered in the next chapter. Certainly, the privatisation programme reduced the overall number of monopolies in the British economy during 1979–2007, and individual shareholders also increased. There are question marks over the process, however, whereby privatisation actually concentrated wealth in the hands of a select number of shareholders, and state-owned enterprises, by being detached from government, became less democratically accountable. The new system allowed politicians to retreat behind the ownership issue when problems emerged. To use one egregious example of recent years, Conservative Secretary of State for Transport Chris Grayling, despite being the target of much of the public anger over the issue,[31] attempted to blame the numerous problems with Britain's trains on the "rail industry",[32] Network Rail[33] and "militant unions".[34] Grayling's approach was a recipe for inaction but indicative of the convoluted ownership structure put in place by successive governments.

Financial services and the City of London

One of the key trends of the 1979–2007 period was the shift towards a more service-orientated economy, in particular the rise of finance. A number of wider factors were at play here, most significantly the acceleration of globalisation and technological innovation. US President Richard Nixon's decision to close the 'dollar–gold' window in August 1971, thereby bringing the curtain down on the Bretton Woods 'system',[35] certainly had a profound impact on the global economy, forcing Germany and its EEC partners to start the long quest for monetary stability that led to the European single currency. This caused a mushrooming of finance, which was now decoupled from fixed exchange rates backed by gold.[36] Other economic historians, such as Helen Thompson, posit the Eurodollar and Eurobond innovations of the late 1950s and early 1960s—allowing the creation of dollars and their subsequent trading outside the purview of the US Federal

Reserve—as a gradual catalyst for capital to seek ever more deregulated havens, a situation pioneered in London.[37] This in turn would cause governments to increase financial incentivisation.

Against this backdrop, we can see the Thatcher government and its successors as reacting to external trends as much as trailblazing wild west capitalism. In terms of actual policies, however, the ending of exchange controls in 1979 was significant for Britain in particular, ending a long period of caution towards capital flows, while the October 1986 'Big Bang' had greater ramifications for international finance, which then started to make London its home.[38] Big Bang entailed a liberalisation of roles in the City of London, ending the separation of 'jobbers' and 'brokers' (or market makers and stockbrokers), as well as lifting the rules on foreign ownership.[39] The reform proved a huge success for the Thatcher government and a fillip for the British economy. There are various statistics that can demonstrate the growth of UK financial services during this period. For instance, between 1984 and 1990, an estimated 84,000 jobs were added in London's financial services sector, and employment in the industry as a whole in the wider South East region grew by 88% during the 1980s.[40] Trading activity in stock and shares also ballooned; a year after Big Bang, customer trade in UK shares had almost doubled, and stock prices rose by almost 50% in the first half of 1987.[41]

UK government data have shown how, from the 1990s, the financial services sector has contributed 5.5–6.5% of GDP to the British economy, then rising under the Blair government to around 8%.[42] The figures demonstrate how reliance on finance grew during this period, particularly as globalisation accelerated, including under the centre-left New Labour government. Clearly, services in South East England have generated a significant amount of UK GDP, and, by the turn of the century, financial services in particular accounted for about a quarter of corporation tax receipts.[43] The country as a whole, buoyed by finance as well as the decline of heavy industry and manufacturing, has seen an increase in services as a proportion of the economy. Services accounted for 60% of the total in 1979, 65% in 1986 before Big Bang, 69% in 1990, 74% in 2000 and 78% in 2007.[44]

So successful did the liberalisation of the City prove that subsequent governments have been loath to criticise or penalise the sector. In fact, the government worked to bolster banking and finance—for instance, in the expansion of Canary Wharf. The London Docklands area was in long-term decline when the Thatcher government came to power in 1979 but was earmarked for one of Chancellor of the Exchequer Geoffrey Howe's signature policy proposals: enterprise zones.[45] The zones would be exempt from certain planning regulations and receive tax incentives. It was in conjunction with a scheme led by Secretary of State for the Environment Michael Heseltine, to set up urban development corporations, that the Docklands area became revitalised. The corporation cleared parts of the area and subsequently built infrastructure such as the Docklands Light Railway. This combination of deregulation and state assistance transformed the area, turning it into a hub of global finance.[46] The flagship section of the Canary Wharf development, One Canada Square, began construction in 1988 and was opened in 1991.[47]

Financial services in the London Docklands went from strength to strength in the Major and Blair eras, and the sector as a whole occupied a crucial position in the UK economy.

John Major initially oversaw a revival in the Conservative government's fortunes after he took office in 1990. Despite a recession, high interest rates and inflation, Major beat the odds to win the 1992 election in what proved a crushing disappointment for Labour—then led by Neil Kinnock, who had gradually won a long struggle against far-left elements in the party—and the catalyst for a group of young modernisers such as Gordon Brown, Tony Blair and Peter Mandelson to seize the party's agenda. The job of opposition became somewhat more straightforward, however, during the 1992–97 Parliament. Major's government struggled to pass the Maastricht legislation that transformed the EEC into the EU, opening up a wound that festered within the party until, and beyond, the 2016 Brexit referendum. Crucially, however, Major's government lost its reputation for economic competence during the 'Black Wednesday' debacle in September 1992, when sterling came under pressure from investors who forecast, correctly, that Britain's currency would need to be devalued. The Treasury used £3.3 billion of reserves in an attempt to keep sterling within its ERM limits, while Chancellor of the Exchequer Norman Lamont increased interest rates from 10% to 12% and then 15%, desperately trying to deter traders from selling pounds.[48] It was to no avail; Britain suspended, permanently as it transpired, its membership of the ERM. The seeds of deep animosity towards European integrationist projects were sown, particularly for those on the right. The Major government was humiliated and never recovered, losing in a 1997 landslide to Tony Blair, who had become leader after John Smith died in 1994.

There are other points to consider, however, in the demise of the Conservatives during the 1992–97 Parliament. With a devalued currency, British exports picked up during the 1990s. Mainly under the stewardship of Lamont's successor as Chancellor of the Exchequer, Ken Clarke, alongside the Bank of England's 'inflation targeting' strategy, Britain began a period of unprecedented economic growth—lasting until the 2008 financial crisis—one for which the Conservatives would gain virtually no credit. By the mid-1990s, the British economy was registering consistently impressive growth figures.[49] This was fuelled by the boom in services, particularly banking and finance, during a period of growing global trade set against the geopolitical backdrop of a 'peace dividend'—that is to say, reduced military spending and international tensions after the end of the Cold War. Ken Clarke described the economic climate of the era as "extremely benign" and said in his memoirs that, after Black Wednesday, the British economic recovery had almost been taken for granted by the public:

> By the time we got to the general election of 1997, the economy was the only subject upon which the government was miles ahead in the opinion polls. Unfortunately, the political world was obsessed with other issues, mainly divisions over Europe and scandals within the Conservative Party.[50]

New Labour, however, worked tirelessly to present itself as a safe pair of hands on the economy, as well as not deviating drastically from the status quo, including cultivating the City. If the party's left-wing supporters and members thought that the Blair government would repeal the Thatcher programme, they would be proven mistaken. New Labour moderated the economic approach it inherited, adapting it to social democratic, rather than socialist, goals. As Carstensen and Matthijs set out in a 2018 article, New Labour, rather than replacing what they describe as Thatcherite neoliberalism, during the Blair and Brown governments "bridged" the gap between the Thatcherite approach and its progressive objectives by bringing "social democratic elements into a broadening neoliberal tent".[51] We can observe this in New Labour's lack of appetite to roll back Conservative trade union legislation or privatisation—with the exception of Railtrack—and in how it extended a number of social reforms, such as the NHS 'internal market' and the choice in schools agenda. However, Gordon Brown used his 10 years as Chancellor—without increasing the top rates of income tax—to introduce Britain's first national minimum wage and a complex web of welfare interventions to alleviate poverty, such as working tax credits. In some respects, this approach was better described as social democratic or even in keeping with the tradition of European Christian democracy, in so far as the government was focused on ensuring, to use Brown's favourite term, "prudent" economic growth to guarantee state revenues could pay for redistribution and other social goals.[52] To paraphrase post-war German Finance Minister and then Chancellor Ludwig Erhard, a well-known Ordoliberal, "the cake must get larger" before you can divide it up through redistribution.[53] As part of New Labour's strategy, therefore, a thriving financial services sector could bring in revenues and provide jobs.

New Labour politicians were keen to have good relations with City firms and powerbrokers. Gordon Brown did establish a new regulatory regime, the Financial Services Authority (FSA), alongside giving the Bank of England operational independence in 1997. The watchword for regulation during this period, however, was 'light touch'.[54] Brown's advisor, Ed Balls, later an MP and City minister, also made statements about the success of Labour's approach.[55] Over the course of its time in office, New Labour gained a reputation for being too close to the financial services sector, insinuating that tougher regulation between 1997 and 2008 could have attenuated the worst effects of the financial crash. Balls disputes this in his memoirs, saying that Brown "had never been a great fan of banks".[56] Although recognising that the period is seen as too lightly regulated, and supporting the light touch approach in office,[57] Balls said that the "reality was that the financial services industry saw the establishment of the FSA as being a toughening of banking regulation", also pointing to a Tony Blair speech from 2005, where the prime minister—not very presciently—called for relaxation of some rules, criticising the FSA as "hugely inhibiting of efficient business by perfectly respectable companies that have never defrauded anyone".[58]

Gordon Brown outlined how he had a battle with Bank of England Governor Eddie George when setting up the FSA, initially proposing complete independence from the bank, but having his efforts watered down, with the bank keeping some powers.[59] Brown said his "tripartite system" (the Bank of England, FSA and government) was a "compromise, it was far less definitive on who did what than it should have been. It was an unhappy start for what proved to be a strained set of relationships".[60] Far from the laissez-faire attitude that has been levelled at New Labour towards financial services, the Chancellor and his close advisor set out that, although their system of regulation was intended to be tougher, it came up against politics. Characteristically, given their long-running rivalry and at times internecine warfare, Brown goes much further in his criticism of Blair's 2005 speech:

> Only a few days after the election, again out of the blue, Tony redefined the whole basis of our approach ... he called for massive deregulation and a bonfire of controls. He appeared to be defending a financial sector 'free-for-all' and denounced the City's regulatory body ... His timing, only two years away from the biggest meltdown in modern financial history, was unfortunate to say the least. [the speech] could be seen in retrospect as a defence of the City's 'non-cooperation culture' when it came to proper supervision.[61]

In this way, Blairites, or the more centrist—or right wing to use the party's parlance—Labour politicians, are lambasted as being soft on the city rather than the more responsible Brownites. Both Balls and Brown were writing after the financial crisis had sunk the New Labour government and their party's own economic credibility and electoral chances.[62] During the period, Thatcherite economic liberals—such as Nigel Lawson, in 2006—were calling for less regulation, setting out how Big Bang had been too bureaucratic and implying the City was too tightly controlled.[63] Other likeminded intellectuals later set out how the 2007–08 crash was caused, and made worse, by excessive government rules and perverse incentives.[64] That the combined approach of Brown, Blair, Balls and other New Labour politicians might have represented a moderate financial services regulatory path between 1997 and 2008 was lost among the financial meltdown and the recriminations that lasted several years. It has been impossible for the Blair and Brown governments to shake the criticism that they were too relaxed towards the practices of the financial sector.

The steep trajectory of global finance and its place in the British economy dovetails this book. One of the Thatcher government's first significant moves was to abolish exchange controls, exposing the UK to the winds of external forces and, in some respects, importing instability—capital inflows buttressed sterling and accelerated the process of factory closures and bankruptcies—but also providing a shot in the arm to the City of London, where international finance started to congregate once more. The UK finance sector was further internationalised and stimulated by the 1986 Big Bang, while the nearby Docklands area also became a finance hub thanks to a combination of the Conservatives' enterprise zones concept and the development corporation that put in place necessary infrastructure. Both the Major and Blair governments rode the waves of finance-led globalisation in the 1990s and 2000s, seeing ever greater employment numbers and tax receipts generated by this growth. The tumult of 2007–08, however, proved to be the end of an era. Shortly after Tony Blair stepped down as prime minister, to be succeeded by Gordon Brown, the world's banking sector started to wobble as a speculative bubble long in the making—supported by helpful central banks— prepared to burst. This it did, in September 2008, with the collapse of Lehman Brothers investment bank. The immediate cause was 'securitised' debt packages such as 'subprime mortgages' in the US. Mortgage defaults spread through the globalised finance system, uncovering a trail of repackaged 'toxic' debt previously sold as investment-grade products.

The post-mortem of the 2008 crash was protracted, and blame spread far and wide. Although the catalyst was in the form of mortgages in the US, the City of London and UK financial sector as a whole came under scrutiny and severe criticism. This was partly because some of the most vulnerable and overleveraged banks were in the UK—most notoriously the Royal Bank of Scotland—but also because the City was a lodestar for the global financial sector. Its practices, remunerations, hubris and, ultimately, incompetence were indicative of what was a global crash. In the eyes of the general public, when the music stopped in September 2008, the British government, alongside its counterparts elsewhere, 'bailed out' the banks to the tune of billions of pounds, pouring money on to their balance sheets in order to keep cash flowing amid a 'credit crunch' and looming depression.[65] Central banks subsequently began a massive programme of quantitative easing, or helicopter money, to reflate the economy. All this caused sovereign debt to skyrocket and leave governments facing painful austerity measures into the 2010s and a long-lasting stagnation in the real economy. The financial sector, meanwhile, after a short pause, continued to boom, despite (unheeded) calls to cap bankers' bonuses[66] and intermittent attempts to impose stricter rules on the sector, such as the Basel III capital rules and the Dodd–Frank Act in the US.[67] A number of other key points, however, need to be considered regarding the crisis.

The first-hand accounts of Gordon Brown and his Chancellor of the Exchequer, Alistair Darling, appear to show that the process, at least for key bankers, moved through three phases. The first was denial that anything seriously was wrong during 2007–08,[68] the second was a stage of increasing concern over a lack of liquidity and capital,[69] and the third involved conceding the severity of the situation and accepting government bailouts.[70] The last was tarnished in the eyes of the politicians by the bankers insisting on maintaining lucrative personal financial arrangements; this was later seized upon by the British press and used to heavily criticise the Brown government. In the longer term, the response to the 2008 crash can be seen as prioritising the well-being of the banking and financial sector at the expense of those lower down the income ladder, who saw paltry rises in wages and living standards while post-2010 UK governments initiated cuts in public spending. The financial sector, meanwhile, has gone from strength to strength, a long stock market bull-run only being halted by the 2020 coronavirus crisis.[71] As the damage of the 2008 financial crisis fades into the distance, voters have nevertheless turned to populist parties and politicians, exemplified by the UK's 2016 referendum to leave the EU. The 'Leave' campaign was led by right-wing nationalists such as Boris Johnson and Nigel Farage and nominally liberal Conservatives such as Michael Gove, who proclaimed "people in this country have had enough of experts".[72] Whereas populists on the right tapped into widespread public grievances that the current economic system was not working for them, if not necessarily directly linking this with concentration in the finance sector, radical voices on the left such as Paul Mason had no such reservations. In his book *Postcapitalism*, Mason outlined how economies that historically have become increasingly dominated by "financial capitalism", are often heading for decline.[73] Whether those kinds of prediction come to pass remains to be seen, but certainly the argument seizes on the notion that power has been increasingly concentrated in finance, despite repeated crashes.

Having taken all this into account, what concentration trends can we see in the financial sector during the 1979–2007 period? As we have seen, the size of the financial and banking sector in the UK increased under the Thatcher, Major and Blair governments. This was partly owing to external forces in the global economy and partly down to government reforms such as Big Bang. By the early 2000s, it accounted for one in ten jobs in the country and, depending on the measurement, up to a quarter of the UK's tax income. Finance was the most lucrative of the growing number of service-based jobs generated during this period. But is the situation in the UK so different from its contemporaries? Manufacturing makes up a significant proportion of the German economy, known for its exports and *Mittelstand* of innovative tech-orientated small and medium-sized businesses. Then there are 'national champions', businesses that are specifically backed, boosted or created by the state. Airbus is one particular example that has received significant pan-EU support. On these terms, the concentration of finance within the British economy perhaps does not look as ominous. Yet, although finance often pays handsome salaries and bonuses, jobs are—in keeping with Thatcherism— not unionised, and the industry has helped increase inequality, even producing a runaway top 1%, 0.1% or 0.01% of wealth.[74] The sector also helped accelerate another, related trend in Britain between 1979 and 2007: the concentration of service jobs and their associated wealth in South East England.

Regional inequalities: London and the South East

During the Thatcher, Major and Blair governments, the wealth of South East England, and in particular London, has galloped away at the same time as other parts of the country have only modestly grown. In actual fact, the population of London was in decline from the Second World War until the 1980s, just as the City began to boom.[75] Over the modern period, however, the statistics paint a stark picture of the region's economic dominance.

During Thatcher's decade in power, the South East began to pick up as services jobs expanded, while manufacturing, which had been the mainstay of employment in many other areas of the country, dwindled. Between 1979 and 1993, an estimated 2.7 million jobs were lost in the manufacturing sector owing to high interest rates and the value of sterling, external trends such as overseas competition and the shifting structure of the world economy, as well as the sometimes gradual withdrawal of state support.[76] The new 'property-owning democracy' model was most enthusiastically taken up in the South East as a boom, some would say fetish, for home ownership took place. The impact of all this was to amplify the divide between South East England and the rest of the UK. The vast disparities continued until the end of Tony Blair's time in office.[77] Unemployment figures were consistently higher outside the South East,[78] property prices were higher,[79] and even public spending per person in areas such as transport were greater within the more affluent capital region.[80]

Political devolution itself will be discussed in a later chapter, but it is worth noting here how the trend towards economic concentration in the South East led to a particular approach by successive governments. The regional structure inherited by the Thatcher government in 1979 was one of various sectors, including heavy industry and manufacturing, spread out across the country. Central government provided significant subsidies and support for this arrangement. As part of the Thatcher government's departure from corporatism, it moved away from this regional policy and towards incentivising private enterprise, as well as shifting the focus towards more transferable, mobile skills.

Britain was, and is, one of the world's more centralised democracies. Central government had been involved in many areas of the economy before 1979. The Thatcher government in particular wanted to break the direct link between the state and regions by putting in place various incentives and providing the tools for the market, and society, to operate more 'efficiently'. Geoffrey Howe's enterprise zones idea was implemented in 1980, with the scheme initially being rolled out to 6 areas, followed by 23 more between 1981 and 1986 and particularly targeting those that were in post-industrial decline, such as Glasgow, Liverpool and the West Midlands.[81] In its initial design, the idea namechecked the likes of Singapore and Hong Kong as low-regulation trading hubs where entrepreneurs and businesses were relatively free from state oversight. British enterprise zones included relaxed building regulations and tax incentives. It has been a favourite Conservative policy, as shown by the David Cameron-led coalition government's adoption of new enterprise zones. Yet, outside the special case of the London Docklands, the evidence to show the efficacy of the zones is patchy.

Enterprise zones were intended to stimulate economic activity and create jobs and wealth. Instead of generating significant numbers of jobs and new businesses, however, the schemes may have simply moved them around, from outside to inside the zones. A study by the think-tank Centre for Cities claimed that enterprise zones were expensive and a poor use of government funds: "On average, one additional job in the EZs [enterprise zones] cost the public purse £26,000 (in 2010–11 prices), which was significantly more expensive than other policies of the time".[82]

Other critics have suggested that enterprise zones favoured larger, more mobile firms rather than smaller businesses and entrepreneurs, somewhat defeating one of the scheme's aims.[83] Perhaps the most general point was that, outside London, enterprise zones were a—not particularly successful—Thatcherite version of regional policy and government subsidisation.

If mobility was a key element in businesses moving to enterprise zones, it also proved crucial in exacerbating regional differences during the 1979–2007 period. Labour mobility was often touted as an important ingredient of the post-1979 economy. The Thatcher government and its successors prioritised home owner-ship, through initiatives such as Right to Buy, or council house sales, and tax breaks such as mortgage interest relief at source (MIRAS), which was only abol-ished by Gordon Brown in 2000.[84] Brown described the combination of perverse incentives on tax relief and housing that New Labour inherited in 1997: "It was entirely unfair to poorer families who rented their homes, and added to inflation by contributing to higher house prices—which in turn, led to higher mortgages, negating its benefits to homeowners."[85]

Although the process of buying and selling property in the UK can be rela-tively swift, prioritising home ownership hardly encouraged labour mobility. In addition, the rental housing market was not significantly reorganised, notwith-standing price deregulation in 1988, and received only piecemeal reform, such as the Blair government's 2004 Housing Act.[86] Biographers of Margaret Thatcher have noted the resistance to reform of the rental market.[87] Along with the rise of the peculiarly British Nimbyism[88] that saw resistance towards new house building in some areas, as well as the disempowering of local councils to build new social housing and housing stock in general,[89] this combination of factors had the effect of limiting regional mobility.[90]

For those who did want to embrace the ethos of the times, and even for those who did not, travelling further afield often required education and skills. The Thatcher government introduced training schemes such as the 1978–83 Youth Opportunities Programme, the 1983–89 Youth Training Scheme (YTS) and its successor Youth Training as alternatives to more traditional apprenticeships. Likewise, the various school reforms of the era essentially attempted to reverse, or at least dampen, the impact of the post-war comprehensive movement. From the late 1980s, the Thatcher government sought to simultaneously ensure uni-form standards in schools while initiating 'choice' by broadening the range of institutions, including technological colleges, available to parents, who now became 'consumers'.[91] This was one trend extended by New Labour as part of its academy programme. Universities, meanwhile, experienced a boom in the later stages of the 1979–2007 period as governments sought to bring ever greater numbers of students into the sector. Changes in higher education were driven by a two-pronged agenda, of student-orientated funding and greater choice. Student fees had been debated during the 1980s but actually introduced by the incoming Blair government, although it accepted the 'cost-sharing' recommen-dations of the Dearing Report commissioned by Major.[92] The vast expansion of universities took place under the Major government after the 1992 Further and Higher Education Act. The 1992 reforms removed the divide between tradi-tional universities and polytechnic colleges, granting the latter degree-awarding status.[93] Although university participation hovered around 15% for most of the

Thatcher years, it soared in the 1990s towards 40% and then, under New Labour, approached 50%.[94]

Whereas youth training schemes were criticised from various quarters—for their "inadequacy" and the difficulty of making businesses invest in transferable skills and even attracting young people in the first place—the success of the Major and Blair governments in getting more young people into university-level education is beyond doubt.[95] Tony Blair's goal was "50% of young adults progressing to higher education by 2010",[96] a figure reached in 2019.[97] The increasing rate of university participation appears to have accelerated some of the trends mentioned above. University graduates have moved into service-based sectors in larger cities, adding to the north–south divide as well as dislocation between urban centres and towns and the countryside. Although lasting well beyond the end of the New Labour period, the changes set in motion over the previous decades appear to have played a crucial role in the vote to leave the EU in 2016. The sense that power and wealth were concentrated in London, the South East and a number of other large cities played into the grievances against the 'establishment' and policymakers more generally.[98] Data from the 2016 referendum illustrate how Remain-voting areas were concentrated in London and other metropolitan areas and university towns, as well as Scotland.[99] There was also a strong correlation between university education and voting Remain, whereas the proportion of those who voted Leave increased in areas with lower numbers of graduates.[100] This aligns Euroscepticism and the Leave campaign with populism, a charge not explored in detail here.[101] Nevertheless, the Thatcher, Major and Blair governments presided over changes to regional economies that were exacerbated by a 'brain drain' of an increasing number of university graduates moving to larger cities with the hope of finding better paid jobs in the burgeoning services sector.

Conclusion

This chapter has examined the changes in ownership in the British economy since 1979, the trend towards services at the expense of manufacturing and heavy industry, the rise of finance, particularly in the City of London, and a shifting approach towards skills and higher education. Many of the trends explored in this chapter have been driven by, or initiated in response to, globalisation. Britain's response to the explosion of international finance has been to try and lead and profit from it, exemplified by the 1986 financial deregulation of Big Bang. The globalised economy has impelled British governments to try and compete by focusing on services, including for export, rather than the more national economy that existed in the 1970s.

In particular, this chapter has looked at financial services, a sector the British economy has increasingly relied on for tax revenues after exchange controls were removed in 1979 and, in particular, Big Bang. Financial services have been treated almost like a bloc in this analysis, which has viewed how power has accumulated in the sector and, as a result, meant that British governments have been unwilling to overly regulate the industry. Despite the widespread condemnation of banking and finance after the 2008 financial crisis, while the sector occupies such a significant portion of the country's economy, British governments are essentially locked in a Gordian knot with the bankers.

Likewise, Britain has invested in skills and especially higher education as a means of supplying skilled labour to do better-paid jobs in the economy. As well as the external changes taking place owing to globalisation, many of these shifts were a result of government choices and decision-making. The Thatcher government's approach to monetary policy, leading to high interest rates in the early 1980s, as well as its relaxation of capital controls, had the effect of hollowing out British industry and accelerating the shift towards the service economy. This aligned with the longer-term Thatcherite policy agenda but has been essentially maintained by successive governments. The governments of both Major and Blair sought to regulate the financial sector lightly and keep the city booming to contribute ever higher tax receipts. The incentivisation of home ownership at the expense of the rental market has led to regional inertia for many, and the push for greater university participation, actively sought by the Major and Blair governments, has led to profound changes in regional mobility and comparative opportunity and wealth. Taken as a whole, we can see a number of events and trends that have led to changing economic concentration in industry and location.

Notes

1 Margaret Thatcher Foundation (hereafter MTF), MTF 104210, "TV Interview for London Weekend Television Weekend World", 6 January 1980.
2 MTF 108353, Margaret Thatcher, "Keith Joseph Memorial Lecture ('Liberty and Limited Government')", 11 January 1996.
3 Noel W. Thompson, *Political Economy and the Labour Party: The Economics of Democratic Socialism, 1884–2005* (Abingdon: Routledge, 2006), 193.
4 Kathleen Burk, *The First Privatization. The Politicians, the City, and the Denationalization of Steel* (London: The Historians' Press, 1988), 140.
5 Charles Moore, *Margaret Thatcher. The Authorized Biography. Volume One: Not for Turning* (London: Allen Lane, 2013), 508–509, 538–540.
6 See: Robert Ledger, *Neoliberal Thought and Thatcherism: "A Transition from Here to There?"* (Abingdon: Routledge, 2017), 88–101.
7 C.G. Hanson, *Taming the Trade Unions. A Guide to the Thatcher Government's Employment Reforms, 1980–90* (Basingstoke: Macmillan, 1991), 74.
8 Nigel Lawson, *The View from No.11* (London: Corgi Books, 1993), 239–240.
9 See: Ledger, *Neoliberal Thought*, 102–116.
10 Ibid.
11 Conservative General Election Manifesto 1983, MTF 110859.
12 Ibid.
13 Nikolaos Zahariadis, "The Rise and Fall of British State Ownership: Political Pressure or Economic Reality?", *Comparative Politics*, 31:4 (1999), 445–63, 460.
14 Colin Robinson, *Competition in Electricity? The Government's Proposals for Privatizing Electricity Supply* (London: IEA, 1988), 7, 18.
15 BBC, "What Has Happened to Energy Since Privatisation?", 16 May 2019, www.bbc.com/news/business-48284802 [accessed 10 March 2020]; David Parker, *The Official History of Privatization. Volume 1: The Formative Years 1970–87* (London: Routledge, 2009), 325.
16 Cecil Parkinson, *Right at the Centre* (London: Weidenfeld and Nicolson, 1992), 260.

17   Ofgem, "State of the Energy Market 2019", 3 October 2019, www.ofgem.gov.u k/publications-and-updates/state-energy-market-2019 [accessed 10 March 2020]; Sylvia Pfeifer, "UK Energy 'Challengers' Face Tough Times", *Financial Times*, 11 February 2018, www.ft.com/content/bbee8de6-0ce5-11e8-839d-41ca06376bf2 [accessed 10 March 2020].

18   John Campbell, *Margaret Thatcher Volume Two: The Iron Lady* (London: Vintage, 2008), 207–252.

19   Geoffrey Howe, *Conflict of Loyalty* (Basingstoke: MacMillan, 1994), 460.

20   George Eaton, "The Conservatives Are in Crisis because 'Popular Capitalism' is no Longer Possible", *New Statesman*, 30 May 2018, www.newstatesman.com/politics/ economy/2018/05/conservatives-are-crisis-because-popular-capitalism-no-longer-po ssible [accessed 10 March 2020].

21   Lawson, *View*, 238.

22   Jeffrey Sachs, *Poland's Jump to the Market Economy* (Cambridge: MIT Press, 1994), 84.

23   Robert Saunders, "Thatcherism and the Seventies", eds. Ben Jackson, and Robert Saunders, *Making Thatcher's Britain* (Cambridge: Cambridge University Press, 2012, 25–42), 41.

24   Thatcher is alleged to have said, "Rail privatisation will be the Waterloo of this gov- ernment. Never mention the railways to me again". In: Christian Wolmar, "Transport Policy", eds. Kevin Hickson and Ben Williams, *John Major: An Unsuccessful Prime Minister? Reappraising John Major* (London: Biteback, 2017, 181–196), 182.

25   Richard Seymour, "A Short History of Privatisation in the UK: 1979–2012", *The Guardian*, 29 March 2012, www.theguardian.com/commentisfree/2012/mar/29/short -history-of-privatisation [accessed 6 March 2020].

26   David Denver, "From Hegemony to Ignominy: Elections and Public Opinion under John Major", eds. Kevin Hickson and Ben Williams, *John Major: An Unsuccessful Prime Minister? Reappraising John Major* (London: Biteback, 2017, 3–20), 15.

27   Robert Jupe, "Public (Interest) or Private (Gain)? The Curious Case of Network Rail's Status", *Journal of Law and Society*, 34:2 (2007), 244–265, 245; Warwick Funnell, Robert Jupe and Jane Andrew, *In Government We Trust. Market Failure and the Delusions of Privatization* (London: Pluto Press, 2009), 148–150.

28   The Guardian, "The Guardian View on Rail Privatisation: Going Off the Tracks", 5 December 2017, www.theguardian.com/commentisfree/2017/dec/05/the-guardian -view-on-rail-privatisation-going-off-the-tracks [accessed 12 March 2020].

29   BBC Radio 4, "The Briefing Room: Is It Time to Renationalise the Railways?", 16 February 2017, www.bbc.co.uk/programmes/b08dmkl6 [accessed 12 March 2020].

30   Gywn Topham, "Completion of London's Thameslink Rail Project Delayed Until December 2019", *The Guardian*, 23 November 2017, www.theguardian.com/uk -news/2017/nov/23/thameslink-rail-completion-delayed-london-december-2019 [accessed 12 March 2020].

31   Jim Pickard, "Chris Grayling Takes Flak for Southern Rail Strikes", *Financial Times*, 13 December 2016, www.ft.com/content/8495a28a-c132-11e6-9bca-2b93a6856354 [accessed 12 March 2020].

32   *BBC News*, "Chris Grayling Says Rail Industry 'Has Failed Passengers'", 30 May 2018, www.bbc.com/news/uk-england-44299902 [accessed 12 March 2020].

33   Josh Spero, "Chris Grayling Blames Network Rail for Timetable Chaos", *Financial Times*, 23 May 2018, www.ft.com/content/63eed0d8-5ea7-11e8-9334-2218e7146b04 [accessed 12 March 2020].

34   Rowena Mason and Rajeev Syal, "Chris Grayling Criticised for Blaming Rail Delays on 'Militant Unions'", *The Guardian*, 10 January 2018, www.theguardian.com/polit ics/2018/jan/10/chris-grayling-criticised-for-blaming-rail-delays-on-militant-unions [accessed 12 March 2020].

35 For an extended account of Nixon's rationale behind the move and the European response, see Luke A. Nichter, *Richard Nixon and Europe: The Reshaping of the Postwar Atlantic World* (Cambridge: Cambridge University Press, 2015), 36–67.

36 Servaas Storm, "Financialization and Economic Development: A Debate on the Social Efficiency of Modern Finance", *Development and Change*, 49:2 (March 2018), 302–329, 304.

37 Helen Thompson, "How the City of London Lost at Brexit: A Historical Perspective", *Economy and Society*, 46:2 (2017), 211–228, 215; Talking Politics, "Moneyland", 26 September 2018, www.talkingpoliticspodcast.com/blog/2018/117-moneyland [accessed 7 July 2020].

38 Ledger, *Neoliberal Thought*, 76–87.

39 Ibid., 81–82.

40 John Allen, Doreen Massey and Allan Cochrane (with Julie Charlesworth, Gill Court, Nick Henry, Phil Sarre), *Rethinking the Region: Spaces of Neo-Liberalism* (Abingdon: Routledge, 1998), 19.

41 Virginia Preston, "'Big Bang': Chronology of Events", *Contemporary British History*, 13:1 (1999), 95–99, 99.

42 Chris Rhodes, "Financial Services: Contribution to the UK Economy", House of Commons Briefing Paper, 6193, 31 July 2019, https://commonslibrary.parliament.uk /research-briefings/sn06193/ [accessed 16 March 2020].

43 Alistair Darling, *Back from the Brink. 1,000 Days at Number 11* (London: Atlantic Books, 2012), 100.

44 Office for National Statistics, "Changes in the Economy Since the 1970s", 2 September 2019, www.ons.gov.uk/economy/economicoutputandproductivity/output/articles/c hangesintheeconomysincethe1970s/2019-09-02 [accessed 16 March 2020].

45 See: Ledger, *Neoliberal Thought*, 64–75.

46 Sue Brownill and Glen O'Hara, "From Planning to Opportunism? Re-examining the Creation of the London Docklands Development Corporation", *Planning Perspectives*, 30:4 (2015), 537–570.

47 Julia Kollewe, "Canary Wharf Timeline: From the Thatcher Years to Qatari Control", *The Guardian*, 28 January 2015, www.theguardian.com/business/2015/jan/28/canary -wharf-timeline-london-building-docklands-thatcher [accessed 16 March 2020].

48 Matthew Tempest, "Treasury Papers Reveal Cost of Black Wednesday", *The Guardian*, 9 February 2005, www.theguardian.com/politics/2005/feb/09/freedomof information.uk1 [accessed 17 March 2020].

49 Roger Blitz, "Brexit, Black Wednesday and Lessons in Trading the Pound", *Financial Times*, 15 September 2017, www.ft.com/content/7f68b50a-9a16-11e7-b83c-9588e51 488a0 [accessed 17 March 2020].

50 Ken Clarke, *Kind of Blue: A Political Memoir* (Basingstoke: Macmillan, 2016), 345.

51 Martin B. Carstensen and Matthias Matthijs, "Of Paradigms and Power: British Economic Policy Making Since Thatcher", *Governance*, 31:3 (July 2018), 431–447.

52 Jon Davis and John Rentoul, *Heroes or Villains? The Blair Government Reconsidered* (Oxford: Oxford University Press, 2019), 179.

53 Ludwig Erhard, *Prosperity Through Competition* (New York: Frederick A. Praeger, translated by Edith Temple Roberts and John B. Wood, 1958), 163.

54 Gordon Brown, "Mansion House Speech", 22 June 2006, *The Guardian*, www.thegua rdian.com/business/2006/jun/22/politics.economicpolicy [accessed 27 February 2020].

55 *BBC News*, "Ed Balls 'Deeply Sorry' over Banking Crisis", 12 September 2011, www .bbc.com/news/uk-politics-14888933 [accessed 18 March 2020].

56 Ed Balls, *Speaking Out* (London: Arrow Books, 2016), 300.

57 Jill Treanor, "Balls Intervenes on LSE to Remove Fears of a US Takeover", *The Guardian*, 14 September 2006, www.theguardian.com/business/2006/sep/14/politics. economicpolicy [accessed 18 March 2020].

58 Balls, *Speaking Out*, 302–303; Tony Blair, "Full Text: Tony Blair's Speech on Compensation Culture", *The Guardian*, 26 May 2005, www.theguardian.com/politics /2005/may/26/speeches.media [accessed 18 March 2020].
59 Gordon Brown, *My Life, Our Times* (London, Bodley Head, 2017), 120–121.
60 Ibid., 121.
61 Ibid., 188–189.
62 *BBC News*, "Ed Balls 'Deeply Sorry'".
63 Nigel Lawson, "Foreword", *Big Bang 20 Years On. New Challenges Facing the Financial Services Sector. Collected Essays* (London: CPS, 2006, i–v), iv.
64 Philip Booth, "More Regulation, Less Regulation or Better Regulation?", ed. Philip Booth, *Verdict on the Crash. Causes and Policy Implications* (London: IEA, 2009, 157–170), 169.
65 Reuters stated the figure as £137 billion in 2016. Andrew MacAskill and Lawrence White, "British Taxpayers Face 27 Billion Pound Loss from Bank Bailout", *Reuters*, 23 November 2016, https://uk.reuters.com/article/uk-britain-eu-budget-banks/br itish-taxpayers-face-27-billion-pound-loss-from-bank-bailout-idUKKBN13I1FJ [accessed 8 July 2020].
66 Andrew Rawnsley, *The End of the Party: The Rise and Fall of New Labour* (London: Penguin, 2010), 607–611.
67 Archives of the Obama White House, "Wall Street Reform: The Dodd–Frank Act", https://obamawhitehouse.archives.gov/economy/middle-class/dodd-frank-wall-street -reform [accessed 23 March 2020].
68 Brown, *My Life*, 309–310.
69 Darling, *Back from the Brink*, 61–62.
70 Ibid., 172–173.
71 Graeme Wearden, "Wall Street and FTSE 100 Suffer Worst Week Since 2008—As It Happened", *The Guardian*, 28 February 2020, www.theguardian.com/business/live/2020 /feb/28/british-airways-easyjet-coronavirus-stock-markets-ftse-dow-global-recession -business-live [accessed 24 March 2020]; Robin Wigglesworth, "US Stocks' Record Bull Run Brought to Abrupt End by Coronavirus", *Financial Times*, 12 March 2020, www.ft .com/content/6b987f46-644f-11ea-b3f3-fe4680ea68b5 [accessed 24 March 2020].
72 Henry Mance, "Britain Has Had Enough of Experts, Says Gove", *Financial Times*, 3 June 2016, www.ft.com/content/3be49734-29cb-11e6-83e4-abc22d5d108c [accessed 23 March 2020].
73 Mason notes "the decline of all economic superpowers begins with a spectacular turn to finance" and quotes historian Fernand Braudel. Paul Mason, *Postcapitalism: A Guide to Our Future* (London: Allen Lane, 2015), 19; Fernand Braudel, *Civilization and Capitalism, 15th–18th Century: The Perspective of the World* (Los Angeles: University of California Press, 1992), 246.
74 Jonathan Aldred, "The Long Read: Socialism for the Rich': The Evils of Bad Economics", *The Guardian*, 6 June 2019, www.theguardian.com/inequality/2019/jun/ 06/socialism-for-the-rich-the-evils-of-bad-economics [accessed 24 March 2020]; *The Economist*, "The Rich v the Rest: A Rare Peep at the Finances of Britain's 0.01%", 29 June 2019, www.economist.com/britain/2019/06/29/a-rare-peep-at-the-finances- of-britains-001 [accessed 24 March 2020]; Aditya Chakrabortty, "The Super-Rich Have Made Britain into a Nation of Losers", *The Guardian*, 6 August 2019, www .theguardian.com/commentisfree/2019/aug/06/britain-super-rich-wealthy [accessed 24 March 2020].
75 Census data show London's population steadily declined from 1939 to 1981, par- ticularly the Inner London population. The trend reversed in 1991, and, by 2015, the figure had exceeded the 8.6 million recorded at the start of the Second World War. In: Office of National Statistics, "Historical Census Population", https://data.london.gov .uk/dataset/historic-census-population [accessed 25 March 2020].

76 Julian Coman, "Margaret Thatcher: 20 Ways that She Changed Britain", *The Guardian*, 14 April 2013, www.theguardian.com/politics/2013/apr/14/margaret-thatc her-20-changes-britain [accessed 25 March 2020].

77 John Carvel, "North–South, East–West Wealth Divides in Survey", *The Guardian*, 10 November 2005, www.theguardian.com/money/2005/nov/10/northsouthdivide. uknews [accessed 25 March 2020].

78 Andrew Powell, "Labour Market Statistics: UK Regions and Countries", House of Commons Briefing Paper (No. 7950, 9 March 2020), 21.

79 Donna Ferguson, "Twenty Years On—The Winners and Losers of Britain's Property Boom", *The Guardian*, 23 January 2016, www.theguardian.com/money/2016/jan/23 /britain-property-boom-losers-winners-housing-market-renting [accessed 25 March 2020].

80 Luke Raikes and Rosie Lockwood, "Revealed: North Set to Receive £2,389 Less per Person than London on Transport", *IPPR*, 19 August 2019, www.ippr.org/news -and-media/press-releases/revealed-north-set-to-receive-2-389-less-per-person-than-london-on-transport [accessed 25 March 2020].

81 Sir Geoffrey Howe, *Enterprise Zones and the Enterprise Culture* (London: Bow Group, 1988), 17.

82 Dmitry Sivaev, "Enterprise Zones: The Forgotten Legacy of Lady Thatcher", *Centre for Cities*, 22 April 2013, www.centreforcities.org/blog/enterprise-zones-the-forgo tten-legacy-of-lady-thatcher/ [accessed 26 March 2020].

83 S.M. Butler, *Enterprise Zones. Greenlining the Inner Cities* (London: Heinemann, 1982), 127.

84 Brown, *My Life*, 143–144.

85 Ibid.

86 Nigel Keohane and Nida Broughton, "The Politics of Housing", Hot House (Social Market Foundation, and National Housing Federation, 2018), www.smf.co.uk/wp-con tent/uploads/2013/11/Publication-The-Politics-of-Housing.pdf [accessed 27 March 2013].

87 Robin Harris, *Not for Turning. The Life of Margaret Thatcher* (London: Bantam Press, 2013), 245.

88 NIMBY is derived from 'not in my back yard'.

89 Campbell, *Iron Lady*, 174.

90 Richard Vinen, *Thatcher's Britain. The Politics and Social Upheaval of the 1980s* (London: Simon & Schuster, 2009), 201.

91 Charles Moore, *Margaret Thatcher: The Authorized Biography, Volume Three: Herself Alone* (London: Allen Lane, 2019), 70.

92 Sonia Exley, "Education Policy", eds. Kevin Hickson and Ben Williams, *John Major: An Unsuccessful Prime Minister? Reappraising John Major* (London: Biteback, 2017, 231–247), 244.

93 Ibid.

94 Susan Lee Robertson, "Globalising UK Higher Education", *Globalisation Societies and Education*, 8:2 (2012), 191–203.

95 David Raffe, Andy Biggart, Joan Fairgrieve, Cathy Howieson, John Rodger and Stephen Burniston, "Thematic Review of the Transition from Initial Education to Working Life" (OECD, July 1998), 38, www.oecd.org/unitedkingdom/1908270.pdf [accessed 27 March 2020].

96 Tony Blair, "Full Text of Tony Blair's Speech on Education", *The Guardian*, 23 May 2001, www.theguardian.com/politics/2001/may/23/labour.tonyblair [accessed 30 March 2020].

97 Sean Coughlan, "The Symbolic Target of 50% at University Reached", *BBC News*, 26 September 2019, www.bbc.com/news/education-49841620 [accessed 30 March 2020].

98 Sara B. Hobolt, "The Brexit Vote: A Divided Nation, a Divided Continent", *Journal of European Public Policy*, 23:9 (2016), 1259–1277.

99 *BBC News*, "EU Referendum: The Result in Maps and Charts", 24 June 2016, www .bbc.com/news/uk-politics-36616028 [accessed 30 March 2020].

100 Martin Rosenbaum, "Local Voting Figures Shed New Light on EU Referendum", *BBC News*, 6 February 2017, www.bbc.com/news/uk-politics-38762034 [accessed 30 March 2020].

101 See: Evgeniia Iakhnis, Brian Rathbun, Jason Reifler and Thomas J. Scotto, "Populist Referendum: Was 'Brexit' an Expression of Nativist and Anti-Elitist Sentiment?", *Research & Politics* (April 2018), https://journals.sagepub.com/doi/10.1177/20531 68018773964 [accessed 30 March 2020].

4 Concentration and regulation

This chapter will focus on the role of government and regulators in fostering competition in markets, a key concern of the early neoliberals and one of the subjects alluded to in the title of this study. The government's competition watchdogs will be examined during the 1979–2007 period. Although, over the longer term, economic concentration has increased, regulation of economic competition has gone through waves of activism, and, therefore, a simple narrative that concentration increased during a 'neoliberal era', that New Labour was ideologically similar to Thatcherism and that regulators quiesce to market power and vested interests is insufficient.

As we saw in previous chapters, a system of economic competition and enforcement was established in Britain after the Second World War. Both Labour and Conservative governments essentially built upon previous legislation, with the focus differing slightly between restrictive practices and the impact on the consumer, as well as concern about mergers. By the time Margaret Thatcher came to office in 1979, competition was monitored by the Monopolies and Mergers Commission (MMC) and the Office of Fair Trading (OFT). One of the key elements of the British system, however, was that launching an investigation into a particular merger or practice required a 'reference' from the Secretary of State; in the late 1970s, this meant at the Department of Trade and Industry (DTI) and, prior to that, the Board of Trade. The system continued during the Thatcher and Major governments, which meant the discretionary element of competition policy left politicians open to criticism, particularly in the highest-profile cases.

Thatcherism and competition

The incoming Thatcher government inherited, as we have seen, a so-called corporatist system of economic organisation involving coordination between government, business and trade unions. This was in acute crisis during the 1970s, first during the coal-mining strikes of 1972–74 and then the widespread stoppages during the 1978–79 'Winter of Discontent'. By the late 1970s, amid a worsening economic picture, the OFT was mainly focused on supervising price controls rather than investigating mergers and competition.[1]

The 1980 Competition Act abolished the Price Commission, which had been set up in 1973, and extended the powers of the MMC and OFT.[2] The 1979 Conservative election manifesto, and a number of Tory MPs, supported the promotion of competition through the MMC and OFT.[3] Although then-Secretary of State at the DTI Norman Tebbit did formulate rules for controlling mergers in 1984, these were still essentially non-binding and subject to political discretion.[4] The key moves towards promoting competition by the Thatcher government in these early years were the declining use of state aid and so-called 'supply-side' reforms: privatisation, deregulation and the general abandonment of corporatism.[5] This was not the same as antitrust enforcement, concern about economic concentration or oversight of mergers and monopolies. In the early 1980s, the Thatcher government was interested in promoting competition in so far as it wanted to stimulate private enterprise. In some respects, this was no small feat considering the challenges it inherited in 1979, but, for much of its time in office, the Thatcher government was essentially pro-business rather than pro-market.[6] There were some Conservatives who wanted to pursue something more akin to European Christian democracy, ensuring competition as an objective in itself, sitting alongside conservative (and sometimes liberal) values. This strand of conservatism also had some overlap with the social market economy concept pioneered in West Germany in the 1950s and 1960s and attracted interest from politicians in the Liberal Party, the moderate wing of the Labour Party as well as the breakaway Social Democratic Party (SDP) from 1981. For these politicians, the MMC and OFT could be vehicles for overseeing competition and preventing monopolies. Over the course of the decade, however, a separate group emerged within the Conservative Party that cleaved to a more radical version of economic liberalism, more in keeping with American ideas and even the Chicago School thinkers such as Milton Friedman. This group, who were often deemed Thatcherites, wanted ever greater deregulation to promote business and private ownership.[7] For them, competition would be the result of liberalisation and deregulation; antitrust was a form of regulation that would impede markets and stifle competition.

The Thatcher government went about promoting business, private enterprise, entrepreneurship and wealth creation in a number of ways. As we have seen, it shifted the terms of ownership within the British economy—for instance, with its privatisation programme as well as reforms such as Right to Buy. A number of sectors were deregulated, notably financial services. Reductions in tax rates acted as another means to incentivise wealth creation and the private sector. This reached its epoch in Nigel Lawson's 1988 budget, reducing the headline top income tax rate to 40%, while corporation tax fell over the Thatcher years from 52% to 34%. Trade union reforms reduced the impact of organised labour—the bête noire of both Conservative and Labour governments in the 1970s—on the economy both in individual sectors and more generally. From an economic liberal point of view, macroeconomic discipline—although this was achieved only intermittently during the Thatcher and early Major years—provided business with more certainty and confidence to invest. Nevertheless, competition was a watchword of neoliberalism. Matthew Eagleton-Pierce, in his book *Neoliberalism: The Key Concepts*, identifies competition as a key principle of a contemporary neoliberal economy not only as "one of the most important words in the neoliberal lexicon", but also "as a kind of governing ethic for all individuals and organisations".[8] Ordoliberals saw competition as a means of preventing overweening power, whereas opposing voices saw competition as creating winners and losers, including in the labour market.

The Thatcher government did acknowledge the concept, but this translated little into concrete antitrust policy. The 1979 election manifesto mentioned enhanced roles for the MMC and OFT, but, besides abolishing the Price Commission in the 1980 Competition Act, the core features of the UK regime were retained, with little in new reforms or enforcement mechanisms. The 1987 election manifesto returned to the subject. Dedicating a section of the manifesto to competition, it outlined the party's broad thinking:

> Competition forces the economy to respond to the needs of the consumer. It promotes efficiency, holds down costs, drives companies to innovate and ensures that customers get the best possible value for money.[9]

To this end, the manifesto promised to remove monopolies or deregulate sectors such as coach travel and professions such as opticians, as well as introducing competition in broadcasting. After Margaret Thatcher won the June 1987 general election, however, there was little in concerted policy regarding competition policy, with a couple of exceptions.

As we noted in the previous chapter, the Thatcher government's privatisation agenda in the third term, 1987–90, such as in water and electricity, came under more scrutiny regarding competition. Conservative politicians such as Cecil Parkinson and Nigel Lawson, in particular, were keen to present the process as not simply moving a state-owned monopoly into the private sector to continue as a monopoly. This meant more discussions over splitting the state monopoly into smaller units and more rigorous regulation. The outcome of water privatisation, however, could hardly be said to have introduced significant competition. The term natural monopoly applied to the supply of water more than any other sector. Electricity was more successful, although this has gone through waves in the three decades since privatisation.[10] Competition was also hampered by the industry's split into supply and distribution, which saw rival companies vie for customers, and generation, which did not. Nevertheless, Secretary of State at the DTI between 1987 and 1989, David Young (usually known as Lord Moore), despite not significantly changing the competition regime, did have an approach to the topic that could be described as 'neoliberal'. Young was much heralded as a businessman who had lent his expertise to the Conservative Party, as if he sat slightly outside the fray of day-to-day politics. He might have been expected to toe the pro-business line that had held sway for most of the 1980s. Indeed, Young claimed that he "came into Government to be the great deregulator" but, in fact, "my legacy will include a vastly increased system of regulations".[11] Young, who was involved in broadcasting reform, privatisation and putting together the European Single Market while at the DTI, continued:

The more a Government professes to be non-interventionist, the more it has to intervene. This marks the difference between a laissez faire system and open markets. Open markets are controlled markets, with all the controls that are necessary to create a competitive economy. A free-for-all would inevitably lead to the growth of monopolies. My job was to ensure the growth of competition. This was invariably unpopular with the managements of companies, for the real beneficiary would be, not them, but the ultimate consumer.[12]

Young's comments, made in his memoirs, are interesting because they demonstrate how competition was taken into consideration by the Thatcher government in its final phase. First, the concern with the rise of monopolies and attempts to promote competition chime with the tenets of Ordoliberalism or the social market economy—that is to say, the European variant of neoliberalism—rather than its more deregulatory American counterpart. Second, it also showed that, when a nominally liberal economic approach came into contact with the reality of governance, even deregulation meant some kind of intervention. This in fact resonates with later critiques of neoliberalism from other parts of the ideological spectrum—for instance, Jamie Peck's *Constructions of Neoliberal Reason*, which notes how neoliberalism is in effect "regulation in denial".[13]

Major government and competition

The Thatcher government brought about huge changes in the British economy between 1979 and 1990 and opened many markets up to greater competition. Yet Thatcherism was focused on liberalising and deregulatory reforms, rather than pursuing competition per se. This can be seen in the limited changes to the competition regime of the MMC and OFT. A number of trends towards economic concentration accelerated during the 1980s, although the government liked to say it was spreading power through 'popular capitalism'. The 1990–97 Major government pursued a similar approach to competition policy—that is to say, only limited reform of bodies such as MMC and OFT, but with some key differences caused by both external factors, most notably the move towards the EU, and the singular approaches of key ministers, such as Michael Heseltine.

The Major government included a number of strains of conservatism. As we saw in the previous chapter, the Thatcherite flame still burned in the government's quest to find more candidates for privatisation, leading to the problematic sale of British Rail. A number of Thatcherite ministers sat in cabinet, such as Michael Portillo, Chief Secretary to the Treasury in 1992–95 and later both employment and defence secretary, and Peter Lilley, who was Secretary of State for Trade and Industry in 1990–92 and then for Social Security in 1992–97. In the 1990s, however, Thatcherism seemed to morph into primarily an anti-EU vehicle, opposed to the Maastricht process; this Euroscepticism was enthusiastically supported behind the scenes by the former prime minister herself. Thatcherites, however, were in a minority during the Major years. The government included a preponderance of liberal Tories, such as Douglas Hurd, Chris Patten, Malcolm Rifkind and

Ken Clarke (although Clarke himself is slightly more difficult to categorise), who represented a more moderate strain of conservatism, aligning in some respects with the continental Christian democratic approach.

However, despite these different strains of liberal conservatism apparently being present, the Major government was not overly focused on competition policy. In fact, notwithstanding pressure from within the regulatory authorities for more oversight and enforcement powers, the UK retained its discretionary system well into the 1990s.[14] The longstanding Liesner Committee, for instance, urged the government to put more effort into reforming competition policy, increase supervision of mergers and look again at the reference system that required action from the Secretary of State at the DTI.[15]

The Maastricht process, the period after the Maastricht Conference of 9–10 December 1991, including the signing of the Maastricht Treaty on 7 February 1992 and culminating in the treaty taking effect on 1 November 1993, bedevilled the Major government. The 1991 conference called for further integration, from a European economic community to a European union. The process would include a more formalised 'pillar' structure, more competencies for the European Commission and a transition towards a single currency. The commission would expand much of its EEC role, including in competition policy, which would come under the Directorate General for Competition (known as DG COMP), both as a standalone institution as well as helping to 'complete' the single market process that had started after Margaret Thatcher signed the 1986 Single European Act. John Major appeared to have navigated the conference astutely, gaining opt-outs for Britain on the single currency as well as the 'social charter' of rights, including employment rights that concerned more market-orientated Tories. Yet the Maastricht process caused Major seemingly unending problems as wave after wave of backbench Thatcherite Conservative rebellions threatened to derail the process and forced the prime minister himself to use unorthodox tactics such as calling a vote of confidence in his government—essentially goading his own MPs to push him out of office.[16]

It was pro-European Conservatives, however, who were in the key positions during this period. As well as Major himself, who famously said he wanted Britain to be at the "heart of Europe", Ken Clarke was Home Secretary in 1992–93 and Chancellor of the Exchequer in 1993–97, Michael Heseltine was Secretary of State at the DTI in 1992–95 and deputy prime minister in 1995–97, and Douglas Hurd was Foreign Secretary in 1989–95.[17] These politicians may have been sympathetic to the European project, but they were not necessarily either the most pro-market Conservatives or particularly interested in the kind of Ordoliberal competition policy being pursued in Brussels. By the end of its time in office, the Major government had left Britain, according to Gregory Baldi, with one of the weakest antitrust regimes in Europe.[18] In particular, Baldi cites how "the ministers who were supporters of stronger competition generally express[ed] scepticism about Europe, and supporters of Europe generally express[ed] uncertainty about the merits of greater competition".[19] Michael Heseltine was a case in point while at the helm of the DTI. A believer in close cooperation between government and business, Heseltine worked with the Confederation of British Industry (CBI) on competition policy, with representatives sitting in DTI working groups and the CBI's competition commission.[20] Baldi said Heseltine was "not a deep believer in antitrust", and *The Economist*, in 1994, stated that he had "more interest in nurturing national champions than championing the interests of the nation's consumers".[21]

For many other EU members, however, particularly the newer ones, antitrust principles were novel ideas. As a result, it may have been easier for countries that did not have a domestic competition policy like Britain's to adopt new EU standards.[22] The UK system had developed after 1945 in an incomplete and fitful fashion, meaning the British business lobby had the opportunity to shape it to its preferences.[23] The key feature of the British competition framework, however, was its discretionary 'reference' practice that meant pressure could be applied to politicians to drop competition concerns or enter into negotiations. It was one feature of corporatism that survived Thatcherism.

New Labour and competition policy

By 1997, the Major government was tired, engulfed in ongoing disputes over European integration and beset by scandals dubbed 'sleaze' by the press.[24] A retrospective view of the Major government, for instance in Kevin Hickson and Ben Williams's book, *John Major: An Unsuccessful Prime Minister?*, is less withering than much of the criticism at the time. The government had overseen an impressive economic recovery after the calamitous exit from the ERM in September 1992 and made a number of domestic reforms, such as Major's Citizen's Charter initiative.[25] Yet, after 18 years being governed by Conservatives, the public had had enough of them. Meanwhile, the Labour Party, after four successive election defeats, chose John Smith to lead its modernisation efforts. When Smith died in 1994, he was succeeded by 41-year-old Tony Blair, from the moderate wing of the party. Blair, alongside politicians Gordon Brown and Peter Mandelson, press secretary and former journalist Alastair Campbell, and pollster and focus-group expert Phillip Gould, forged 'New Labour'. Adopting a number of liberal economic positions, or at least promising not to reverse Conservative reforms such as lower income rates, privatisation and Right to Buy, New Labour built a highly professional communications machine, presenting an ultra-modern, socially liberal and forward-looking political project. Blair was a hugely talented communicator; Brown developed a number of innovative policy ideas while endlessly reinforcing that Labour would be 'prudent' with the public finances in an attempt to address the party's perceived key weakness. The public were impressed. Labour won a landslide in May 1997.

The Major government had by and large been inactive towards competition policy. This would quickly change under Tony Blair's government. New Labour had a somewhat more economically liberal approach in comparison with its predecessors in the post-war period, led by Clement Attlee in 1945–51, Harold Wilson in 1964–70 and 1974–76 and James Callaghan in 1976–79. As we saw in the previous chapter, New Labour wanted economic growth, even if that meant relatively 'light-touch' regulation of financial services, as a means to fund its other programmes and also in an attempt not to alienate middle-income voters. The party's approach to competition included previous concerns about consumers and restrictive practices, but also included a more objective view of monopolies, mergers and concentration more generally. This embodied New Labour's position as an honest broker in the economy and less a representative of trade unions in Whitehall, a position that had so damaged the party during the 1970s and had lived on in the public imagination in the years since, fuelled by hostile elements in the media. It was also a signifier of how New Labour was much more techno-cratic compared with its ideological predecessors. For Margaret Thatcher, New Labour's approach to markets and lack of appetite to repeal most of her government's reforms was proof that she had won the battle of ideas.[26]

Labour, under Tony Blair, adopted an approach to competition that had echoes of social market economy thinking, even of the Ordoliberal principles embraced by Social Democrats in European countries such as Germany. In fact, the European dimension is key to understanding why the Blair government quickly passed leg-islation in this area, the Competition Act, introduced in late 1997 and completed the following year. As we have noted, Britain sat outside a number of areas of European policy convergence, such as the single currency and the Social Chapter, but also lagged behind in European competition law.[27] Blair moved quickly to catch up with his European counterparts, signing up to the Social Chapter in 1998, to the chagrin of the now much-weakened Conservative Party, and sought to per-suade his colleagues of the benefits of UK membership of the single currency. This latter issue dragged on for several years, running up against resistance from the Treasury and Gordon Brown's "five tests", before it was finally, and perma-nently, side-lined.[28]

Implementing changes in competition policy, however, proved more straight-forward for Labour. Its 1997 manifesto promised "Gains for consumers with tough competition law", while either promoting competition or ensuring "tough, efficient regulation in the interests of customers" in utilities.[29] One section of the document provides a good example of the background of the era, of economic competition in a globalising economy, but also Labour's unusual focus on eco-nomic concentration and competition:

> Competitiveness abroad must begin with competition at home. Effective competition can bring value and quality to consumers. As an early priority we will reform Britain's competition law. We will adopt a tough "prohibitive" approach to deter anti-competitive practices and abuses of market power.

The 1998 Competition Act was the most wide-ranging piece of competition leg-islation passed by a British government since 1945. The MMC was abolished and replaced by a new Competition Commission, whereas the OFT was retained and given greater independence. Crucially, the discretionary role of the Secretary of State was reduced.[30] The bill sought to bring together all the features of post-1945 competition policy, aligning and streamlining them, while jettisoning out-of-date practices. One of the most interesting features of the 1998 Act was the benchmark used to gauge concentration in a particular market. As we saw in Chapter 2, the post-war competition framework deemed that a market share of more than one-third was worthy of potential examination as a monopoly or cartel; this was later reduced to 25%. By the late 1990s, however, British antitrust policymakers had a number of possible measures available to gauge concentration. The legislation stated that a market share greater than 40% was a "threat to competition" and mentioned indices such as the Herfindahl-Hirschman Index (HHI).[31] HHI uses the market share of the 50 largest firms in a particular market, providing a figure between 0 and 10,000 (a figure less than 1,000 is considered low concentration; above 2,000 is highly concentrated) to gauge how concentrated that market is, notably after a proposed merger.[32] Other commonly used measures are concentration ratios of the market share of, for instance, the four largest firms in a sector (CR_4) or the eight largest (CR_8). That the British government invoked a measure such as HHI suggests a different approach to concentration compared with its predecessors, as well as a desire to align with European Commission, rather than US, practice. Typically, the figures stated by US antitrust regulators set out higher limits to be considered moderately or highly concentrated.[33] The Blair government's competition legislation aligned British antitrust enforcement with the EU both ideologically and in practice. The OFT and the Competition Commission were in place for issues of domestic monopolies, mergers and restrictive practices, while the EU Competition Directorate would investigate high-profile cases that had a cross-border impact within the single market.

The OFT and Competition Commission regime now had a clarity and some level of enforcement that had been missing for most of the rest of Britain's attempts at antitrust policy. It even included prison sentences for cartel behaviour in follow-up legislation, the 2002 Enterprise Act, whereby a "cartel offence"—when someone "dishonestly" enters into a horizontal cartel agreement—could face an unlimited fine and up to 5 years in prison or, in the case of directors, 15 years.[34] The Enterprise Act also set out special rules for "media mergers", which would be subject to the law unless the Secretary of State issued an intervention notice that could take "public interest" into consideration. The Act intended the OFT and media regulator Ofcom to advise politicians whether to refer a case to the Competition Commission.[35] As we shall see, media concentration has often been an issue that attracts the interest of government ministers, who more often than not appear to be acting out of political necessity. Therefore, despite the appearance of a more objective, less politicised competition regime under New Labour, some of the old discretionary practices endured.

In its design, however, by the early 2000s, British competition policy was aligned with EU law and processes. The national and supranational regulators had a range of tools at their disposal, such as fines, divestiture, prevention of mergers and even imprisonment. At the EU level, divestiture was the favourite policy tool of the Commission, impelling firms to sell parts of their business, to prevent monopolies and concentration.[36] In more recent years, Brussels has used fines fairly liberally in an attempt to alter the behaviour of large multinationals. The Competition Commissioner has also been involved in a number of high-profile cases, including, since 2000, with the likes of Microsoft and Google.[37] It is widely considered that EU antitrust enforcement is more activist than its American counterparts.

Nevertheless, there is evidence that, despite the UK-level and EU-wide competition regimes, concentration has been rising regardless of regulation. This is partly owing to globalising markets that have allowed large multinational companies to form, making it difficult for national antitrust bodies to effectively enforce anti-monopoly measures. In addition, the modern world economy creates incentives for investment from large companies, whereby many countries are loath to punish the firms they need for jobs and trade. An example of this kind of situation in recent years was demonstrated when EU Competition Commissioner Margrethe Vestager mandated Ireland to collect unpaid tax from tech giant Apple, which had been enticed to set up operations in Dublin. The tax incentives were effectively state aid, according to the EU.[38] Yet the Irish government initially refused to collect any extra tax from Apple, afraid it would lose the firm's high-skilled jobs from the country and its reputation as a burgeoning tech hub operating in a low-tax environment. The same, longer-term, pattern can be seen with international banking and finance in London, which has allowed light-touch regulation to persist despite the calamitous events of 2007–08 and the fact that the vast majority of the British population would happily see measures such as curbs on bonuses and higher taxes, exactly the kind of actions that could force companies to relocate.

Concentration since privatisation: energy markets

In the last chapter, we examined how privatisation had liberalised some markets while moving monopolies from state to private sectors in others. Energy markets have attracted intermittent attention in Britain, following the gas and electricity privatisations of 1986 and 1990, respectively. Such was the negative public perception of energy privatisation that Gordon Brown felt confident enough, despite his attempts to show that New Labour was dissimilar to its tax-and-spend predecessors, to levy a one-off 'windfall tax' on energy companies in 1997 on "excess profits".[39] Energy markets in Britain, however, have not followed a linear progression towards more concentration, like many other sectors in the modern era. As a broad figure, the number of electricity suppliers in the domestic sector has increased from a sole provider during the nationalised period to double figures by 2000s, and rising further in the 2010s. HHI figures for the UK electricity sales market show increasing concentration until around 2002, before the trend reversed and then plateaued for the rest of Labour's time in office.[40] A report by free market think-tank the Institute of Economic Affairs (IEA) suggested that the energy regulator had indeed made a concerted effort to reduce barriers to entry at the turn of the century, although companies were, according to one IEA study, subsequently prone to collusion with the watchdog.[41] Nevertheless, data show that the HHI in the electricity markets oscillated between 1,500 and 2,000 for most of

New Labour's time in office—closer to the latter figure at the beginning and end of the 2000s—suggesting moderate concentration.

The privatised gas market has followed a similar, more marked, trajectory to electricity. Since the early 2000s, the UK gas market has become less concentrated,[42] and in recent years the HHI for gas supply is the least concentrated in Europe, with a figure under 1,000, and, for retail markets, the UK is also an EU leader in terms of competition, with HHI at around 1,700.[43] British energy markets made a further shift after New Labour left office, with HHI figures decreasing in both gas and electricity markets during the 2010s. British energy regulators seem clear that lower concentration is primarily a result of reducing barriers to entry and encouraging new market participants.[44]

Looking at the evidence for UK energy markets appears to validate the privatisation process. Despite intermittent public disquiet about energy prices and the conduct of some companies, particularly over long-term pricing, the 'Big Six' cartel and the ease of switching suppliers, these markets seem to be functioning as well as could have been predicted. The regulatory structure has led to an activist regime that encourages new market entrants, lowering concentration as a result. The energy markets show the interplay between competition, consumer choice and promotion of lower concentration. Nevertheless, it is not as simple to say that increased competition leads to lower prices in markets as complex and dependent on external factors as commodity prices and even geopolitics. At certain points in the 1990s and 2000s, UK energy regulators imposed price controls to prevent spikes in payments. Prices have increased even as concentration fell, and, although in the longer term British households have spent less of their household income on energy costs, 'fuel poverty' has persisted and, at times since 2000, even increased.[45] Therefore, even when a market operates relatively freely and competition is promoted, its benefits cannot be enjoyed by a significant proportion of the population. UK government data show that 10–12% of households in England suffered fuel poverty in the 2000s. Although clearly not working for everyone, and some would say even failing many, energy markets are somewhat of an outlier among other trends in the British economy and demonstrate the most successful results in lowering concentration and promoting competition.

Media and broadcasting

An issue that has long animated observers of British politics, as well as political scientists, is concentration in the media and broadcasting. This has become seemingly more acute with the acceleration of globalisation, which has generated large multinational media companies that own newspapers and broadcasters and are often owned outside the jurisdiction being reported on.[46] The development of new technologies, such as the use of satellites and the internet, has also been crucial in how this sector has evolved.

Concentration in the media has not developed in a linear fashion, and government policy towards the sector has often been contradictory. Recent data show that concentration in television and radio broadcasting and newspaper publishing is decreasing in terms of CR_5, or the five largest firms in a particular market.[47] This is at odds with public perceptions of powerful media moguls controlling large amounts of the newspaper and television markets, causing politicians to seek support from proprietors such as Rupert Murdoch and the Barclay Brothers and editors such as Paul Dacre. It may be, in fact, that technology has simply out-paced firms' desire to maintain high market shares. Nevertheless, the story of the 1979–2007 period is punctuated by sporadic attempts to liberalise media markets and open them to competition, while simultaneously encouraging concentration.

The situation in the newspaper industry when Margaret Thatcher came to power in 1979 was one of, in some respects, limited competition. The British press was, and is, sufficiently rowdy and untameable to suggest there was compe-tition aplenty in the sector. It was also, however, highly unionised, and the previ-ous Callaghan government had failed to effectively deal with practices such as 'blacking' of work produced by non-unionised workers.[48] The Thatcher govern-ment's first major decision on newspaper publishing was whether the Secretary of State at the DTI, John Biffen, should refer the proposed takeover, in 1981, of *The Times* and *The Sunday Times* by Rupert Murdoch's News Corporation to the MMC. A referral seemed sensible on the grounds that Murdoch's companies would own a significant proportion of daily circulation.[49] Murdoch threatened to pull out of the deal if the case was referred to the MMC. The acquisition was sub-sequently waived and went ahead, allowing News Corporation to indeed accrue a powerful chunk of Britain's daily newspapers (including the previously acquired *The Sun* and *News of the World*). It was later revealed that Murdoch had met with the prime minister before a decision was made, and even Conservative colleagues thought she had leant on Biffen over the matter.[50]

If the Thatcher government seemed to be relatively laid back about increasing concentration in the newspaper business, particularly regarding titles that broadly shared the Thatcherite agenda, it made more effort to break monopolies in broad-casting, albeit with limited success.[51] When it took office, television broadcasting was limited to the BBC's two channels and ITV. A state-owned broadcaster paid for by compulsory licence fee and an 'independent' channel with a monopoly on advertisements hardly made a competitive market. The idea for a new chan-nel had been around for some years and was finally agreed to by the Thatcher government in the 1980 and 1981 Broadcasting Acts. The Conservatives were somewhat reluctant, because Channel 4, as it became known, was intended to satisfy more fringe—that is to say, potentially left-wing—tastes not catered for by the existing channels. Therein lay the core tension in the Tory approach to the media. Thatcherism suggested a liberal, if not libertarian, impulse for competi-tion and choice, juxtaposed with a small-c conservatism concerned about taste, standards and departure from the status quo. Nevertheless, Channel 4, launched in 1982, was not a great leap forward in terms of competition. The government then turned its attention towards the real behemoth of broadcasting in Britain: the BBC. As has repeatedly been the case, governments—particularly Conservative ones—turned their gaze towards the corporation when the licence fee came up for renewal. When the BBC sought a large increase in the licence fee in 1984, the government set up an inquiry, led by liberal economist Alan Peacock, to investigate the issue.[52] By this point, the prime minister had developed a thinly veiled animosity towards the BBC, believing it was too critical of her government and too accommodating to those hostile to it.

If the Thatcher government's hope was that an inquiry led by a pro-competition liberal such as Peacock would recommend radical reform of the BBC and even abolition of the licence fee, it was to prove unfounded.[53] The report, published in 1986, proposed retaining the licence fee, with some reform of the BBC and liberalisation of commercial television. Disappointed, the government then turned its attention away from the BBC and towards ITV and the burgeoning satellite television sector.

The 1990 Broadcasting Act, which took some of the recommendations from the Peacock Report, was an attempt to open commercial broadcasting up to more competition. The Act also paid lip service to broadening ownership of media outlets in an attempt to break the essential BBC–ITV duopoly in television. Part of this arrangement was that newspaper owners should not own more than a 20% market share in television. This quickly came unstuck with the growing satellite television sector. In the early 1990s, the medium was dominated by the early entrants into this relatively new market: Rupert Murdoch's Sky and British Satellite Broadcasting (BSB). The former proved much more popular than the latter, however, leading to a proposed takeover that would give Sky far more than the mandated 20% market share.[54] Faced with another possible monopoly case, the Conservatives, now led by John Major, again waived concentration concerns, allowing BSkyB to launch in 1991 and dominate the satellite broadcasting markets during the 1990s and 2000s.[55] Nevertheless, criticism over concentration is less clear-cut in this instance. Few companies were willing to invest in satellite technology or gamble on untested public enthusiasm for packages that, in the case of Sky, partly consisted of re-runs of old shows. On the other hand, it was not disagreeable to the Conservative government, particularly for Thatcherites, that Murdoch's companies, generally pro-Tory, had increased their presence in the newspaper and television sectors.[56]

New Labour and the media

By the mid-1990s, Conservative deregulation of publishing and broadcasting had not significantly decreased concentration. In fact, the idea that Rupert Murdoch's companies owned too much of the British media was one that concerned many in the country, particularly on the left.[57] This sentiment was exacerbated by the often noisy coverage of politics by Murdoch publications such as *The Sun*. Notoriously, the newspaper claimed it had tipped the balance of the 1992 general election in favour of John Major's Conservatives after it lambasted and lampooned Neil Kinnock's Labour Party. "It's The Sun Wot Won It" was emblazoned on the red top's front page the day after the election. Whether newspapers make much of a difference in elections, and to what extent *The Sun* played a role in 1992, is open to debate. What was important, however, was that a group of Labour modernisers thought *The Sun*'s 11 April 1992 headline might have contained some substance. When Tony Blair became Labour leader 2 years later, his approach to the media was markedly different from his predecessors'.

Blair's New Labour team, including the media-savvy Peter Mandelson, Alastair Campbell and Philip Gould and, to a lesser extent although still keenly aware of the importance of presentation, Gordon Brown, took a vastly different approach to public relations to many in the party. The press team would present a stream of new initiatives and challenge and rebut negative coverage. Seeking to highlight elements of stories that put New Labour in a more positive light became known as 'spin', and its practitioners 'spin doctors'.[58] None of this was new in itself, only that the Labour Party professionalised its approach to the media. In particular, the media strategy sought to change opinions in the Murdoch press and prevent any 1992-esque effect shifting the dial for the Tories at the next election. As part of this quest, Tony Blair flew to Australia for a meeting with Rupert Murdoch in July 1995, a move that attracted opprobrium from many in the party, including, unsurprisingly, former leader and subject of *The Sun*'s negative campaign in 1992, Neil Kinnock.[59] Having an audience with the media mogul was quite a turnaround after some of the vitriol aimed at Murdoch by Labour politicians in the previous years. From Blair's point of view, however, the gambit paid off. Along with a number of policies directed more at 'Middle' England rather than the Labour rank and file, such as the 'tough on crime, tough on the causes of crime' rhetoric, the focus on education and Brown's insistence Labour would not raise the highest income tax rate, New Labour attempted a 'broad church' strategy. A number of policies emanated from the, for the time novel, use of Gould's focus groups, such as reluctance to increase the top rate of income tax.[60] On 18 March 1997, shortly before the general election, *The Sun* came out in support of Labour.[61] It was a dramatic volte face after 1992. Blair won a landslide in 1997 and again in 2001, also winning in 2005, albeit with a reduced majority. The Murdoch press supported Blair through this entire period. It is impossible to gauge how much influence this backing actually had. Perhaps newspapers such as *The Sun*, in actual fact, just wanted to be seen to be backing a winner, responding to, rather than leading, public opinion. Indeed, the paper changed horses in 2009, abandoning Gordon Brown's Labour Party for David Cameron's Tories. Cameron won the most seats, if not a majority, in the 2010 general election. Moreover, the actual influence of the media on government decision-making is debatable. For an operation so in tune with the press, the Blair government was highly activist in responding to negative stories and also sensitive to focus groups. These forces probably helped define the parameters of what was possible politically. Blair was wary of how the Eurosceptic elements of the press, including Rupert Murdoch's titles, would portray his government. Murdoch's "voice was rarely heard but his presence was always felt", according to one insider.[62] In this respect, the media reflect the UK's ideological parameters as well as simply reporting day-to-day news stories.

Throughout the era, much was made of the influence of newspapers and broadcasters on politicians, and the impact of these relationships on politics. As well as the Conservatives', then Blair's, proximity to Murdoch's newspapers, Gordon

Brown was known for his contacts with *Daily Mail* editor Paul Dacre, despite that publication's consistent criticism of Brown's government.[63] One could point to the provisions of the 2002 Enterprise Act, whereby political discretion was maintained over media mergers. Following the demise of New Labour, David Cameron was criticised for his close relationship with Murdoch lieutenants Andy Coulson, once editor of the *News of the World* and subsequently Cameron's chief of staff, and Rebekah Brooks, chief executive of Murdoch's company News International.[64] After Gordon Brown left office, the issue of the media's relationship with politicians, and other public institutions, came to a head in 2010–11 during the 'phone hacking scandal', with tabloids such as *News of the World* in the eye of the storm. The paper closed following public outcry in 2011, and News International subsequently withdrew its proposed takeover bid to acquire full control of BSkyB—in 2010, the company owned 39%. The Cameron government appeared to be following the pattern seen in earlier takeover bids, such as with *The Times* in 1981 and BSB in 1991, with Conservatives unenthusiastic about referring the deal to the regulator. This was a slightly different situation, however, as the Secretary of State at the renamed Business, Innovation and Skills Department during the coalition government was Liberal Democrat Vince Cable, who attempted to block the bid, before the decision was passed to the Secretary of State for Culture—a Conservative—Jeremy Hunt. The issue provoked a furore in other parts of the media and from the opposition Labour Party, now led by Ed Miliband. It was the phone hacking scandal, however, that probably tipped the balance in News International withdrawing its bid in July 2011.

In fact, it was technological advances that really opened publishing and broadcasting up to competition. Despite claims that New Labour was too close to the press, including Murdoch titles, and that its policymaking was in hock to public opinion, by the end of his time in office, Tony Blair seemed perfectly content to be unpopular if he thought he was pursuing the most appropriate form of action. Gordon Brown, although also seeking to control the media narrative, was not particularly close to, or popular with, the British media. Although David Cameron's Conservatives appeared to be on good terms with right-leaning newspapers and News International itself, his governments came under a tsunami of criticism, in particular over Britain's relationship with the EU. Although we can see concentration increasing at certain points in the 1979–2007 period, sometimes facilitated by governments' refusal to refer merger cases to the competition watchdog, and with the satellite television market highly concentrated in its early years, one could also say that UK media markets were deregulated enough to allow new entrants and maintain the generally rowdy atmosphere of the British press to continue.

What the established outlets, either in publishing or broadcasting, could not prevent, either through mergers, anticompetitive practices or political pressure, however, was the march of globalisation and technology. The rise of the internet, online platforms and faster fibre and Wi-Fi speeds meant the British no longer needed to rely on daily printed newspapers, or terrestrial or established satellite television stations, to receive news and information. Available on laptops, phones and other devices, news can be received from a smorgasbord of providers, start-ups and niche channels. Some may follow the same rules of journalism, if not political persuasion, of established titles, such as the *Huffington Post*, while space has also opened up for channels—often using social media as a gateway—peddling populism and conspiracy theories. The result of all this is that, despite the efforts of British governments and the established publishers and broadcasters, British media markets are now less concentrated. Nevertheless, this trend is connected with another development, the rise of tech companies such as Google and Facebook, which have facilitated some of these trends. Concentration has emerged in these new markets, including internet search engines and social media, leading some critics to talk about a new 'Gilded Age', dwarfing the scale of some of the other concentration trends covered in this book. We shall look briefly at the rise of the tech giants in the final chapter.

Other sectors

After the 1998 Competition Act and 2002 Enterprise Act, in concert with the European Competition Commission, antitrust academics have generally described how the UK finally had a robust system of competition regulation and enforce-ment in place. Yet, as we have seen, this has not necessarily led to less concentra-tion, for instance in publishing and broadcasting, which needed the advances of technological disruption to promote more competition. On the other hand, led by industry regulators, the British gas and electricity markets have generally become more competitive over the medium term, although still not benefitting all consum-ers. A range of other sectors, however, have managed to evade significant antitrust investigations or serious scrutiny while becoming ever more concentrated. The IMF published a report in April 2019 that outlined how most sectors have been concentrating since 2000:

> market power has increased moderately across advanced economies, as indi-cated by firms' price markups over marginal costs rising by close to 8 percent since 2000.[65]

Here the IMF spotlights how price increases are symptomatic of reduced competi-tion. For many of these sectors, it is perhaps more useful to look at international trends, rather than solely the British example. The IMF data show that, since 2000, in a study of almost 1 million firms in 27 countries, the spoils are increas-ingly going to the top 10% of companies in a given sector, and the rest are left behind.

Globalisation seems to encourage concentration through international mergers and agreements that lead to monopolies or cartels at the national level. Judging by data collected from—as well as the IMF—*The Economist*, the Resolution Foundation and the Social Market Foundation, the results have demonstrated increased concentration. In a 2018 report, the Resolution Foundation showed that, across all sectors of the British economy in the 12 years after 2004, the share of the top five firms in a particular market, as a proportion of total revenue, increased. With some exceptions—for instance, energy—most sectors became more concentrated. This included transport, communications, hospitality and retail sectors, with the most marked rise being in manufacturing.[66] As well as the market shares of the top 5 firms, concentration is also increasing in terms of the top 10 and 20 firms, and these trends appear particularly stark during the latter stages of the New Labour era.[67]

The Resolution Foundation also makes clear one area that has *not* concentrated in recent years, one we have as yet not considered: the labour market. The data show that this measure, the distribution of employees between firms, has flatlined or become less concentrated since 2000. As Bell and Tomlinson note, "A highly concentrated labour market will all else equal mean greater employer power vs employees, with less opportunity for workers to move to other firms or use the threat of moving to push for higher wages".[68] It is perhaps unsurprising that this has occurred in Britain, which is considered to have one of the most 'flexible' labour markets in Europe—that is to say, hiring and firing are more straightforward than in other countries.[69] As countless academic studies have shown, this was in major part thanks to the rolling back of trade union privileges by the Thatcher government and the subsequent reluctance of New Labour to alter the reforms.[70] Nevertheless, this metric shows that large companies are potentially gaining ever more market share without employing significantly more workers. This is obviously linked with technological advances and accelerating globalisation. As Bell and Tomlinson summarise in the Resolution Foundation study:

> The paradox of these two divergent trends in product and labour market concentration may, in part, be explained by the impact of globalisation and growing international trade in the 2000s ... Another possible explanation could be that as big firms have taken a greater share of revenue in sectors that have become more concentrated, they are employing relatively fewer people.[71]

As these studies demonstrate, the modern British economy, set against a backdrop of globalisation, has experienced concentration in many sectors from the New Labour years, despite the regulatory framework put in place in 1998.

Conclusion

This chapter has explored the competition agendas and regulatory frameworks of the Thatcher, Major and Blair governments, as well as examining case studies of the energy markets and the media in some detail. Competition policy was nominally a part of the Thatcher government's programme in 1979, but little was done in terms of activist antitrust policy. For the most part, competition policy was changed at the margins, such as the Tebbit rules on mergers. Crucially, however, political discretion was retained in cases of potential or actual concentration.

Nevertheless, the Thatcher government did stimulate greater competition, reducing concentration in some markets, as a result of its deregulation and liberalisation policies. Crucially, the government did not entertain the kind of corporatism, or coordinated policymaking between business, trade unions and government, that had been a feature of its predecessors. This removed one of the curious features of the previous competition regime, that of price setting and supervision.

The Major government had different priorities in competition policy, namely trying to align British antitrust arrangements with the new European Union system that came into being in the mid-1990s. Led by the interventionist Michael Heseltine, Conservative competition policy appeared to be moving back to a closer relationship between business and government, whereby the competition authorities could promote 'national champions' rather than actively prevent anti-competitive practices. By the time it left office, critics have suggested that the outgoing Major government had left Britain with one of the EU's least effective antitrust regimes.

Tony Blair's New Labour government was unusual in several respects regarding its approach to markets and, even as a centre-left administration, appeared to be in some ways more 'pro-market' than its predecessor. Upon taking office, Labour quickly passed the 1998 Competition Act, providing a more thorough competition policy with more robust enforcement mechanisms and essentially taking a more objective approach to antitrust. The Act allowed Britain to converge with EU standards, which was reinforced by the 2002 Enterprise Act. A Labour government had established Britain's most rigorous competition framework. By 2006, a comparative review rated the UK Competition Commission as one of the world's most effective antitrust agencies, alongside the US and German bodies.[72] That is not to say, however, that antitrust policy was particularly effective over this period or that it prevented concentration in numerous sectors.

Despite the evidence to show many industries have concentrated, notably ones such as manufacturing, this chapter has examined a couple of areas that have seemingly bucked the trend. We have looked at energy markets after the privatisation process and found that, despite waves of increased and decreased concentration, over the longer term British gas and electricity markets have generally become more competitive and less concentrated. This reduction in concentration, however, appears to be a result of the industry regulators paving the way for new entrants to the respective markets, although of course this sits against the background of the broader regulatory and antitrust framework. Concentration has also fallen in recent years in publishing and broadcasting markets, despite the often close (and sometimes tense and adversarial) relationship between media owners, companies and politicians. Here, the key trend that seems to be driving change is technology. Concentration has increased in many other markets, for the most part despite the competitive framework. Globalisation is a key driver for many of these shifts. We shall return to recent trends, such as the rise of tech giants, in the final chapters of this book.

Notes

1 Adrian Kuenzler and Laurent Warlouzet, "National Traditions of Competition Law: A Belated Europeanization through Convergence?", eds. Kiran Klaus Patel and Heike Schweitzer, *The Historical Foundations of EU Competition Law* (Oxford: Oxford University Press, 2013, 89–124), 114.
2 Ibid.
3 Adrian Williamson, *Conservative Economic Policymaking and the Birth of Thatcherism, 1964–1979* (Basingstoke: Palgrave Macmillan, 2015), 155.
4 Kuenzler and Warlouzet, "National Traditions", 114.
5 Ibid.
6 Neil Rollings, "Cracks in the Post-War Keynesian Settlement? The Role of Organised Business in Britain in the Rise of Neoliberalism before Margaret Thatcher", *Twentieth Century British History*, 24:4 (2013), 637–659; Ben Jackson, "The Think-Tank Archipelago: Thatcherism and Neoliberalism", eds. Ben Jackson and Robert Saunders, *Making Thatcher's Britain* (Cambridge: Cambridge University Press, 2012), 47–49.
7 For instance, Keith Joseph, Nicholas Ridley, John Redwood, Norman Tebbit, Michael Portillo and, to a lesser extent, Nigel Lawson.
8 Matthew Eagleton-Pierce, *Neoliberalism: The Key Concepts* (Abingdon: Routledge, 2016), 33.
9 Conservative Party 1987 Election Manifesto, www.conservativemanifesto.com/1987/1987-conservative-manifesto.shtml [accessed 2 April 2020].
10 Colin Robinson, *From Nationalisation to State Control. The Return of Centralised Energy Planning*, IEA Discussion Paper No. 49 (London: IEA, 2013), www.iea.org.uk/sites/default/files/publications/files/From%20Nationalisation%20to%20State%20Control_web.pdf [accessed 6 April 2020], 11.
11 Lord Young, *The Enterprise Years: A Businessman in the Cabinet* (London: Headline, 1991), 287.
12 Ibid.
13 Jamie Peck, *Constructions of Neoliberal Reason* (Oxford: Oxford University Press, 2010), xiii.
14 Gregory Baldi, "Europeanising Antitrust: British Competition Policy Reform and Member State Convergence", *British Journal of Politics and International Relations*, 8:1 (2006), 503–518, 511.
15 Tony Freyer, *Regulating Big Business: Antitrust in Great Britain and America; 1880 – 1990* (Cambridge: Cambridge University Press, 1992), 316.
16 Owen Bowcott, "John Major Had a 'Full Gloat' after Defeating Rebels on Maastricht", *The Guardian*, 24 July 2018, www.theguardian.com/politics/2018/jul/24/john-major-full-gloat-defeating-rebels-maastricht-european-union [accessed 7 April 2020].
17 John Major, "Mr Major's Speech at the Inauguration of the European Bank for Reconstruction and Development", 15 April 1991, www.johnmajorarchive.org.uk/1990-1997/mr-majors-speech-at-the-inauguration-of-the-european-bank-for-reconstruction-and-development-15-april-1991/ [accessed 8 April 2020].
18 Baldi, "Europeanising Antitrust", 504.
19 Ibid., 512.
20 Ibid.
21 *The Economist*, 21 May 1994; Baldi, "Europeanising Antitrust", 512.
22 Baldi, "Europeanising Antitrust", 516.
23 Ibid.
24 Bruce Pilbeam, "Social Morality", eds. Kevin Hickson and Ben Williams, *John Major: An Unsuccessful Prime Minister? Reappraising John Major* (London: Biteback, 2017, 215–230), 218.
25 Ben Williams, "Social Policy", eds. Kevin Hickson and Ben Williams, *John Major: An Unsuccessful Prime Minister? Reappraising John Major* (London: Biteback, 2017, 197–214), 208–209.

26 Charles Moore, *Margaret Thatcher: The Authorized Biography, Volume Three: Herself Alone* (London: Allen Lane, 2019), 801–802.

27 Nicholas Crafts, "Creating Competitive Advantage: Policy Lessons from History", University of Warwick Working Papers, No. 91 (2012), https://warwick.ac.uk/fac/soc/economics/research/centres/cage/manage/publications/91.2012_crafts.pdf [accessed 9 April 2020]; Baldi, "Europeanising Antitrust", 503.

28 Gordon Brown, *My Life, Our Times* (Bodley Head, 2017), 173–184; Ed Balls, *Speaking Out: Lessons in Life and Politics* (London: Arrow Books, 2016), 155–167.

29 Labour Party 1997 Manifesto, "New Labour: because Britain deserves better", www.labour-party.org.uk/manifestos/1997/1997-labour-manifesto.shtml [accessed 9 April 2020].

30 Baldi, "Europeanising Antitrust", 513.

31 UK Government, "Competition Act 1998", www.legislation.gov.uk/ukpga/1998/41/contents [accessed 10 April 2020].

32 The OFT and the Competition Commission set out merger assessment guidelines that "indicate that a market with an HHI exceeding 1,000 may be regarded as concentrated, and an HHI exceeding 2,000 may be regarded as highly concentrated". Competition Commission & Office of Fair Trading, "Merger Assessment Guidelines", September 2010, https://assets.publishing.service.gov.uk/government/uploads/system/uploads/attachment_data/file/284449/OFT1254.pdf [accessed 10 April 2020].

33 The US Department of Justice states, "The agencies generally consider markets in which the HHI is between 1,500 and 2,500 points to be moderately concentrated, and consider markets in which the HHI is in excess of 2,500 points to be highly concentrated". US Department of Justice, "Herfindahl–Hirschman Index", 31 July 2018, www.justice.gov/atr/herfindahl-hirschman-index [accessed 10 April 2020].

34 Andrew Scott, "The Evolution of Competition Law and Policy in the United Kingdom", LSE Working Papers 9/2009, 13, http://eprints.lse.ac.uk/24564/1/WPS2009-09_Scott.pdf, 24; UK Government, "Enterprise Act 2002", www.legislation.gov.uk/ukpga/2002/40/contents [accessed 14 April 2020], section 188.

35 Scott, "Evolution", 24.

36 Stephen Davies and Bruce Lyons, *Mergers and Merger Remedies in the EU: Assessing the Consequences for Competition* (Cheltenham: Edward Elgar, 2007), 243.

37 Maurice Stucke and Allen Grunes, *Big Data and Competition Policy* (Oxford: Oxford University Press, 2016).

38 Foo Yun Chee, "Apple Spars with EU as $14 Billion Irish Tax Dispute Drags On", *Reuters*, 18 September 2019, www.reuters.com/article/us-eu-apple-stateaid/apple-spars-with-eu-as-14-billion-irish-tax-dispute-drags-on-idUSKBN1W31FE [accessed 13 April 2020].

39 Brown, *My Life*, 127, Gordon Brown, House of Commons Debates (10 July 1997) vol. 297, col. 1055.

40 UK Department for Business, Energy and Industrial Strategy, "Energy Trends: September 2016, Special Feature Article—Competition in UK Electricity Markets", 29 September 2016, https://assets.publishing.service.gov.uk/government/uploads/system/uploads/attachment_data/file/556310/Electricity_competition.pdf [accessed 14 April 2020], 89–90.

41 Robinson, *From Nationalisation to State Control*, 8–12.

42 Scott Corfe and Nicole Gicheva, "Concentration not Competition: The State of UK Consumer Markets", Social Market Foundation (October 2017), www.smf.co.uk/wp-content/uploads/2017/10/Concentration-not-competition.pdf [accessed 15 April 2020], 9.

43 Energy UK, "Powering Europe", June 2015, www.energy-uk.org.uk/publication.html?task=file.download&id=5334 [accessed 15 April 2020].

44 Ofgem, "State of the Energy Market: 2017 Report", www.ofgem.gov.uk/system/files/docs/2017/10/state_of_the_market_report_2017_web_1.pdf [accessed 15 April 2020], 20.

45 Tom Rutherford, "Energy Prices", House of Commons Library, Briefing Paper Number 04153, 9 February 2018, http://researchbriefings.files.parliament.uk/documents/SN041 53/SN04153.pdf [accessed 15 April 2020].

46 Keith Cowling and Philip R. Tomlinson, "Globalisation and Corporate Power", *Contributions to Political Economy*, 24:1 (2005), 33–54, 35–36.

47 Torsten Bell and Dan Tomlinson, "Is Everybody Concentrating? Recent Trends in Product and Labour Market Concentration in the UK", Resolution Foundation, July 2018, www .resolutionfoundation.org/app/uploads/2018/07/Is-everybody-concentrating_Recent -trends-in-product-and-labour-market-concentration-in-the-UK.pdf, 38–39, [accessed 1 November 2020].

48 John Gennard and Peter Bain, *SOGAT: A History of the Society of Graphical and Allied Trades* (London: Routledge, 1995), 109.

49 At this stage, the law stated that a merger leading to daily circulation above 500,000 newspapers required consent by the Secretary of State. UK Government, "Fair Trading Act 1973", www.legislation.gov.uk/ukpga/1973/41/enacted [accessed 16 April 2020].

50 Records of the Prime Minister's Office: Correspondence and Papers, 1979–1997. Held at the National Archives, Kew, London, PREM 19/1063, Murdoch met with Thatcher on 27 March 1981; Ken Clarke, *Kind of Blue: A Political Memoir* (London: Macmillan, 2016), 259.

51 See Robert Ledger, *Neoliberal Thought and Thatcherism: "A Transition from Here to There?"* (Abingdon: Routledge, 2017), 117–124.

52 Andrew Crisell, *An Introductory History of British Broadcasting* (London: Routledge, 2002), 234; John Campbell, *Margaret Thatcher. Volume Two: The Iron Lady* (London: Pimlico, 2004), 404.

53 Jean Seaton and Anthony McNicholas, "It Was the BBC Wot Won It. Winning the Peacock Report for the Corporation, or How the BBC Responded to the Peacock Committee", eds. Tom O'Malley and Janet Jones, *The Peacock Committee and UK Broadcasting Policy* (Basingstoke: Palgrave Macmillan, 2009, 121–145).

54 John Campbell, *Margaret Thatcher. Volume Two: The Iron Lady* (London: Pimlico, 2004), 572.

55 Crisell, *British Broadcasting*, 231, 259–260.

56 Campbell, *Margaret Thatcher*, 572.

57 Torin Douglas, "Analysis: Murdoch and Media Ownership in UK", *BBC News*, 22 December 2010, www.bbc.com/news/uk-12062176 [accessed 20 April 2020].

58 Will Woodward, "Spin and Scandal: How New Labour Made the News", *The Guardian*, 13 June 2007, www.theguardian.com/media/2007/jun/13/politicsandthemedia.pressan dpublishing [accessed 21 April 2020].

59 Alastair Campbell, *The Diaries: The Blair Years* (Reading: Arrow Books, 2008), 73–83 (entries 13 July 1995–2 August 1995).

60 Martin Powell, "New Labour and Social Justice", ed. Martin Powell, *Evaluating New Labour's Welfare Reforms* (Bristol: The Policy Press, 2002, 19–38), 33.

61 Roy Greenslade, "It's the Sun Wot's Switched Sides to Back Blair", *The Guardian*, 18 March 1997, www.theguardian.com/politics/1997/mar/18/past.roygreenslade [accessed 21 April 2020].

62 Director of Communications Lance Price, cited in Oliver Daddow, "Margaret Thatcher, Tony Blair and the Eurosceptic Tradition in Britain", *British Journal of Politics and International Relations*, 15 (2013), 219; Helen Parr, "European Integration", eds. Matt Beech, Kevin Hickson, and Raymond Plant, *The Struggle for Labour's Soul: Understanding Labour's Political Thought Since 1945* (Abingdon: Routledge, 2018, 159–171), 167.

63 Peter Wilby, "Paul Dacre of the Daily Mail: The Man Who Hates Liberal Britain", *New Statesman*, 2 January 2014, www.newstatesman.com/media/2013/12/man-who-hates-l iberal-britain [accessed 22 April 2020]; Brown, *My Life*, 368.

64 Tom Peck, "Ken Clarke: David Cameron May Have 'Done Some Sort of Deal' with Rupert Murdoch", *Independent*, 23 November 2017, www.independent.co.uk/news/uk/politics/ken-clarke-rupert-murdoch-deal-2010-election-rebekah-brooks-a8072456.html [accessed 22 April 2020].

65 World Economic Outlook, "Chapter 2: The Rise of Corporate Market Power and Its Macroeconomic Effects", IMF (April 2019, 55–76), www.imf.org/en/Publications/WEO/Issues/2019/03/28/world-economic-outlook-april-2019#Chapter%202   [accessed 14 January 2020], 55.

66 Bell and Tomlinson, "Is Everybody Concentrating?", 14.

67 Ibid., 11.

68 Ibid., 18.

69 *The Economist*, "British Immigration. You're Welcome", 21 December 2013, www.economist.com/news/leaders/21591865-open-letter-citizens-bulgaria-and-romania-youre-welcome [accessed 24 April 2020].

70 Carole Thornley and Dan Coffey, *Globalization and Varieties of Capitalism: New Labour, Economic Policy and the Abject State* (Basingstoke: Palgrave Macmillan, 2009), 12.

71 Bell and Tomlinson, "Is Everybody Concentrating?", 27.

72 Citing the Global Competition Review, in Scott, "Evolution", 2.

5 Devolution, nationalism and the British state

Separating economic from political power can be somewhat of a false dichotomy. By dividing the two, however, we can examine a number of diverse themes that evade a simple narrative outlining how power is concentrating in Britain. Even when considering political power specifically, academics have described a trend in the modern era whereby the state has become increasingly centralised, accumulating power by exercising 'managerialism' or technocratic control over more layers of society.[1] Yet this narrative risks playing down a number of key trends in British politics since the 1970s, albeit uneven ones. Political power has, at various points, been devolved from central government. The two issues that particularly preoccupied British politicians, and the general public, during this time were European integration and devolution in Scotland, Wales and—in a more multifaceted way—Northern Ireland. As well as these political changes, we have seen a profound shift in power caused by the move to grant operational independence to the Bank of England in 1997. In some ways, these shifts have fuelled populism; in others, they might have pacified its rise. Taken together, they demonstrate the complex shifts in concentration of power in Britain over the past decades.

1970s Britain: a crisis of political power?

The decade before Margaret Thatcher became prime minister, in which several of the core ideas that would guide her government were developed, was seen by many as one lacking a coherent central authority. This is perhaps better articulated as an era where the status quo was fiercely contested owing to ongoing crises. Many on the left thought the turmoil of 1970s Britain was proof that its capitalist system was broken and an opportunity to seize more of the 'commanding heights' of the economy, nationalise more industries and expand the power of the unions.[2] This was encapsulated by Labour's 'alternative economic strategy', backed by the party's far left. On the right, however, the strikes that crippled the economy, the chaotic and often violent secondary pickets, soaring inflation and impotency of government were all evidence of a crisis of central authority and power. For economic liberals on the right of the Conservative Party, such as Keith Joseph, the attitude of the left was indicative of the post-1945 trend, that since the Second World War, Britain had been increasingly statist and shifting towards ever greater intervention. Joseph famously called this the "ratchet effect", a shift that Conservatives had failed to roll back when in government or even colluded in accelerating.[3] It was the Conservatives, however, who seized upon these issues in their 1979 election manifesto, setting out as one of its five tasks "To uphold Parliament and the rule of law"; invoking chaos in industrial relations: "Labour have given a minority of extremists the power to abuse individual liberties and to thwart Britain's chances of success", and, more generally:

> Attempting to do too much, politicians have failed to do those things which should be done. This has damaged the country and the authority of government.[4]

Other trends multiplied. The far right gained popularity, and its political manifestation, the National Front, caused, and was met by, street violence.[5] There were even shadowy discussions about a military coup.[6] Questions of power also revealed themselves as ones of representation. The decade saw an increase in support for the Scottish National Party and the stirrings of Welsh cultural nationalism. Northern Ireland's challenges on these issues were far more acute during the 1970s, which proved to be the most violent decade of the 'Troubles' in the province. It was against this backdrop that the Thatcher government, and its opponents, developed answers to the questions of the era that would resonate over at least two decades.

Despite the competing narratives that Britain lacked a competent central authority, that more power should be dispersed, that economic power should be concentrated in the name of the workers, or that individuals should be liberated from overweening interference from Whitehall, Britain *did* have one of the most centralised political systems in the West by the 1970s. Compared with federal systems or countries that delegated more power to regions and municipalities, London exercised an overwhelming proportion of decision-making in the UK. Although a 'union', the constituent nations of the UK had little say over their own affairs. Regional assemblies and city mayors were alien to the British conception of political organisation. At the same time, the Conservatives sought to curb local councils, who they considered to be bastions of leftism and incompetent with public funds. The Tories, therefore, were more likely to concentrate power than give it away, despite their rhetoric suggesting the opposite. This was borne out over the subsequent period of 18 years of Conservative governments.

Rising nationalism in the union

The second half of the 20th century saw the rise of nationalism in the smaller nations of the UK. This continued beyond the millennium and, to take one view of the 2016 Brexit referendum, was joined later by English nationalism. How did this profound shift happen? It is a central theme of this study that concentrating power inevitably leads to a backlash, which can manifest itself as populism. Therefore, lack of representation in Northern Ireland (for the minority Catholic or nationalist population), Wales, Scotland and, later, regions in England has played a part in the rise of nationalism pushing back against the status quo. This is to suggest, perhaps too simplistically, that nationalism is a variety of populism. Nevertheless, both populists and nationalists often fish in the same waters, feeding on grievance and promoting figures that represent the 'people' in opposition to corrupt and out-of-touch elitist decision-makers.[7]

Demonstrations by the Catholic population erupted in Northern Ireland during the 1960s against the discriminatory practices of the majority Protestants, or Unionists, who occupied local positions of power. What started as civil rights protests descended into violence, leading the British government to suspend the regional assembly at Stormont in 1972 and deployed the army to pacify the situation. What followed was, despite being known by the understated sobriquet 'the Troubles', more than two decades of essentially civil war. The 1970s were particularly bloody, with more than 200 people killed in the province in each year between 1972 and 1976. Nevertheless, the situation in Northern Ireland is clearly not particularly helpful as a comparison with other political devolution because of the security component. The bloodshed played into the narrative during the 1970s that the UK was becoming ungovernable and increasingly violent. Likewise, the negotiations to end the conflict, culminating in the 1998 Good Friday Agreement, emphasised the importance of a workable, equitable local assembly. Northern Ireland, however, was different from the other examples we consider in this chapter.

Welsh and Scottish nationalism

It is sometimes easy to forget, given the salience of Welsh and Scottish nationalism in contemporary British politics, how these forces, at least in terms of political representation, seemingly came from nowhere in the second half of the 20th century. The main political vehicles for Welsh and Scottish nationalists emerged during the interwar era: Plaid Cymru (the Party of Wales) had been formed in 1925, and the Scottish National Party (SNP) was founded in 1934. Yet they both failed to make their mark on the electoral landscape. In the 1951 election, for example, Plaid Cymru fielded only four candidates and won a meagre 10,920 votes, and the SNP did even worse, fielding two candidates and winning 7,299 votes. Labour was the dominant force in Wales and Scotland and had been for decades. Socialism, or at least Labour's variant of social democracy, seemed to have appeal in every corner of Britain and could override nationalist considerations. This was also the height of Britain's political duopoly: in the 1951 election, Labour and the Conservatives took a combined 96% of the vote, winning 616 of 625 seats between them.

The 1960s and early 1970s saw increased support for Plaid Cymru and the SNP. Plaid focused on preserving and promoting the Welsh language, whereas the SNP pursued a more political and economic strategy, concentrated around the recent discovery of hydrocarbons under the North Sea. The core component of the SNP's early 1970s' electoral strategy was the "It's Scotland's oil" campaign. The gambits appeared to work, as both Plaid and the SNP picked up voters and seats, primarily at by-elections at first, and then won broader support at general elections. The October 1974 election provided a narrow victory for Harold Wilson's Labour Party, as well as a new high for Welsh and Scottish nationalists. The SNP, led by William Wolfe, secured 839,000 votes and 11 MPs, which equated to 30% of the vote in Scotland.[8] Plaid Cymru, meanwhile, won 166,000 votes and three MPs, taking 11% of the Welsh vote.[9] This was a steep rise since the 1950s and aligned with the period when Britain entered into industrial decline and there was a shift towards a more service-orientated economy. The loss of heavy industry particularly affected established sectors, such as mining, steel works and shipbuilding, in Wales and Scotland.[10] The apparent neglect of Wales and Scotland by decision-makers in London fuelled nationalist fires.

Labour was sufficiently concerned by the rise in nationalism to offer a referendum on forming devolved administrations in Scotland and Wales after 1974. The decision was driven by political practicality. Jim Callaghan's 1976–79 government relied on first the Liberal Party and then the SNP to maintain a working parliamentary majority. The plebiscites were held on 1 March 1979, and, although 51.6% in Scotland voted in favour of a devolved assembly, the result failed to pass a minimal threshold of 40% of the total electorate voting yes. The Welsh electorate was much less enthusiastic about a national assembly, with only 20% voting in favour. As a result, the Callaghan government shelved the devolution process, leading to the SNP withdrawing its support from the government and Labour finally losing a vote of no confidence on 28 March 1979. A general election was called, which Margaret Thatcher won. Therefore, the rise of nationalist sentiment can be seen as having a direct role in the Conservatives' returning to power. Nevertheless, in the 1979 election, support for the SNP and Plaid Cymru actually declined. The SNP was down 14 points in Scotland to 17%, losing all but two of its MPs, and Plaid fell 2.7% to 8.1%, losing one seat. On the face of things, the surge in nationalism during the 1970s petered out when Margaret Thatcher came to power, despite her government's reputation for paying little attention to locations outside South East England. Electoral support for the SNP and Plaid Cymru continued to fall during the 1980s, only picking up again at the 1992 election. By the end of the 1990s, support for nationalists hovered around 20% and 10% for the SNP and Plaid, respectively. This was not an overwhelming level, but was nevertheless eating into the major parties' vote share.

Although the Thatcher years did not see any immediate electoral surge for Welsh and Scottish nationalists, the nature of the movements and their rhetoric took on a new character. With the focal point of Welsh nationalism on language and culture, a row emerged over a possible new Welsh language television channel. Demand for a permanent Welsh language station had grown in the 1960s and 1970s—Plaid Cymru said it was "essential"—and the Conservatives had made positive noises about establishing one before the 1979 election.[11] Upon taking office, however, Home Secretary Willie Whitelaw quickly backtracked on the idea. A rapid chain of events would change his mind. Enraged by the abandoning of their cherished Welsh language channel, nationalists started a civil disobedience campaign of refusing to pay the television licence fee. Plaid Cymru leader Gwynfor Evans threatened to go on a hunger strike in September 1980 unless a channel was established.[12] Given the Thatcher government's subsequent reputation as stubborn and unlikely to change course, including its attitude to hunger strikers in Northern Ireland, we may have expected the campaign to have had little impact. In fact, Whitelaw executed a sharp U-turn and set in motion the founding of the Welsh language channel, Sianel Pedwar Cymru (Channel 4 Wales). S4C, as it was known, launched a day before the UK-wide Channel 4, in September 1982.[13]

Welsh nationalism even included a violent fringe: Meibion Glyndŵr (Sons of Glyndŵr). Formed in 1979 and aggrieved about the diminution of the Welsh language and culture within the UK, Meibion Glyndŵr conducted a firebombing campaign of English-owned properties in Wales.[14] More than 200 homes were attacked during the 1980s. The group's main targets were estate agents facilitating property sales from England, as well as the Conservative Party more generally. It planted a number of bombs at the party's offices in England, even sending letter bombs to Tory MPs, which led to prison sentences. Plaid Cymru leaders "condemned" the group's methods, if not their nationalist motivations.[15] Meibion Glyndŵr activities had petered out by the mid-1990s, and the violence only ever involved a small number of assailants. Nevertheless, by the time New Labour took office in 1997, Welsh cultural nationalism was established as a force in Welsh politics.

Events in Scotland during the Thatcher era more acutely animated Conservative politicians, and it is hard to imagine now, but the party had once been well represented in the country. Historians have outlined how flagship Thatcherite policies such as Right to Buy had relatively slow take-up in Scotland.[16] Moreover, as we have noted, the decline of heavy industry, although predating the Thatcher government, particularly damaged the Scottish economy. Nevertheless, the Conservatives contrived to alienate a significant section of the Scottish population during the decade, none more so than with the 'poll tax', or community charge. The system inherited by the Thatcher government, the 'rates', was highly unpopular with Conservative activists and party members. Yet an alternative evaded the government until the community charge was proposed in 1985, which would be levied on individuals, rather than households, for local services. The idea appealed to Margaret Thatcher because it was framed as a charge that would better connect local councils with their voters; payment would be based on the electoral register, hence the moniker the 'poll tax'. The prime minister thought that, once a direct link was made between spendthrift local councils and individuals, they would more likely abandon far-left Labour administrations and choose Tory alternatives, reigning in public spending in the process.[17]

The poll tax was planned to be rolled out gradually, with Scotland first in line. The chaotic results suggested that the government viewed Scotland as a laboratory for its new policy.[18] Despite the government's rhetoric that the charge was more 'democratic', its application seemed to be highly inequitable, causing monthly bills for many to rise sharply.[19] After the poll tax was rolled out in Scotland in

1989, one year ahead of England and Wales, it quickly became a public relations disaster. When the community charge came into force in April that year, 25,000 Scots marched through Edinburgh in protest.[20] Further demonstrations and civil disobedience followed, including refusal to pay the new tax by around 15–20% of those registered.[21] Events in Scotland could not budge the prime minister on the issue, who was by now in fully-fledged 'not for turning' mode. With disquiet growing from Conservative MPs and the public more generally, however, Number 10 appeared to be under siege regarding the issue. As the poll tax was about to be introduced in England, a riot ensued in central London in March 1990. This in itself did not move the dial for Thatcher, but the catastrophic presentation and public perception of the poll tax undoubtedly impacted other Tory ministers. When Margaret Thatcher was ousted in November that year, her refusal to change path on the poll tax was high up on the plotters' list of complaints.

The poll tax was dropped by her successor, John Major, and his Secretary of State for the Environment, Michael Heseltine, who had posed the initial challenge to her leadership in 1990. Nevertheless, the political damage of the poll tax would cast a long shadow in Scotland and provide impetus to the nationalist cause. It was a good example of how decision-making was concentrated in London without taking local, regional and national considerations into account. This was somewhat ironic, as the poll tax was intended to increase local accountability, even potentially having an empowering impact. However, neither the details of the policy implementation nor the philosophical impression of the tax more generally came near to matching that goal of the design phase. As Margaret Thatcher's biographer Charles Moore has written, "although the community charge was intended to be decentralising, related measures were intended to centralise. The non-domestic rate, paid by business, was now to be made uniform and set centrally".[22]

Future SNP leader Nicola Sturgeon said that she joined the party in the first instance (in 1986) because the policies of Thatcherism were imposed on a Scottish population: "it was wrong for Scotland to be governed by a Tory government that we hadn't elected".[23] Although the Conservatives still had a significant vote share in Scotland—declining from 31% in 1979 to 24% in 1987—it lost half of its MPs during the Thatcher years. In this way, Sturgeon draws the direct comparison between lack of representation and an increase in antipathy to the UK government, through the vehicle of nationalism. Other studies have been sceptical of any relationship between devolution and anti-Conservatism or anti-Thatcherism during the 1980s, highlighting how histories of Welsh and Scottish devolution have tended to be written retrospectively by proponents of the process.[24] Nevertheless, where political representation has been deemed to be weak, a populist reaction has often stirred, applicable to all parts of the UK.

The Major government was more conciliatory and less confrontational in general than its predecessor. It sought to pacify nationalists throughout the 'Celtic fringe' of the UK—Wales, Scotland and Northern Ireland—while maintaining the public spending principles of Thatcherism.[25] Nevertheless, the legacy of Thatcherism was difficult to shake off. As Richard Finlay has written, the die had been cast: "For many Scots, Thatcher's Britishness was indistinguishable from

Englishness. To some extent this lesson was learnt in the Major era, but by then the damage had been done".[26] What's more, John Major was a committed unionist and opposed to devolution, seeing it as a halfway house to separation.[27] Major did look at other means of improving government relations in Scotland through a Scottish Office White Paper exploring alternatives to devolution, but these would be swept away with the post-1997 constitutional changes.[28]

Calls for Welsh and Scottish devolution grew during the 1990s, attracting broad-based popular support. Where nationalists such as the SNP and Plaid Cymru had led, now other, less radical-minded people followed. This time, Labour was determined to get out in front of nationalist demands. The Labour leader from 1992 to 1994 John Smith, himself a Scotsman, was committed to devolution. Labour believed that, by supporting Welsh and Scottish assemblies, it could pacify nationalism and bring voters back who may have once voted for it, but had since moved to Plaid Cymru or, particularly, the SNP.

Labour's embrace of devolution

In March 1989, at the height of the poll tax controversy in Scotland and just before the policy was about to be rolled out there, the Scottish Constitutional Convention (SCC) was established by political parties and civil society groups. Although the Conservatives rejected the SCC, and the SNP was lukewarm towards the forum, it received support from Labour and the Liberal Democrats. The convention helped articulate a framework for a devolved administration in Scotland and also gave Labour a key role in this development. Labour's 1992 election manifesto made provision for a Scottish Parliament and Welsh Assembly.[29] Although Neil Kinnock lost that election, his successor, Smith, reinforced Labour's moves in this direction. Smith had brought the devolution process through the House of Commons for the Callaghan government in the late 1970s and, despite some disquiet within the party, promoted devolution as leader, emphasising how Labour was at the forefront of the campaign to establish a "Scottish Assembly".[30] Smith was a signatory to the SCC and saw a Scottish Parliament or Assembly as "the settled will of the Scottish people".[31]

John Smith died of a heart attack in May 1994. He was replaced as leader by Tony Blair, who worked closely with Smith's protégé Gordon Brown as Shadow Chancellor and architect of domestic policy. Blair was far less enthused by devolution than Smith, but by then the party had generated enough momentum on the issue that Blair continued to pursue the pledge in opposition.[32] Nevertheless, New Labour had a taste for modernisation, change and renewal in seemingly every sphere. Devolution, an inherited policy, could align with the rest of the New Labour programme because it represented something different, a break from the past. Politically, national governments in Wales and Scotland had the potential to satiate nationalist desires and let Labour reap the electoral reward, although to date this is not how the process has transpired. Devolution became a pillar of a radical New Labour constitutional overhaul, embracing the European Union,

House of Lords reform, city mayors and even electoral reform. The 1997 election manifesto outlined Labour's thinking:

> Subsidiarity is as sound a principle in Britain as it is in Europe. Our proposal is for devolution not federation. A sovereign Westminster Parliament will devolve power to Scotland and Wales. The Union will be strengthened and the threat of separatism removed.[33]

Labour won a landslide in May 1997. Gaining 418 seats, an increase of 145 from 1992, with 43% of the vote, Tony Blair had swept away the moribund Major government and now enjoyed a colossal parliamentary majority of 179. What part had the devolution pledge played in electoral terms? Labour saw a jump in support in Wales from 1992 by 5 percentage points to 54%, a gain of seven seats, while seeing a similar trend in Scotland: a 6-point rise to 45.6% of the vote, gaining seven seats. Nevertheless, it should be noted that Labour's gains came at the expense of the Conservatives in Wales and Scotland. Votes for both Plaid Cymru and the SNP actually went up in 1997.

New Labour duly fulfilled its pledge for national assemblies, holding referendums on the issue in September 1997—this time needing only a simple majority of votes. Scotland, with 74% voting in favour, was, as in 1979, more enthusiastic than Wales, which just passed with 50.3% backing devolution. Legislation was passed the following year, and the Scottish Parliament and Welsh Assembly were established in 1999. Tony Blair, meanwhile, saw his party's share of the vote decline in both Wales and Scotland in 2001 and 2005. After initially forming governments in both national legislatures, Labour also lost its primacy in Scotland to the SNP in the 2007 Scottish elections. After first governing as a minority administration, the SNP won a majority in 2011 and forced a referendum on independence in 2014, which was lost by 45% to 55%. At the time of writing, the SNP is the dominant party in Scotland, whereas Labour has retained its support in Wales. Clearly, events did not work out as imagined for Labour, and some may see John Major's view as prescient—of devolution being the stepping stone to separation—but, with the process still in its infancy, it is perhaps still too early to draw many conclusions between devolution and the long-term future of the union.

Taken in its maximalist form, New Labour's constitutional revolution was always likely to fall short. Electoral reform fell at an early stage. Blair tasked former Labour heavyweight and by now Liberal Democrat peer Roy Jenkins with compiling a report on electoral reform soon after the 1997 victory. Jenkins had formed the breakaway Social Democratic Party in 1981, was a biographer of Liberal Prime Minister Herbert Asquith and had long sought to 'realign' the left and "unite the strands of social democracy and liberalism".[34] Published the following year, the Jenkins Report, rather than recommend proportional representation as most—including Blair—had expected, proposed a hybrid system, "AV Plus".[35] The proposals were quickly shelved by Blair on the basis that he would not achieve cabinet approval of the plan.[36] In actual fact, having achieved a huge landslide the previous year, there was no incentive for Labour to alter the voting system that delivered such an overwhelming outcome. It would be the devolved administrations that saw a break from first past the post, all using a version of proportionality. Yet, the voting system may well have played a long-term role in the rise of populism in the UK. The Gallagher index measures the gap between votes and seats, acting as a proxy for proportionality. The index shows how, since the 1990s, a significant gap has emerged in Westminster elections, with the main parties generally gaining fewer votes but still most of the seats, compared with elections under devolution.[37] The gap in English constituencies is particularly stark, demonstrating a lack of democratic responsiveness between votes cast and MPs elected. The result was that the 2016 Brexit referendum offered many people in England the chance to vote and, unlike in other elections in the modern era, for that choice to be actually heard.

New Labour delivered on other aspects of constitutional reform. Its 1997 manifesto promised to "End the hereditary principle in the House of Lords" and establish "Elected mayors for London and other cities".[38] House of Lords reform proceeded in Blair's first term, reducing the numbers of hereditary peers but stalling before further, more democratic changes were initiated.[39] Devolution was also extended beyond Wales and Scotland. The Blair government's efforts to secure peace in Northern Ireland are widely considered one of its most significant achievements. After marathon talks between all sides in the province, a number of which had been initiated by the Major government, the Good Friday Agreement was signed in 1998 and then endorsed by referendum. As part of the process, the Northern Ireland Stormont assembly was to resume, having been suspended almost three decades previously, in a power-sharing format. This was to prove fiendishly difficult for the British government to put into practice, but, by the end of Blair's time in office, a power-sharing compromise of sorts had been reached, and Stormont operated for several years without the interruptions of its early phase.

English devolution

English devolution was the least pressing element of New Labour's constitutional programme, and only the re-establishment of a London city mayoralty, as well as a number of local unitary authorities, was achieved during the 1997–2010 period. London had traditionally had a mayor and a city administration, but the latter, the Greater London Authority (GLA), was abolished by the Thatcher government in 1986.[40] Led by Ken Livingstone and dominated by 'hard left' or, to use the media's derisory label from the era, 'loony left' activists and administrators, the GLA was part of a left-wing bloc of local councils that Margaret Thatcher despised.[41] Her objective, to dilute the power of big-spending local councils, caused the government to centralise political power in several instances, such as with the abolition of the GLA, despite the liberalising rhetoric of Thatcherism.

The tide began to turn in the 1990s. Although the Major government was generally unenthusiastic about devolution, it nevertheless sought to delegate more competencies back to local councils, after the centralisation of the Thatcher years.

The 'Citizen's Charter' could even be viewed as a mechanism to empower the individual, granting certain rights regarding public services and shifting power somewhat from the centre. Michael Heseltine, who was involved in a number of the key policies of the Major government, was more open to elected city mayors than other Conservative politicians.[42] Nevertheless, it was Tony Blair's government that brought back the mayoralty to London. A referendum was held on the issue in 1998, and 72% voted in favour, although on a low turn-out, and the first elections for the new body, which incidentally used the (proportional) supplementary vote system, were held in 2000. In an interesting twist, Ken Livingstone stood to get his old job back and won, despite opposition from Tony Blair himself. The mayor of London, therefore, has a strong personal mandate, although with competencies limited to areas such as transport and policing.

Following the first wave of devolution in the late 1990s, Labour subsequently sought to expand the policy. The 2000 Local Government Act made provision for more city and local mayors, although this was then limited to 11 unitary authorities in 2002. Before long, however, and with the government distracted by mounting problems—not least in foreign policy—the devolution agenda ran into the sand. The set piece for extending devolution in England was a plan to bring in elected mayors and administrations to three areas of the North East. Led by Deputy Prime Minister John Prescott, the North East devolution proposal fell flat with local voters. Amid widespread cynicism about the government's motivations as well as the likely impact, 78% voted against the idea in a referendum held in 2004. The overwhelming rejection of devolution in the North East caused Labour to shelve further devolution for the remainder of its time in office.

The constitutional changes introduced by Labour proved dynamic, setting forces in motion that clearly have not found an endpoint. Devolution outside London was rejected in England in 2004, but English voters did now appear dissatisfied with the political status quo, although this was also related to longer-term political trends. Critics, in line with Gallagher index data, talked about a democratic deficit in England outside London.[43] The rise of the UK Independence Party (UKIP) was most marked in provincial England during the 2000s and 2010s. As the SNP gained ground in Scotland, and a significant number—although not yet a majority—favoured independence north of the border, English nationalism also grew. After the 2014 Scottish independence referendum, Conservative Prime Minister David Cameron promised to look at ways to increase English voters' political clout, although Westminster politicians have generally stepped back from the idea of an English parliament.[44] In the 2010s, we have seen a situation whereby nationalism has grown both with (in Scotland) and without (in England) significant devolution. Nevertheless, the principle seems here to stay. The 2010–15 Conservative–Liberal Democrat coalition government was keen on extending devolution in England, most notably Chancellor of the Exchequer George Osbourne's 'Northern Powerhouse' concept. A number of 'metro mayors' were subsequently established, attracting Westminster figures such as Andy Burnham, in Manchester, to run for city hall. The Brexit referendum in 2016 also had implications for devolution. It was noteworthy how some of the largest votes to leave the EU occurred in areas with the lowest levels of local devolution. This point seems to have been taken up in the aftermath of Boris Johnson's landslide victory in the December 2019 general election, where the Conservatives picked up seats in former Labour strongholds, the so-called 'Red Wall', many of which voted heavily for leave.

In summary, after centralisation under the Thatcher government, political devolution has been one area where politicians have sought to disperse power since the 1990s. The results have been uneven. Whereas, in Scotland, the trend appears to be away from UK-centric parties towards the SNP and independence sentiment, Wales has focused on cultural concerns and increasing the use of the Welsh language. Labour's support in Wales has more or less held up. In England, London, with its city mayor, has increasingly looked like an island amid a country at various degrees of dissatisfaction with the established political parties. Devolution is now being extended in England. Policymakers seem keen to extend the agenda started by Labour in the late 1990s and disperse more political power.

European integration

Decentralisation of power from Whitehall has followed a somewhat uneven trajectory since 1979. Whereas the Thatcher and Major governments were resistant to dispersing power, the Blair government initiated the process of devolution that has since gathered momentum. During the same period, the composition and role of the European Union has also dramatically changed. From her early days in office, Margaret Thatcher embarked on a confrontational relationship with the European Economic Community (EEC) and its national leaders. From Britain's budgetary contributions in the early part of her premiership to German unification at the end, Thatcher proved an awkward 'partner' in 'Europe'. Nevertheless, despite her Eurosceptic positions after leaving office, most would consider Britain to have been an active and engaged EEC member during the 1980s. Indeed, the 1986 Single European Act included the framework for the 'single market' and an acceleration of intra-bloc trade. The single market demonstrated Britain's clout in moving the EEC policy agenda forward. The single market, however, also led to expanded rules and bureaucratic oversight from Brussels, developments far further from Thatcher's objectives.

As the Cold War ended, EEC leaders, particularly German Chancellor Helmut Kohl, moved quickly to alter the geopolitical status quo. Alongside the remarkably quick unification of Germany in 1990, policymakers in Brussels and national capitals, including France but also Britain, developed several far-reaching ideas. The countries formerly part of the Soviet Union's sphere of influence in Central and Eastern Europe were dramatically brought into the Western orbit with promises of trade and development funds if they committed to 'European' ideals and practices. The bloc also incorporated long-standing allies such as Sweden and Austria as full members. From 12 members at the end of the Cold War, membership grew to 25 by 2004. Even the EEC itself changed, becoming the European Union (EU) after the Maastricht Treaty was agreed in late 1991. The EU had three 'pillars', which included foreign policy, and four 'freedoms', of goods, capital, services and labour. The latter would mean free movement of people within the bloc. By now led by John Major, the British were concerned about the rush to create a single European currency and managed to gain an opt-out from the project. Nevertheless, these developments—the single market and its associated bureaucratic changes, expanding membership and single currency—caused disquiet for some in Britain.

Euroscepticism in Britain has a long history. After all, the debates about joining the 'Common Market' in the 1960s and 1970s were often bitter. The development of the EEC and then EU in the 1990s generated a new wave of Euroscepticism, predominantly on the right, which found fuel in the trends and events linked with European integration. Britain's membership of the European Exchange Rate Mechanism (ERM), the precursor to the single currency, proved contentious and then disastrous when the government was forced to suspend membership on Black Wednesday in 1992. The experience of Black Wednesday was proof for many that Britain should not involve itself in European monetary schemes. The establishment of the single currency, the euro, caused further disputes and a campaign by William Hague's Conservative Party at the 2001 general election to 'save the pound'.[45] Eurosceptic Tories would rail against Britain's budgetary contributions, 'diktats' from Brussels and rulings by the European Court of Justice. The thread that bound these complaints together, particularly prominently during the Maastricht process in the Major era, was a 'loss' of British sovereignty. Hostility towards the EU took a more xenophobic turn when the Blair government declined temporary freedom of movement restrictions for the new member states in 2004. This combination of issues fed into UKIP's nationalistic and sometimes distasteful offering—David Cameron once described the party as "fruit cakes and loonies and closet racists mostly"[46]—that was particularly appealing to the kinds of areas in England mentioned earlier, where devolution was thin and where proximity to decision-making already seemed distant. The result of this variant of Euroscepticism was a rise in English nationalism, which manifested itself in the vote to leave the EU in 2016. A map of the areas that voted to leave in the greatest numbers closely matches UKIP support in the elections leading up to the referendum; they are located in provincial England, away from the largest cities.[47]

Many of these trends, however, are due to structural changes in the UK and global economy. As we have seen in previous chapters, the make-up of the British economy changed over several decades, shifting towards services and away from heavy industry and manufacturing. Many of these jobs in services were located in cities, notably London, and South East England. Wealth accumulated in these areas, linked with other trends such as in the property market. The EU's single market implied a number a rules and oversight that could only be supervised from Brussels. One example we have seen in a previous chapter is the expanding competencies of the EU's Competition Directorate within the European Commission. The design of the single market, in which Britain played a key role, included the need for a 'level playing field' to equalise trading conditions and standards across the bloc. This all required supranational oversight, and surrendering national powers to Brussels was the crucial grievance for Eurosceptics. The trends seen in the EU were of a piece with others taking place in the world economy.

Globalisation and sovereignty

Perhaps the core focus of populists' anger towards the status quo in the early years of the century, particularly after the 2007–08 financial crisis, has been globalisation. Although the process did not start during the 1979–2007 period, it certainly accelerated in these years and appeared to be turbo-charged by UK government decision-making. Economic relationships were increasingly managed at a supranational level, and multinational corporations had enough clout to circumvent national government rules and regulations. Globalisation has led to material benefits, accompanied by a feeling of powerlessness, for millions.

Broadly speaking, globalisation is the expanding network of international trade and of a rising level of global trade as a proportion of all trade. Put a different way, globalisation indices frame this as the combined total of imports and exports divided by world GDP.[48] The trend is not new and has increased at various points in history. The global trade proportion measure is a useful metric because, seen over the longer term, it acts as a proxy for rising or falling globalisation. For instance, this figure fell in 1914 and only started to pick up after the Second World War. Moreover, we can see it accelerate from the early 1970s, which coincides with the end of the Bretton Woods system of fixed exchange rates tied to the US dollar and backed by gold. US President Richard Nixon closed the 'gold window', bringing in a new era of floating rates not anchored by gold, in one of the most consequential decisions of his time in office, in August 1971.[49] Modern globalisation has been underpinned by dramatic advances in technology, allowing finance firms to rapidly expand as money flows around the world in seconds. As well as the financial and trade implications of globalisation, academics and critics have identified how culture, language and relationships have been transformed by the greater interconnection encouraged by these processes. By the 1990s, those more sympathetic to globalisation talked about a 'global village',[50] whereas, to critics, the trends represented cultural 'homogenisation' and even the neo-imperialism of unchecked modern capitalism.[51]

Where did Britain fit into all this? UK governments have been buffeted by the new economic reality at certain points, including financial crashes, while also helping to accelerate these trends. As discussed elsewhere in this study, the Thatcher government's abolition of exchange controls in 1979 and liberalisation of the City of London in 1986 gave a boost to the finance sector, cementing London's place as a world financial hub. In this respect, Britain moved into the vanguard of new economic trends during the 1980s. In foreign policy, the Thatcher government pursued a pro-trade agenda, pushing the development of the European single market through the 1986 Single European Act and also the reductions in tariffs achieved during the General Agreement on Trade and Tariffs (GATT) Uruguay Round.[52] The Conservatives reduced corporation tax, liberalised the labour market through its tough stance towards trade unions and generally pursued the kind of light touch regulation of the financial sector continued by the Major and Blair governments.[53] Taken together, these programmes favoured big business and helped it thrive in the new globalised economy.

The growing size of companies became an issue. By the 1990s, the terms multinational corporations (MNCs) and transnational corporations became widely used for corporations whose revenues and capital exceeded that of some sovereign states. Therein developed a key issue regarding the structure of the global economy: sovereignty. The world economy shifted throughout the final decades of the 20th century. National governments sought to attract foreign direct investment by incentivising companies' presence in their territories. Much of these pro-business components were put in place by the Thatcher government: reduced taxes, openness to trade, deregulation and labour market flexibility through trade union reform. Multilateral organisations such as the World Trade Organization (WTO), from 1995 the successor to the GATT, encouraged an orthodoxy on trade based around these principles. This policy toolbox was dubbed the Washington Consensus during the 1990s, although the lineage of the term was somewhat more specific than the 'market fundamentalist' derision it received from the left.[54]

The 1990s saw the high point of globalisation. After the end of the Cold War, trade barriers came down, with the United States, and the West more generally, in the ascendency. Market-based liberal democracy was now hegemonic; political economy had reached the "End of History".[55] Against this backdrop, the incoming New Labour government did not fundamentally swim against the tide of the times. Perhaps the crucial area that disappointed its traditional supporters was the failure to reverse Conservative trade union legislation and, to a lesser extent, privatisation.[56] In some respects, Labour rode the economic gains in the spirit of the times. While Gordon Brown and Ed Balls, counter to claims that New Labour was simply a continuation of neoliberalism, worked out complex ways of redistributing growth at the Treasury, other ministers such as Peter Mandelson made quite un-Labour pronouncements about being 'intensely relaxed' over individual wealth.[57] As we have already seen, at the time, New Labour figures tended to make a virtue of light-touch regulation of the financial sector.

There were real gains in the 1990s and 2000s. Economic growth after Black Wednesday in 1992 and when the financial crisis intensified in 2008 was impressive: 15 years of sustained expansion.[58] At the same time, and as we shall see, the Bank of England oversaw a monetary environment of low inflation and low interest rates. The housing market grew, and the proportion of homeowners increased.[59] The prices of many consumer items fell in relative terms, particularly as a result of technological advances. To give one example that captured the zeitgeist, the forerunner to the Apple Mac home computer, the NeXTcube, was launched by Steve Jobs in 1988 during his stint away from Apple. With much of the functionality that would become familiar to Apple users, the then state-of-the-art machine retailed in 1988 at US$6,500 (equivalent to $14,000 in 2020 prices).[60] When Jobs launched the iMac home computer in 1998, after his return to Apple, it cost US$1,299 (equivalent to $2,000 in 2020). An iPhone, launched in 2007, which performed many of its predecessor's tasks and was essentially a portable computer, cost $499 (equivalent to $620 in 2020). This represented a staggering fall in price over the space of two decades. The functionality of the NeXTcube, affordable only to the well-off or institutions in 1988, looked almost quaint in comparison with subsequent computers and devices available by the turn of the century; its capacity and features—although not cheap compared with Apple's competitors—were available to many more consumers as a result of complex globalised trading patterns and a revolution in technology. With development galloping along and the size and cost of key components such as microchips shrinking, these markets benefitted from globalisation. Many of the parts of consumer goods, including Apple's products, were produced in developing countries, sometimes deemed emerging economies—in particular, China.[61]

Despite the benefits to consumers of reduced prices, not every product or item has followed the same pattern. Global supply chains are susceptible to shocks, which can cause the prices of commodities and food, for example, to oscillate.[62] Critics of globalisation also articulate a long list of downsides to the process and decision-makers that have facilitated the process, particularly focused on the impact of trade and the associated rapid changes on some communities.[63] Although much of this has emanated from the left, in recent years these themes have been incorporated by the nationalist right and processed as anti-migration sentiment. Whereas protests against globalisation, for instance at WTO meetings—notably the 1999 'Battle for Seattle'—and the more recent Occupy movement, have tended to focus on weakened labour rights and 'outsourcing', environmental degradation and the threat to indigenous populations, at the ballot box, anti-globalisation feeling has appeared more likely to benefit the nativist right.

Political scientist Dani Rodrik has identified a number of the core themes of 'hyperglobalisation' in his work. The 'paradox' of globalisation, according to Rodrik, is that economic gains are increasingly outweighed by political losses.[64] One of the focal points for Rodrik is the interplay between democracy and globalisation, whereby power is increasingly yielded to regional and international organisations that weaken national governments and generate disquiet among disenfranchised populations. Making the direct link between globalisation and the rise of populism, Rodrik noted, "The rise of populism forces a necessary reality check. Today the big challenge facing policy makers is to rebalance globalization so to maintain a reasonably open world economy while curbing its excesses".[65]

Yet, although globalisation has been questioned by academics, protestors and eventually voters, for decades an increasingly integrated world economy was seen as inevitable. Thatcherite ministers explained their programme, of pro-enterprise and stable monetary conditions, as TINA (there is no alternative).[66] Tony Blair, meanwhile, thought that globalisation was a reality that had to be accepted. In his 2005 Labour Party conference speech, Blair said, "I hear people say we have to stop and debate globalisation. You might as well debate whether autumn should follow summer".[67] The view that government should play a more technocratic role, providing stable conditions for trade to operate, can be seen in particular in the decision to grant the Bank of England independence in 1997.

Bank of England independence

When the incoming Labour government announced it would grant operational independence to the Bank of England in May 1997, it was presented and reported as a great departure from orthodoxy. This was an unusual example of central government giving away power. Gordon Brown and Ed Balls go into much detail in their respective memoirs about the policy and the amount of resistance it came up against politically and institutionally. Some critics suggested that monetary policy was now run in the interests of big business, and not with the concerns of voters in mind.[68] Others have posited the move as another piece of the neoliberal agenda underpinning and driving globalisation and, as a result, being fundamentally anti-democratic.[69] An independent central bank was indeed a neoliberal concern, albeit for particular strands of neoliberalism, but it was in fact Britain that was out of step with its contemporaries by 1997. A number of other developed economies, notably Germany and the US, had had independent central banks for decades by the 1990s.

Inflation was the Thatcher government's primary focus when it came to office in 1979. The attempts to reduce it between 1979 and 1983 were a tortuous series of efforts to control the money supply and reduce public spending. The task was made all the more difficult by the impact of North Sea oil, accompanied by the removal of exchange controls, which caused sterling to appreciate. The first Thatcher government, with Geoffrey Howe as Chancellor of the Exchequer, was bitterly divisive for many in Britain, as the tight monetary policy and rising prices of British exports accelerated industrial decline, causing widespread factory closures and levels of unemployment not seen since the 1930s. By 1983, Howe was claiming a victory of sorts when inflation fell to 5%.

To understand the turmoil of British monetary policy during the Thatcher years—the issue re-emerged during the third administration, in 1987–90—one needs to look at UK inflation figures during the 1970s. Having hovered at or around 5% during the 1960s, inflation leapt to almost 10% in 1971, then an eyewatering 23% in 1975 and was still 14% in 1979.[70] Inflation had been a key issue for neoliberals for years.[71] There was some disagreement over the role of trade unions, with some, such as Friedrich Hayek, stating that union wage demands were a driver of inflation, whereas others, including Milton Friedman, thought unions were responding to inflation in the rest of the economy.[72] Friedman was the best-known neoliberal thinker during this era, famously describing inflation as "always and everywhere a monetary phenomenon", and he articulated the view that government spending and market intervention led to inflation.[73] In this way, the neoliberal critique formed in the 1970s that government should reduce subsidies to ailing firms and public spending more generally. By and large, it would be the approach taken by the Thatcher government. Others, particularly in retrospect, have pointed to the (external) oil price shocks of 1973 and 1979 as crucial, pushing up prices and, therefore, playing down the neoliberal argument.[74]

During the years spent attempting to tame inflation in the 1970s, 1980s and 1990s, attention was often on the base interest rate. Ultimate authority over this rate lay with the Chancellor of the Exchequer, and, although it was usually coordinated with the Bank of England, the level often took on a political dimension. Chancellors were accused of crafting 'election budgets' and lowering the interest rate in the run-up to a general election.[75] Margaret Thatcher, supposedly a true believer in free markets, would continually pressure her chancellors to reduce interest rates to benefit mortgage payers—that is to say, core Conservative voters. Indeed, Charles Moore has described how "such disagreements were endemic in the relationship between Chancellor and Prime Minister".[76] Thatcher also wanted central bank intervention to prevent sterling falling to parity with the dollar in the mid-1980s, seemingly owing to the loss in British prestige such a level would represent.[77] In summary, politicians used interest rate decisions for more than simply the control of inflation.

For neoliberals, politicised monetary policy was seen as a crucial component in chronic inflation. In Germany, this problem was particularly salient, and the analysis that inflation was directly linked with interwar political instability is one that has endured. The Ordoliberal-inspired 1949 German constitution, the Basic Law, made provisions for an independent central bank, the Bundesbank. The Chicago School also saw the importance of an independent Federal Reserve, established in 1913, for maintaining price stability. For Milton Friedman, this would manifest itself in monetarism. Not all neoliberals thought central banks were useful or that they could function independently. Friedrich von Hayek thought attempts at monetary control through central banks were inherently political and another form of government intervention that would ultimately distort the workings of free markets. Hayek advocated 'choice' in currency, to let the market decide which currency was the most secure.[78]

Despite the Thatcher government's professed economic liberalism, there was little appetite to give up the discretionary power over interest rates in the 1980s. Nevertheless, there is evidence to show that the more independent the central bank, the lower inflation over the medium term. Studies showing the degree of independence compared with average inflation rates between the 1950s and 1980s indicate that the UK experienced higher inflation and lower central bank independence compared with its contemporaries.[79] Although many Conservative politicians, including several chancellors, seemed attracted to, or wholeheartedly supportive of, Bank of England independence, Margaret Thatcher and John Major were reluctant to surrender control over interest rates.[80] In addition, a new arrangement during the 1990s, without central bank independence, finally brought inflation under control.

1990s: inflation targeting and independence

After two decades of oscillating inflation, including a rise to 7% in 1990, the Major government oversaw a period of low inflation. From 1993, the relationship between Chancellor Ken Clarke and Bank of England Governor Eddie George was portrayed as so cordial that the press dubbed the pair's monthly meetings the "Ken and Eddie Show".[81] Clarke took over from Norman Lamont several months after the humiliation of Black Wednesday in September 1992, when Britain suspended its membership of the ERM. At the same time, the Bank of England adopted a new method in its monetary policy: inflation targeting. The bank initially adopted a target range of 1–4% until 1995 and involved forecasts for the exchange rate—essentially devalued after Black Wednesday—and interest rates.[82] Nevertheless, the bank was not formally independent. Ultimate responsibility for interest rates still fell to the chancellor.

The UK economy appeared to have finally tamed inflation in the mid-1990s. Labour Party modernisers, however, were still highly sensitive to accusations that they could not be trusted with the public finances, a charge that seemingly cost them the 1992 election. Between 1992 and 1997, Gordon Brown, alongside his advisor Ed Balls and other New Labour figures, worked tirelessly to show how the party was now a sober, competent government-in-waiting, not the spendthrift throwback to the past. A part of this programme, which included promises not to increase the top rate of income tax and even to stick to Conservative spending limits for the first 2 years of a Labour government, was Bank of England independence. Balls and Brown worked through the concept in opposition, Balls later stating that he thought the move would "transform the party's economic credibility",[83] while Brown said, "it would give both the public and the markets confidence that we had put in place a framework to ensure stability and keep inflation low".[84] Wanting to make a bold move upon taking office, Brown announced the bank's operational independence the day after the 1997 general election victory. The actual practicality of implementing the change led to some tension between the Treasury and the bank. As part of the shift, Labour wanted to set up a regulator, the Financial Services Authority, outside the remit of the Bank of England. Ultimately, this was watered down by Eddie George and the bank, and Brown had to settle for a compromise that, according to his memoirs, "was far less definitive on who did what than it should have been".[85] The new monetary policy arrangements were an extension of the previous set-up: an inflation target of 2.5%, led by a monetary policy committee that met monthly, and a letter from the bank governor to the chancellor if inflation strayed from its target range. The new system appeared to be a success. Inflation did not rise above 3% until 2008.

Subsequently, UK monetary policy has come in for criticism owing to its narrow focus on inflation. After the financial crash, commentators complained that this approach, including its quantitative easing programme, was benefitting the well-off, including shareholders, at the expense of those in the real economy. Operational independence occurred as globalisation accelerated during the 1990s and as opinions about what government could and should do were changing. As free markets were the only game in town, the role of government seemed to become more technocratic. Maintaining a benign monetary environment was necessary to allow business and trade to proceed in a stable economic system. Therefore, Bank of England independence can be seen as a move that prioritised business and finance in a rapidly globalising world. Although the arrangement continued to function as intended regarding inflation, financial regulation—as discussed elsewhere in this book—in hindsight was too light-touch to acknowledge the structural dangers within the banking system. In the after-math of the 2008 crash, the Bank of England acted to prevent a depression through asset buying. Nevertheless, there has been criticism about this arrangement, crucially regarding accountability. As one retrospective remarked in the British press, "the Bank has become more powerful and more political but not more accountable".[86] Some of the discussions revolve around arguments made before independence, that the central bank is both unaccountable and essentially anti-democratic.[87] Others suggest that the mandate of the bank should be altered to include targets for employment and environmental outcomes. Even Ed Balls has called for a rethink, writing, "the new powers it has acquired since the financial crisis require a new framework to reconcile operational independence with effectiveness and accountability".[88]

Conclusion

This chapter has looked at several seemingly disparate case studies: devolution, European integration, globalisation and Bank of England independence. The thread that ties these topics together, however, is the shift in power in modern Britain the trends represent. After resistance from the Thatcher and Major governments, New Labour devolved powers to Scotland, Wales, Northern Ireland and London. In the years since this constitutional upheaval, devolution has been increasingly—although unevenly—rolled out to other areas of England. The results have included a surge in pro-independence sentiment in Scotland, while lack of devolved power in England may also be linked to a rise in English nationalism in some areas. The latter trend was important in voters abandoning traditional parties and embracing populist outfits such as UKIP and subsequently voting to leave the EU. European integration accelerated after the end of the Cold War, leading to constitutional changes that drew criticism from, in particular, the right-wing press and Conservative politicians. The perception was that Britain had surrendered sovereignty to an undemocratic set of institutions in Brussels. These assertions were debated during the Brexit referendum campaign and, in particular, its aftermath.

In part, the forces of nationalism and populism in recent years have demonstrated the fragility of the UK's constitutional arrangements. Globalisation, and related trends such as the rise of the independent central bank, seemed to create a new normal of dominant MNCs operating almost beyond the purview of the nation-state, with little oversight from global institutions. The contemporary economic system and its enablers have been accused of hostility towards trade unions and non-economic concerns. Importantly, globalisation has become a central part of the argument that national governments are no longer accountable to their citizens, and democracy is not responsive enough. A combination of these trends is implicated in the rise of populism. Political devolution is one way to counter the populist surge, although, judging by the results in Scotland, one could also see—without knowing the counterfactual impact of denying devolution—the process as being a catalyst for renewed nationalism. Nevertheless, the period since 1979 has seen power reconfigured, moving from central government in several directions. A number of groups have reacted against these trends, fuelling the rise of populism.

Notes

1 Frank Bealey, *Power in Business and the State: An Historical Analysis of Its Concentration* (Abingdon: Routledge, 2001), 149, 178–179.
2 John Callaghan, "The Plan to Capture the British Labour Party and Its Paradoxical Results, 1947–91", *Journal of Contemporary History*, 40:4 (2005), 707–725.
3 Margaret Thatcher Foundation (hereafter MTF), MTF 108353, Margaret Thatcher, "Keith Joseph Memorial Lecture ('Liberty and Limited Government')", 11 January 1996.
4 Conservative Party 1979 Election Manifesto, www.conservativemanifesto.com/1979/1979-conservative-manifesto.shtml [accessed 30 April 2020].
5 Mark Townsend, "How the Battle of Lewisham Helped to Halt the Rise of Britain's Far Right", *The Guardian*, 13 August 2017, www.theguardian.com/uk-news/2017/aug/13/battle-of-lewisham-national-front-1977-far-right-london-police [accessed 30 April 2020].
6 Jonathan Freedland, "Enough of this Cover-Up: The Wilson Plot Was Our Watergate", *The Guardian*, 15 March 2006, www.theguardian.com/commentisfree/2006/mar/15/comment.labour1 [accessed 30 April 2020].
7 Felipe Andrés Orellana Pérez and Pedro Pérez Herrero, "The Shadow of Nationalism in the New Populist Proposals in Europe", *The Conversation*, 19 May 2019, https://theconversation.com/the-shadow-of-nationalism-in-the-new-populist-proposals-in-europe-117127 [accessed 4 May 2020].
8 Lukas Audickas, Richard Cracknell and Philip Loft, "UK Election Statistics: 1918–2019: A Century of Elections", Briefing Paper CBP7529, House of Commons Library, 27 February 2020, 20.
9 Ibid., 18.
10 Richard Finlay, "Thatcherism, Unionism and Nationalism: A Comparative Study of Scotland and Wales", eds. Ben Jackson and Robert Saunders, *Making Thatcher's Britain* (Cambridge: Cambridge University Press, 2012, 165–179), 172–173.
11 Dafydd Hancock, "A Channel for Wales", EMC Seefour, 1 January 2002, https://web.archive.org/web/20090304205140/http://www.transdiffusion.org/emc/seefour/wales.php [accessed 6 May 2020].
12 BBC Radio Wales, "Gwynfor Evans Hunger Strike, 1980", Welsh Experience: Gwynfor Evans, 3 May 2011, www.bbc.co.uk/programmes/p00gpzsf [accessed 6 May 2020].
13 Elain Price, "A Cultural Exchange: S4C, Channel 4 and Film", *Historical Journal of Film, Radio and Television*, 33:3 (2013), 418–433.
14 Helen Carter, "Police Take Fresh Look at Sons of Glyndwr", *The Guardian*, 11 March 2004, www.theguardian.com/uk/2004/mar/11/helencarter [accessed 6 March 2020].
15 *Daily Post*, "Gwynfor 'Was Thinking of Martyrdom'", 9 November 2005, www.dailypost.co.uk/news/north-wales-news/gwynfor-was-thinking-of-martyrdom-2902456 [accessed 6 May 2020].
16 Finlay, "Thatcherism, Unionism and Nationalism", 173.
17 Charles Moore, *Margaret Thatcher: The Authorized Biography, Volume Two: Everything She Wants* (London: Allen Lane, 2015), 359–360; John Campbell, *Margaret Thatcher. Volume Two: The Iron Lady*, (London: Pimlico, 2004), 556.
18 Moore, *Volume Two*, 367; *BBC News*, "Secret Papers Reveal Push to 'Trailblaze' Poll Tax in Scotland", 30 December 2014, www.bbc.com/news/uk-scotland-scotland-politics-30610043 [accessed 7 May 2020].
19 Campbell, *Iron Lady*, 558.

20 Michael Lavalette and Gerry Mooney, "The Struggle against the Poll Tax in Scotland", *Critical Social Policy*, 9:26 (September 1989), 82–100.
21 Campbell, *Iron Lady*, 560.
22 Moore, *Volume Two*, 373.
23 Philip Sim, "Who Is Nicola Sturgeon? A Profile of the SNP Leader", *BBC News*, 26 May 2017, www.bbc.com/news/uk-scotland-25333635 [accessed 5 May 2020].
24 Finlay, "Thatcherism, Unionism and Nationalism", 171.
25 Catherine McGlynn and Shaun McDaid, "'72 Hours to Save the Union': John Major and Devolution", eds. Kevin Hickson and Ben Williams, *John Major: An Unsuccessful Prime Minister? Reappraising John Major* (London: Biteback, 2017, 91–105), 92.
26 Finlay, "Thatcherism, Unionism and Nationalism", 179.
27 McGlynn and McDaid, "'72 Hours'", 92.
28 Ibid., 96–97.
29 Labour Party 1992 Manifesto, "It's Time to Get Britain Working Again", www.labour -party.org.uk/manifestos/1992/1992-labour-manifesto.shtml [accessed 11 May 2020].
30 Paul Sweeney, "'A Great Future Prime Minister Lost to This Country': On the Legacy of John Smith", *New Statesman*, 13 May 2019, www.newstatesman.com/politics/stagg ers/2019/05/great-future-prime-minister-lost-country-legacy-john-smith   [accessed 11 May 2020].
31 Gerry Hassan and Eric Shaw, *The Strange Death of Labour Scotland* (Edinburgh: Edinburgh University Press, 2012), 60.
32 Pauline Schnapper, "New Labour, Devolution and British Identity: The Foreign Policy Consequences", eds. Oliver Daddow and Jamie Gaskarth, *British Foreign Policy* (Palgrave Macmillan, 2011, 48–62).
33 Labour Party 1997 Manifesto, "New Labour: Because Britain Deserves Better", www .labour-party.org.uk/manifestos/1997/1997-labour-manifesto.shtml [accessed 11 May 2020].
34 John Campbell, *Roy Jenkins: A Well-Rounded Life* (London: Jonathan Cape, 2014), 723.
35 Oonagh Gay, "Voting Systems: The Jenkins Report", Research Paper 98/112, 10 December 1998 (House of Commons Library).
36 Campbell, *Roy Jenkins*, 714–715.
37 Kelly Shuttleworth, "Electoral Systems across the UK", Institute for Government, 1 July 2020, www.instituteforgovernment.org.uk/explainers/electoral-systems-uk [accessed 17 August 2020].
38 Labour Party 1997 Manifesto.
39 Deborah Summers, "Labour's Attempts to Reform the House of Lords", *The Guardian*, 27 January 2009, www.theguardian.com/politics/2009/jan/27/house-of-lords-reform [accessed 12 May 2020].
40 Moore, *Volume Two*, 372.
41 Esther Webber, "The Rise and Fall of the GLC", *BBC News*, 31 March 2016, www.bbc .com/news/uk-england-london-35716693 [accessed 13 May 2020].
42 Russell Deacon, *Devolution in the United Kingdom* (Edinburgh: Edinburgh University Press, 2012), 47.
43 Ibid., 55.
44 Ibid., 54.
45 BBC News, "Hague: 'Last Chance to Save Pound'", 31 January 2001, http://news.bbc .co.uk/2/hi/uk_news/politics/1146210.stm [accessed 13 July 2020].
46 Jamie Lyons, "Ukip Are Closet Racists, Says Cameron", *Independent*, 4 April 2006, www.independent.co.uk/news/uk/politics/ukip-are-closet-racists-says-cameron-6104 699.html [accessed 13 July 2020].
47 *BBC News*, "EU Referendum: The Result in Maps and Charts", 24 June 2016, www .bbc.com/news/uk-politics-36616028 [accessed 13 July 2020]; Eric Kaufmann, "Rochester and UKIP: We Shouldn't Leap to the Conclusion that This By-Election

is a Bellwether for 2015", LSE British Politics and Policy Blog, 21 November 2014, https://blogs.lse.ac.uk/politicsandpolicy/rochester-and-ukip-we-shouldnt-leap-to -the-conclusion-that-this-by-election-is-a-bellwether-for-2015/ [accessed 13 July 2020].

48 Esteban Ortiz-Ospina and Diana Beltekian, "Trade and Globalization", *Our World in Data*, October 2018, https://ourworldindata.org/trade-and-globalization [accessed 20 May 2020].

49 Luke A. Nichter, *Richard Nixon and Europe: The Reshaping of the Postwar Atlantic World* (Cambridge: Cambridge University Press, 2015), 36–67.

50 OECD, "A Global or Semi-Global Village? (1990s to Today)", *Economic Globalisation: Origins and Consequences* (OECD Publishing: Paris, 2013), 48–67.

51 For instance, see John Tomlinson, "Homogenisation and Globalisation", *History of European Ideas*, 20:4–6 (1995), 891–897; Johanna Bockman, "Socialist Globalization against Capitalist Neocolonialism: The Economic Ideas behind the New International Economic Order", *Humanity: An International Journal of Human Rights, Humanitarianism, and Development*, 6:1 (2015), 109–128.

52 Lynda Chalker, House of Commons Debates (14 July 1989), vol. 156, col. 1239–308. GATT was one of the Bretton Woods institutions created at the end of the Second World War. It was succeeded by the WTO in 1995.

53 Nigel Lawson, "Tax Reform (The Government's Record) (CPC pamphlet)", June 1988, MTF 109507.

54 John Williamson, "The Strange History of the Washington Consensus", *Journal of Post Keynesian Economics*, 27:2 (2005), 195–206.

55 Francis Fukuyama, *The End of History and the Last Man* (New York: Free Press, 1992).

56 Carole Thornley and Dan Coffey, *Globalization and Varieties of Capitalism: New Labour, Economic Policy and the Abject State* (Basingstoke: Palgrave Macmillan, 2009), 12, 33–34.

57 George Parker, "A Fiscal Focus", *Financial Times*, 7 December 2009, www.ft.com/content/5f0bf460-e36d-11de-8d36-00144feab49a [accessed 25 May 2020].

58 Office for National Statistics, "Changes in the Economy since the 1970s", 2 September 2019, www.ons.gov.uk/economy/economicoutputandproductivity/output/articles/changesintheeconomysincethe1970s/2019-09-02 [accessed 25 May 2020].

59 UK House Price Index, "House Price Statistics January 1991-March 2018", *Land Registry*, https://landregistry.data.gov.uk/app/ukhpi/browse?from=1991-01-01&location=http%3A%2F%2Flandregistry.data.gov.uk%2Fid%2Fregion%2Funited-kingdom&to=2018-03-01 [accessed 25 May 2020].

60 Using comparison website measuringworth.com

61 *The Economist*, "Foxconn and Labour Laws: Using Globalisation for Good", 24 February 2012, www.economist.com/democracy-in-america/2012/02/24/using -globalisation-for-good [accessed 25 May 2020].

62 Chris Arsenault, "Globalization Worsens Food Price Shocks for Importers— Researchers—TRFN", *Reuters*, 12 May 2015, www.reuters.com/article/us-food-climatechange-politics/globalization-worsens-food-price-shocks-for-importers-researchers-trfn-idUSKBN0NX24D20150512 [accessed 26 May 2020].

63 David Held and Anthony McGrew, *Globalization/Anti-Globalization* (Cambridge: Policy Press, 2003), 25–37, 62–63.

64 Dani Rodrik, *The Globalization Paradox: Democracy and the Future of the World Economy* (New York: W.W. Norton, 2011), 157, 231–232.

65 Dani Rodrik, "Populism and the Economics of Globalization", Working Paper 23559, National Bureau of Economic Research (Cambridge, MA, July 2017), 27.

66 Nick Robinson, "Economy: There Is No Alternative (TINA) Is Back", *BBC News*, 7 March 2013, www.bbc.com/news/uk-politics-21703018 [accessed 26 May 2020].

67 Tony Blair, "2005 Labour Party Conference Speech", *The Guardian*, 27 September 2005, www.theguardian.com/uk/2005/sep/27/labourconference.speeches [accessed 26 May 2020].
68 Katie Kedward, "Why It's Time to Abandon the Myth of Central Bank Independence", *Open Democracy*, 1 April 2019, www.opendemocracy.net/en/oureconomy/central-b ank-independence-myth-its-time-abandon-it/ [accessed 13 July 2020].
69 Robert Geyer, Andrew Mackintosh and Kai Lehmann, *Integrating UK and European Social Policy: The Complexity of Europeanisation* (Oxford: Radcliffe, 2005), 144.
70 Office for National Statistics, "Changes in the Economy Since the 1970s".
71 Robert Ledger, *Neoliberal Thought and Thatcherism: "A Transition from Here to There?"* (Abingdon: Routledge, 2017), 23–25, 39–42, 54–55.
72 Milton Friedman, *Inflation and Unemployment: The New Dimension of Politics. The 1976 Alfred Nobel Memorial Lecture* (London: IEA, Occasional Paper 51, 1977), 1–18; Adrian Williamson, *Conservative Economic Policymaking and the Birth of Thatcherism, 1964–1979* (Basingstoke: Palgrave Macmillan, 2015), 170.
73 Milton Friedman and Anna Schwartz, *A Monetary History of the United States* (Princeton: Princeton University Press, 2015, first published 1963).
74 Andy Beckett, *When the Lights Went Out: Britain in the Seventies* (London: Faber & Faber, 2009), 129.
75 Patrick Barkham, "Setting Britain's Interest Rates", *The Guardian*, 10 February 2000, www.theguardian.com/world/2000/feb/10/qanda.interestrates [accessed 29 May 2020].
76 Charles Moore, *Margaret Thatcher: The Authorized Biography, Volume Three: Herself Alone* (London: Allen Lane, 2019), 102–103.
77 Nigel Lawson, *The View From No. 11* (London: Corgi Books, 1993), 468–469.
78 F.A. Hayek, *The Constitution of Liberty* (London: Routledge, 2006, first published 1960), 291; F.A. Hayek, *Choice in Currency. A Way to Stop Inflation* (London: IEA, 1976), 14–22.
79 Ed Balls and Anna Stansbury, "Twenty Years On: Is There Still a Case for Bank of England Independence?", *Vox EU*, 1 May 2017, https://voxeu.org/article/twenty-years -there-still-case-bank-england-independence [accessed 27 May 2020].
80 Ken Clarke, *Kind of Blue: A Political Memoir* (Basingstoke: Macmillan, 2016), 323.
81 Stephen Fay, "What Comes after the Ken and Eddie Show?", *The Independent*, 16 February 1997, www.independent.co.uk/news/what-comes-after-the-ken-and-eddi e-show-1278965.html [accessed 2 June 2020].
82 Andrew Haldane, "Targeting Inflation: The United Kingdom in Retrospect", eds. Mario I. Bléjer, Alain Ize, Alfredo Mario Leone and Sérgio Ribeiro da Costa Werlang, *Inflation Targeting in Practice: Strategic and Operational Issues and Application to Emerging Economies* (Washington, D.C.: IMF, 2000, 52–59).
83 Ed Balls, *Speaking Out: Lessons in Life and Politics* (Reading: Arrow Books, 2016), 146.
84 Gordon Brown, *My Life, Our Times* (London: Bodley Head, 2017), 116.
85 Ibid., 120–121.
86 *The Guardian*, "*The Guardian* View on the Bank of England: Independence and Accountability", 4 May 2017, www.theguardian.com/commentisfree/2017/may /04/the-guardian-view-on-the-bank-of-england-independence-and-accountability [accessed 27 May 2020].
87 Ferdinando Giugliano, Sam Fleming and Claire Jones, "Central Banks: Peak Independence", *Financial Times*, 8 November 2015, www.ft.com/content/f0664634-7c d4-11e5-98fb-5a6d4728f74e [accessed 27 May 2020].
88 Balls and Stansbury, "Twenty Years On".

6   Politics and power

This chapter will further explore the distribution of power in UK politics by examining the trends towards concentration at the top of government, greater income inequality within British society and how governing pressures altered from the 1970s until the 2000s. A number of the themes covered in this chapter developed in an uneven fashion. For instance, concerns over a presidential style of government and concentration of power within the executive have usually depended on the size of a prime minister's parliamentary majority. Others have arisen as a result of specific structural changes to the British economy, such as regulatory 'capture' and income inequality. External developments and events such as accelerating globalisation have been responsible for a number of trends, including the rise of multinational corporations and finance, associated with widening disparities in wealth. Some appear to be more or less consistent regardless of which party is in power, such as the numerous scandals that have plagued British politics since the 1990s, and, although driven in no small part by the rise of a 24-hour media industry, these scandals have accumulated in the minds of the public, ultimately weakening trust and making space for populism.

Executive power

A common criticism during the post-1979 era has been that British prime ministers have accumulated ever greater power. In particular, Margaret Thatcher and Tony Blair were accused of running a presidential style of government. This, in turn, has led to the sentiment that the growing clout of Number 10 Downing Street demonstrates a widening distance between rulers and the ruled and a weakening of democratic accountability. To what extent, then, has power concentrated in the executive since 1979?

Margaret Thatcher was known for bringing in close advisors, much to the chagrin of ministers and the civil service, who were then overruled or opposed. These included her press secretary, Bernard Ingham, economic advisor, Alan Walters and, in particular, foreign policy advisor, Charles Powell. In economic and foreign policy, critics and colleagues alleged that Thatcher was making decisions behind closed doors and disregarding departmental policy, or actively working against them.[1] When John Major came to office in 1990, he declared he would reinstate cabinet government—that is to say, collective decision-making.[2] One particularly well-known demonstration of this occurred during Black Wednesday in September 1992, when he called his key ministers to Admiralty House to oversee the chaos of Britain's eventual departure from the ERM, or, as Ken Clarke put it, 'dip their hands in the blood'.[3] Tony Blair seemed to move in the opposite direction, allegedly running a 'sofa government', whereby key decisions were made outside Cabinet in small groups, using Cabinet itself as a mere rubber stamp.[4] Gordon Brown was also portrayed as a leader who concentrated operations within Number 10, although this has been described as more dysfunctional than Blair's office.

Since the New Labour era, we have seen a selection of unique situations: the Conservative–Liberal Democrat coalition government, David Cameron's short-lived majority administration, the troubled Theresa May premiership either side of the 2017 election and Boris Johnson's already tumultuous period as prime minister. The coalition organised regular 'quad' meetings between David Cameron and George Osbourne and leading Liberal Democrats Nick Clegg and Danny Alexander.[5] Clearly, this was a different power hierarchy to that in Thatcher's or Blair's heyday. Since the coalition, there have been further complaints that the prime ministers have wielded too much power, as have their unelected officials—Nick Timothy and Fiona Hill in Theresa May's case, and Dominic Cummings for Boris Johnson. Yet, in the final analysis, it is difficult to perceive any concentration of power at the top of British politics. The instances described above are highly contingent on a prime minister's parliamentary majority.[6] In the cases of Thatcher and Blair, their success at the ballot box and the size of their majorities gave them significant authority, which they exercised accordingly. Major, Cameron and May all seemed less potent figures owing to the precariousness of their parliamentary position. Indeed, May was forced to jettison her influential advisors after she lost her parliamentary majority. Apart from electoral considerations, the prime minister's office, which is supplemented to some extent by the cabinet office, is a relatively small operation, in terms of staff and resources, compared with Britain's peers in other countries. Consider the scale of the US or French presidencies, or even the German chancellery. Therefore, over the period of 1979–2007 (and beyond), we cannot see a clear trend, unlike in other areas studied in previous chapters, towards concentration of power within the political executive. Where periods have seen greater power in the office of the prime minister, this is primarily owing to the vagaries of both the British electoral system and its unwritten constitution, both of which are important structural factors in other trends covered in this book.

Political authority and trade

Changes in the structures of the British and world economies are also responsible for trends in concentration of power. Most significantly, the acceleration of globalisation since the early 1970s has forced economies such as Britain's to re-orientate from national to regional and global trading networks and modes of production.

The rise of multinational corporations and national governments' thirst for private investment, sometimes framed as foreign direct investment (FDI), have had significant long-term implications. British governments, most notably those of Margaret Thatcher, liberalised the finance sector and capital flows and weakened trade union rights. Partly responding to global changes, partly driving them, Britain was therefore transformed from the post-war, heavily regulated economy with a significant role for the unions to something much more market-orientated and pro-business. The fundamental changes were not rolled back by either the Major or New Labour governments, and, in some areas—for instance, trade policy and privatisation—they actually extended them.

The British economy, during the 1980s, 1990s and 2000s, broadly made a transition towards services and away from heavy industry and manufacturing. As we have already seen, wealth and higher-paying jobs accumulated in certain sectors and parts of the UK, particularly London and the South East. The trade union reforms of the Thatcher government, including the set-piece battle with the miners in 1984–85, enfeebled organised labour and, as a result, collective bargaining, wages and, ultimately, job security. Britain became particularly noteworthy as an economy with a 'flexible labour market'—that is to say, where workers can be hired and fired with greater ease than in comparable countries, save the United States. All this meant that economic power became more concentrated with higher earners and owners of capital. The most obvious proxy for this is the rise in economic inequality during this period.

Wealth inequality

In recent years, there has been an increase in work on, and interest in, economic inequality, most famously set out in French economist Thomas Piketty's 2013 book *Capital in the Twenty-First Century.*[7] There are several measurements to gauge inequality. The Gini coefficient, which calculates distribution of income to provide a figure between 0 (maximum equality) and 1 (maximum inequality), is the longest standing of these. More recently, measures such as the wealth held by the top 1%, 0.1% and even 0.01% have become more prominent. The online repository developed by Piketty and other economists, the World Inequality Database, has collected a huge swathe of country-specific data from the past century, including for the UK.[8] It has become an article of faith that economic inequality started to rise during the years of Thatcherism.[9] Indeed, according to every measure, inequality in Britain fell broadly from the late 1930s, before picking up in the late 1970s and increasing from at least the early 1980s. The figures plateaued somewhat during the New Labour years and dipped after the 2008 financial crash.[10]

As we have seen, globalisation began to accelerate after the demise of the Bretton Woods system in the early 1970s. Under the Thatcher government, economic liberalisation allowed wealth inequality to surge, a process exacerbated by high levels of unemployment. It should also be noted that a similar process took place in most developed countries, and Britain lagged behind developments in the United States. As Labour Chancellor, Gordon Brown managed to offset this, partly through welfare interventions such as working tax credits.[11] Nevertheless, critics complained that a Labour government should have done more to address rising inequality.[12] Certainly, economic inequality is far higher today than during the 1970s and followed an upward trend after 1979. It also seems likely that inequality has created fertile territory for populism.

Globalisation has fractured other elements of British society and its economy, leading to a backlash. As well as the weakening of trade union rights, Britain is now plugged into global supply chains, meaning what is made in the UK is vastly different from in the pre-Thatcher era. Criticism from the left arose during the 1980s and 1990s that British businesses and consumers were benefitting from outsourcing and production by poorly paid workers without, or with few, employment rights. Terms such as 'sweat shops' and 'slave labour' became labels for exploitation in the quest for lower prices in a globalised economy. On the right, there was disquiet that Britain was losing its place as a manufacturing nation and that foreign ownership was on the rise, even—perhaps surprisingly—regarding liberalisation of the City of London.[13] European integration meant that freedom of movement of workers within the EU increased from the 1990s, giving a further boost to the British economy, but infuriated many on the right, including cultural and economic nationalists. All of these themes point to a loss of democratic oversight over the economy during the 1979–2007 period. Successive governments wanted economic growth and were willing to push these concerns down their list of priorities. The real backlash and desire to rebalance these priorities, however, would come in the decade after the 2008 financial crash.

The trends discussed in the previous section directly affected individuals as a result of the structural changes to the British economy, but there were other, less direct changes that also exerted huge influence, including regulation and its 'capture', governing pressures concerning home ownership and 'rent-seeking' more generally.

Regulatory capture

Regulation became increasingly important as Britain shifted from nationalised industries to privatised, or part-privatised, firms under regulatory oversight. With every privatisation, the Thatcher and Major governments set up a regulator—for instance, Ofcom in telecoms, Ofgas for the gas industry, and so on. Each regulator was responsible for monitoring company behaviour, investigating complaints and enforcing competition. This arrangement was not long in place before criticism emerged over weak regulation and regulatory capture, which was the notion that regulation is framed by the regulated and pursued primarily in its interests or under pressure from those interests.[14] It is also worth noting how regulators often operate on scarce resources and staff compared with the corporate interests they oversee. Historians of British antitrust policy have written how regulatory capture seemed to entrench during the 1990s under the Major government and only started to reverse once the Blair government fully signed up to EU competition policy in 1998.[15] Regulatory capture can result in reduced competition, consumer welfare issues and raised prices. One of the central aims for lobbyists is blocking new market entrants.

The shift towards an EU-wide competition policy may have had some impact on larger companies, which was largely the focus of Europe-wide antitrust policy. It should be noted, however, that most competition cases were still under the purview of the UK regulator. That said, with the incorporation of EU standards into British domestic law, competition policy took on a different character after 1998. It followed a trend of much economic policy after 1979, a drift towards a more technocratic style of government. Monetarism, inflation targeting, Bank of England independence, removal of trade union dialogue from top-level decision-making, privatisation and the general ending of corporatism all demonstrated how an economic view of governance replaced a more political style. This had some tangible results. As we have seen, by the late 1990s, inflation was tamed, and the economy went into a long period of expansion. The technocratic solutions of Gordon Brown to welfare, such as tax credits, lifted people out of poverty without setting pulses racing. By embracing globalisation, Britain appeared to be benefitting handsomely and making a transition to a high-tech, service-based economy. European integration assisted these processes by taking on responsibility for some policy, such as competition, from Brussels and consistently expanding trade in the single market through 'level playing field' reforms—reducing non-tariff barriers—and the process of increasing the membership of the EU itself.

Yet, all was not well with this model. As we have seen in previous chapters, deregulation appeared to happen in waves in the UK, where consumers benefitted from lower prices in some sectors at various points, but then, even after 1998, regulation could not prevent increasing concentration in many industries. This suggests that either regulation was not functioning as intended or even that there was some level of regulatory capture. For other sectors, such as financial services, the situation was more systemic and far more serious for the economy as a whole. The reasons for the 2007–08 financial crash are myriad, but clearly the regulatory compact between banks, financial services companies and regulators, in Britain, the US, EU and elsewhere, failed. In Britain, a tacit agreement was made between the government and the City that while the tax revenues flowed into the Treasury, the British government and the financial services regulator would pursue a light-touch approach. The exposure of retail banking to the often reckless operations of their investment arms was, in hindsight, a high-risk strategy. The behaviour of banks in developing financial instruments that repackaged high-risk debt, sold as investment-grade products and backed by the ratings agencies, posed serious questions as to why regulators did not investigate these developments. The recriminations were heated in the wake of the 2008 crisis and cast a long shadow over the economic policy of the Thatcher, Major and Blair governments. Had the financial services sector experienced regulatory capture? Commentators have claimed the City is not unified enough to have organised itself in a fashion to exercise political pressure. Yet, from Big Bang in the 1980s, where the London Stock Exchange managed to turn an antitrust referral into one of the era's defining pieces of deregulation, the City usually knew how to make government and regulators work in its interests.[16] This can also be seen in the benefits the sector reaped from the London Docklands Authority in terms of infrastructure building and tax incentives, light-touch regulation after Bank of England independence in 1997 and even in the aftermath of the crash, during the furore over bonuses and David Cameron's use of his veto at a 2011 EU council to block a financial services tax. Desperate for economic growth and to increase Britain's standing in the world, UK politicians made themselves willing accessories in allowing the financial sector to expose the country's economy to the disaster of 2007–08.

Rent-seeking in the British economy

One of the core structural issues to emerge in British political economy during the 1979–2007 period was 'rent-seeking'. The term came to prominence in academic circles during the 1960s and 1970s through conservative economists such as Gordon Tullock and James Buchanan at the University of Virginia in the United States, known as the Virginia School or 'Public Choice' School. Rent-seeking was used as a critique of the public sector or government more generally.[17] It was the concept that economic actors—in Public Choice's case, these were civil servants or government officials—seek ever greater reward for essentially performing the same tasks. In fact, the principle of rent-seeking is far more appropriate when applied to the private sector.[18] Actors in a market economy, including individual businesses or even entire sectors, more broadly seem to tend to rent-seeking. In its most obvious sense, this could be property owners seeking more rent on the same capital outlay, a trend particularly prevalent in cities such as London, where prices have soared. It can manifest itself when firms seek subsidies or try to block new market entrants, essentially seeking special treatment. The most egregious example was the series of bailouts during the 2008 financial crisis, where banks extracted a gargantuan rent from the British taxpayer, which would have to be borne over the following decade, with few ramifications for those who had instigated the crash. At the individual level, the British press paid particular attention to CEOs and other executives who refused to waive hefty bonuses or pensions after the bailouts, Royal Bank of Scotland's then former chairman Fred Goodwin being the highest profile example.[19]

Lobbying can be a form of rent-seeking, attempting to secure preferable conditions and generate higher profits for a particular business or sector. This has been exacerbated by the 'revolving door' principle whereby politicians continue their careers on executive boards in the private sector. In 2019, the director of the NGO Unlock Democracy told *The Economist* that revolving door-type appointments "contribute to regulatory capture" and "feed the public's perception that money buys access and influence in a cosy process from which voters are excluded".[20] Guy Standing, in his book on the subject, *The Corruption of Capitalism: Why Rentiers Thrive and Work Does Not Pay*, outlines how business is often subsidised and income channelled to capital and intellectual property owners.[21] Standing draws a direct correlation between the trend towards rent-seeking in the private sector and the vote to leave the European Union in 2016 as a "populist vote against the insecurity, inequalities and austerity induced by a system of rentier capitalism that has channelled more of the income to a minority in a global Gilded Age".[22] Standing also highlights how automation and the virtual economy are causing more rent, a subject to which we shall return in the final chapter.[23]

Declining trust in politicians

The structural issues in the British economy, including regulatory capture and rent-seeking, have contributed to a general decline in trust in politicians. Many of these trends are, however, difficult to gauge and not obvious to voters in their everyday lives. Nevertheless, this has been accompanied by a series of scandals involving every political party. Sometimes scandals have centred around individuals or, in the case of the expenses scandal, seemed systemic. Political scandals are part of the terrain and by no means started in the 1980s and 1990s. What has made the scandals more acute, and seemingly more regular, is the rise of an omnipotent news media jostling for the next political scoop. As 24-hour media exploded in the early 1990s with the advent of entire channels devoted to news coverage, the number of political scandals similarly soared. In Britain, this notoriously manifested itself as 'sleaze' during the Major government.[24] While the tabloids seemed to enjoy nothing more than exposing hypocrisy in ministers' private lives, more far-reaching investigations focused on corrupt parliamentary practices such as the 'cash for questions' row.[25] A number of foreign policy scandals also reflected poorly on both the Major and Thatcher governments, including the Pergau Dam 'arms-for-aid' affair,[26] uncovered by a combination of the press and a select committee inquiry, as well as the Scott Report, which looked at arms contractors' dealings with Saddam Hussein's Iraq and very nearly toppled the Major government in 1996.[27]

Tony Blair made political hay with the calamitous conduct of the Major government and promised a new start under Labour, and yet he soon ran into trouble and met cries of hypocrisy. In October 1997, the Blair government waived a ban on tobacco advertising for Formula One (F1) racing, the exemption following a meeting with F1 boss—and (at the time undisclosed) Labour Party donor—Bernie Ecclestone.[28] The government, including the prime minister, was evasive with the media when they picked up the story, initially issuing denials or dissembling. Press secretary Alastair Campbell wrote in his diary that the situation made the government look "shifty and shabby".[29] Ultimately, Blair gave an interview to the BBC apologising for the affair, famously professing to be a "pretty straight sort of guy".[30] The incident, however, had broken the New Labour spell and suggested the incoming government would not mark a significant break from its predecessor's reputation for sleaze.

Blair would act quickly to sack cabinet ministers after the Ecclestone affair, twice firing close ally Peter Mandelson, in 1998 over an undisclosed loan and in 2001 after a row about potentially influencing a passport application for an Indian businessman. Another minister considered close to Blair, David Blunkett, was also forced to resign twice amid media furores. Yet perhaps the most damaging allegation surrounding New Labour occurred at the end of Tony Blair's time as prime minister, in 2006–2007. The 'cash-for-honours' scandal involved allegations that major donors to the Labour Party were promised peerages as a quid pro quo for money. Blair was interviewed three times by the police over the issue while still in office. Although no charges were ever brought, the scandal may well have hastened Blair's resignation in 2007.[31] Andrew Rawnsley, in his political history of New Labour, outlined how the party both attempted to become less reliant on trade union donations while also struggling for cash, coming close to bankruptcy.[32] Rawnsley summarises the descent of Blair's reputation: "It completed a transformation from the first term's Teflon Tony, the Prime Minister to whom nothing really stuck, to the Toxic Tony, whom the voters saw as presiding over a sleazy regime".[33]

Worse was to come for Tony Blair's successors. Gordon Brown was prime minister when the expenses scandal struck in 2009. MPs had helped author a parliamentary code, the Green Book, for claiming expenses, which was partly initiated to prevent a salary increase that would have proved unpopular with the public.[34] After a series of freedom of information (itself a New Labour innovation) requests in 2008, the press—led by the *Daily Telegraph*—uncovered numerous claims that ranged from illegal to embarrassing, with much else in between, and uniformly reflected badly on politicians in the eyes of the general public. As well as the high-profile expense claims for services such as the clearing of a moat, claimed by Douglas Hogg, and installation of a 'duck island' on the grounds of the home of one MP, Peter Viggers, the more common instance was the 'flipping' of second homes. Flipping was the practice of claiming the more costly expenses for a London residence compared with a home in an MP's constituency.[35] The problem with flipping, which was widespread among MPs, as well as other practices such as renting out second homes, overclaiming for council tax, other tax schemes and subsidised property refurbishments, was that it seemed to show MPs behaving in a crafty, borderline corrupt fashion. Following in the slipstream of the bankers' practices that came to light in the 2007–08 financial crisis, MPs were particularly vulnerable to the public's wrath. The crises would weaken support for the main parties in the 2010 general election, but the reckoning would really come during the following years, giving impetus to new or insurgent fringe parties and populist positions.

If the bankers and politicians were in the eye of the storm during this period, public confidence in other institutions was also subsequently shaken. In particular, the phone hacking scandal shocked many for the unethical behaviour of the media, its editors and journalists. Although the basic facts around the scandal, that journalists had 'hacked' celebrities' phones as well as high-profile figures as a means of obtaining scoops, had been known for some time, the breadth of the practice—and its depravity in cases such as the hacking of a murdered schoolgirl and the victims of the 7 July 2005 London terrorist attacks—only emerged in 2011. Rupert Murdoch's News International titles were at the centre of the scandal, in particular *News of the World*, whose former editor, Andy Coulson, was then Prime Minister David Cameron's director of communications at Number

10 Downing Street. The newspaper was forced to close in 2011, and a public inquiry was established by Cameron into the "culture, practices and ethics of the press", chaired by Lord Justice Leveson. Published in November 2012, the Leveson Report recommended a tougher system of press regulation than the Press Complaints Commission (PCC), proposing a self-regulatory watchdog with statutory underpinnings.[36] The Conservatives rejected the legislative element of the Leveson findings, claiming they presented an assault on freedom of the press. Ultimately, it was unsurprising that the report withered on the vine, partly because the media reporting on Leveson's recommendations, the press, were the ones most opposed to a new watchdog. In the end, a new body, the Independent Press Standards Organisation, was set up in 2014 to replace the PCC, falling short of Leveson's suggestions. In the meantime, however, events have overtaken the phone hacking scandal. The rise of social media has allowed an exponential rise of unfiltered news, comment and opinion pieces, along with a torrent of grievances, 'echo chambers' and conspiracy theories that have proven very difficult to regulate. Traditional news and media outlets, meanwhile, have seemingly moved into terminal decline.

A narrative has emerged in recent years that trust in politicians has fallen as a result of numerous sleaze scandals, the expenses scandal and other issues such as the rationale behind why the UK joined the US coalition's invasion of Iraq in 2003. Steve Richards, for instance, has described an 'anti-politics' mood.[37] Yet data suggest that the British public did not significantly alter in its attitudes towards politicians between the early 1980s and the 2010s. In fact, average opinions towards politicians have been consistently poor, without deviating significantly.[38] Nevertheless, research has shown that the British public's trust in the capabilities of what government can do and its ability to spend public funds wisely has fallen.[39] Faith in political institutions has dropped since the early 1980s, as research from the British Social Attitudes survey shows, and this is matched by trust in public institutions such as the police and private ones such as banks.[40] Taken together, these events, and public opinion data, show a system that has increasingly displayed signs of weakness from the latter years of the New Labour era, a process that has accelerated in the decade since. It has been relatively straightforward for populists on the right, such as Nigel Farage, and on the left, such as Jeremy Corbyn, to frame Britain as an inequitable, unequal and unfair society in need of an overhaul. Their prescriptions might be very different, but some of the core diagnosis is markedly similar, much of which in some way revolves around a critique of globalisation and liberal institutions that are not representative of the 'people'. Whereas the Major, Blair and Brown governments all focused on reform, the loudest voices after 2007–08 have demanded much more drastic change.

Conclusion

This chapter has explored a number of themes related to shifting trends of concentration of political power. Not all of these have followed a consistent pattern.

For instance, concerns grew over the 1979–2007 period that increasing power was accumulating in the office of the prime minister, that cabinet government was on the wane, and that a presidential style of government was emerging. This is partly the result of the British constitution, or lack of a written one, which allows a prime minister with a large parliamentary majority to exert power seemingly unopposed. Although a presidential mode of governance appeared to some extent under Margaret Thatcher, specifically after the 1983 election, and more markedly under Tony Blair, the claims that power was being concentrated in Number 10 were exaggerated. Prime ministers with slimmer, or no, majorities, such as John Major, David Cameron and Theresa May, were generally considered weaker prime ministers who have needed the agreement of cabinet and Parliament to execute policy.

The changing structures of the UK economy, operating within a rapidly globalising trading system, have led to profound shifts in economic and political power. Privatisation was intended as a piece of deregulation, and yet patterns of 'regulatory capture' emerged almost as soon as state-owned utilities and companies were moved into the private sector. UK and EU regulators have attempted to punish anti-competitive behaviour, but concentrating power in this way has proven very difficult to reverse. Adopting EU competition law was one mechanism of promoting more robust forms of competition, but, for Britain, this will also end when the country leaves the bloc in the 2020s. Globalisation more generally has unleashed forces that have seemingly concentrated power in the hands of large corporations and away from workers. The global economy, with national governments seeking FDI, has incentivised a flexible labour market, and jobs have often seemed transient and not anchored in a particular location. Uncertain job prospects have been negatively reinforced by growing income inequality. A swathe of data backs up the trend of increasing inequality from the late 1970s until the 2007–08 financial crash. Although the Blair government attempted, successfully, to stall this trend with initiatives such as tax credits, lower trade barriers and globalisation seemingly led to increased aggregate wealth, more unevenly distributed. The result has been a feeling of increased powerlessness. Finally, the number of political scandals appears to have grown during the 1979–2007 period (and beyond), although this is in large part owing to the rise of round-the-clock media coverage. Nevertheless, taken together, we can see a decline in public trust in politicians and British institutions more generally. Many of these trends would manifest themselves at the ballot box during the 2010s. The final chapter will look at how the legacy of the shifts in concentration of economic and political power, which took root between 1979 and 2007, have revealed themselves in the years after the demise of New Labour.

Notes

1 Charles Moore, *Margaret Thatcher: The Authorized Biography, Volume Three: Herself Alone* (London: Allen Lane, 2019), 306–311, 343–348, 732–733.
2 Ibid., 738–739.
3 Ken Clarke, *Kind of Blue: A Political Memoir* (Basingstoke: Macmillan, 2016), 304–305; Andrew Rawnsley, "The Damaging Questions Keep Coming", *The Guardian*,

14 September 2003, www.theguardian.com/politics/2003/sep/14/tonyblair.iraq [accessed 9 June 2020].

4 Jon Davis and John Rentoul, *Heroes or Villains? The Blair Government Reconsidered* (Oxford: Oxford University Press, 2019), 61–63.

5 Nick Clegg, *Politics* (London: Bodley Head, 2016), 79–80.

6 Davis and Rentoul, *Heroes or Villains*, 76, 99–100.

7 Thomas Piketty, *Capital in the Twenty-First Century* (Cambridge: Harvard University Press, 2014).

8 World Inequality Database, "United Kingdom" (2020), https://wid.world/country/united-kingdom/ [accessed 12 June 2020].

9 Simon Rogers, "How Britain Changed under Margaret Thatcher. In 15 Charts", *The Guardian*, 8 April 2013, www.theguardian.com/politics/datablog/2013/apr/08/britain-changed-margaret-thatcher-charts [accessed 11 June 2020].

10 Office of National Statistics, "Household Income Inequality, UK: Financial Year Ending 2019", 5 March 2020, www.ons.gov.uk/peoplepopulationandcommunity/personalandhouseholdfinances/incomeandwealth/bulletins/householdincomeinequalityfinancial/financialyearending2019 [accessed 11 June 2020].

11 Gordon Brown, *My Life, Our Times* (London: Bodley Head, 2017), 146–152.

12 Chris Dillow, "Why Tony Blair and His Critics Are Both Partly Right on Inequality", *New Statesman*, 17 June 2019, www.newstatesman.com/politics/uk/2019/06/why-tony-blair-and-his-critics-are-both-partly-right-inequality [accessed 11 June 2020].

13 Ranald Michie, "City and Government: Changing Relationship", eds. Ranald Michie and Philip Williamson, *The British Government and the City of London in the Twentieth Century* (Cambridge: Cambridge University Press, 2011, 31–56), 51; David Kynaston, *City of London, The History* (London: Chatto & Windus, 2011), 575.

14 Keith Cowling and Philip R. Tomlinson, "Globalisation and Corporate Power", *Contributions to Political Economy*, 24:1 (2005), 33–54, 44.

15 Gregory Baldi, "Europeanising Antitrust: British Competition Policy Reform and Member State Convergence", *British Journal of Politics and International Relations*, 8:1 (2006), 503–518, 516.

16 The OFT launched an investigation into restrictive practices in the City of London in 1979. Nicholas Goodison, chairman of the London Stock Exchange, asked the regulator to call off the probe if the sector undertook reform. The outcome was 1986's Big Bang. See: Nigel Lawson, *The View from No.11. Memoirs of a Tory Radical* (London: Corgi Books, 1993), 398–399; Kynaston, *City of London*, 556.

17 Robert Ledger, *Neoliberal Thought and Thatcherism: "A Transition from Here to There?"* (Abingdon: Routledge, 2017), 25–27.

18 Warwick Funnell, Robert Jupe and Jane Andrew, *In Government We Trust* (London: Pluto Press, 2009), 64.

19 George Mathewson, "Goodwin's Undoing", *Financial Times*, 25 February 2009, www.ft.com/content/dbcc20aa-02a0-11de-b58b-000077b07658 [accessed 16 June 2020].

20 *The Economist*, "The Sweet Hereafter: Cheer Up, Sacked MPs. A Big Payday Awaits", 12 December, 2019.

21 Guy Standing, *The Corruption of Capitalism: Why Rentiers Thrive and Work Does Not Pay* (London: Biteback, 2016), 12, 243–244.

22 Ibid., 9.

23 Ibid., 175, 183.

24 Bruce Pilbeam, "Social Morality", eds. Kevin Hickson and Ben Williams, *John Major: An Unsuccessful Prime Minister? Reappraising John Major* (London: Biteback, 2017, 215–230), 218.

25 Donald Macintyre, "The Cash-for-Questions Affair: Major Rocked as Payments Scandal Grows: Minister Resigns Over 'Cash for Questions' PM Reveals He Knew of Allegations by Harrods Owner Three Weeks Ago", *Independent*, 21 October 1994, www.independent

.co.uk/news/the-cash-for-questions-affair-major-rocked-as-payments-scandal-grows
-minister-resigns-over-cash-for-1444057.html [accessed 23 April 2020]

26 Robert Ledger, "The Road to Pergau Dam: Aid Policy, Ideology and the Thatcher Government", *Diplomacy & Statecraft*, 30:1 (2019), 50–69.

27 Mark Garnett, "Foreign and Defence Policy", eds. Kevin Hickson and Ben Williams, *John Major: An Unsuccessful Prime Minister? Reappraising John Major* (London: Biteback, 2017, 269–286), 283;
   Robin Cook, House of Commons Debates (hereafter HC Deb), 15 February 1996, vol. 271 col. 1145.

28 Rachel Stevenson, "Blair Intervened over F1 Tobacco Ban Exemption, Documents Show", *The Guardian*, 12 October 2008, www.theguardian.com/politics/2008/oct/12 /tonyblair-labour [accessed 18 June 2020].

29 Alastair Campbell, *The Diaries: The Blair Years* (Reading: Arrow Books, 2008), 260.

30 Fran Abrams, "Blair: 'I Think I'm a Pretty Straight Sort of Guy'", *Independent*, 17 November 1997, www.independent.co.uk/news/blair-i-think-im-a-pretty-straight -sort-of-guy-1294593.html [accessed 18 June 2020].

31 Andrew Rawnsley, *The End of the Party: The Rise and Fall of New Labour* (London: Penguin, 2010), 373–374.

32 Ibid., 373.

33 Ibid.

34 Ivor Gaber, "The Lobby in Transition", *Media History*, 19:1 (2013), 45–58.

35 Andrew Sparrow, Hélène Mulholland, Richard Partington and Patrick Wintour, "More than 50 MPs Flipped Second Home, New Expenses Figures Show", *The Guardian*, 10 December 2009, www.theguardian.com/politics/2009/dec/10/mps-expenses-50-fli pped-homes [accessed 21 June 2020].

36 Lisa O'Carroll, "Leveson Report: Key Points", *The Guardian*, 29 November 2012, www.theguardian.com/media/2012/nov/29/leveson-report-key-points [accessed 21 June 2020].

37 Steve Richards, *The Rise of the Outsiders: How Mainstream Politics Lost Its Way* (London: Atlantic Books, 2018).

38 Peter Taylor-Gooby and Benjamin Leruth, "Why British People Don't Trust the Government Any More—And What Can Be Done about It", *The Conversation*, 31 January 2018, https://theconversation.com/why-british-people-dont-trust-the-gov ernment-any-more-and-what-can-be-done-about-it-89627 [accessed 21 June 2020].

39 Ibid.

40 British Attitudes 30, "Trust, Politics and Institutions", *British Social Attitudes*, 2013, www.bsa.natcen.ac.uk/latest-report/british-social-attitudes-30/key-findings/trust-pol itics-and-institutions.aspx [accessed 21 June 2020].

7 A legacy of concentration

This final chapter will observe how some of the trends examined in this book have developed in the years since New Labour's fall from power. A number of hugely important political and economic events have taken place over this time, but the most epoch-changing for the UK were the 2008 financial crisis and the 2016 Brexit referendum. If a number of broad trends seemed to come together in 2008 and its aftermath—the special position of the finance sector and its weak regulation, even 'regulatory capture', the prominence of central banks in navigating a way out of the crisis, the apparent inequity of the austerity that followed in the 2010s—then the 2016 referendum appeared to be the apotheosis of these trends. The referendum was nominally about the UK's membership of the European Union and constitutional issues such as national sovereignty. Although the referendum campaign did contain some discussions around sovereignty, it was not a sober reflection on membership of a supranational union. This was a supremely populist moment, an opportunity for voters, fed up after years of growing disquiet and sentiment that their voices were not being heard, to deliver a political earthquake. As noted in several other parts of this book, the changes set in train by globalisation simmered under the surface during this period. The ease with which capital, goods and services moved across borders had a profound impact on the British economy, in particular on jobs and the longevity of employment. Movement of people was more restricted than money and trade but moved further up the political agenda after the 2008 crash. Right-wing populists, encouraged by the press, fanned the flames of anti-immigrant sentiment during the 2016 Brexit campaign. The backlash during the post-2008 years looked like a counter movement against the economic and social liberalism that had prevailed in the previous period. Yet, for all that, some of the trends observed in this study are marching on apparently untouched by populism. Monopolies and economic concentration have become more marked since 2008, most notably in the new economy dominated by tech giants. On the other hand, having been launched during the first Blair government, devolution also continues to become more entrenched and expanded. Concentration of economic and political power is still a live issue, although it is only being taken seriously in certain spheres.

Economic policy

The years before the 2008 financial crash were known as the 'Great Moderation' as a result of consistently low inflation and steady economic growth. Gone were the wild oscillations of price rises and interest rate fluctuations experienced in Britain during the 1970s and 1980s. Successive governments had embraced the gains of increased global trade, technological advances and the seemingly unending success of key sectors such as finance and banking. For those who thought the Thatcher, Major and Blair governments were 'neoliberal', policymakers had, as a result, become technocratic and almost apolitical. In so far as they were political, it was in the pursuit of leaving as much as possible to the market. Government was mostly non-interventionist and had even initiated 'internal markets' in public services such as healthcare. This kind of analysis, however, works much better on the page than in reality. Both Conservative and Labour governments, as well as the Bank of England, were constantly intervening and tinkering in all aspects of the British economy during this period. Market distortions were the norm, not the exception. In some areas, such as social policy, markets were artificially created in an often-vain attempt to make institutions such as the NHS benefit from market forces or operate more efficiently. Some accounts of British economic policy after 2008 claimed that it became highly discretionary. Yet it was discretionary before the crash. As Philip Cerny described as part of the 'paradox' of neoliberalism in the 21st century, the system has "involved extensive ad hoc re-regulation in response to complex, unforeseen events such as the global financial and Eurozone crises and other market failures and inefficiencies. They have become more regulatory and interventionist".[1] Each decision has the potential to provide benefit but also create inequity or, in liberal economic terms, to distort markets.

Gordon Brown, as Chancellor of the Exchequer in 1997–2007, was the architect of British economic policy for a decade. After becoming prime minister in 2007, he was subsequently left to battle against economic collapse during the financial crisis. The light-touch system of financial regulation, the Financial Services Authority (FSA), was found to have been alarmingly insufficient. It appeared that Brown and his chancellor, Alistair Darling, were completely unaware of the types of practice that had mushroomed in the finance sector over the previous years. Investment bankers had engaged in high levels of risk, which was repackaged as apparently safe financial instruments. Banks had little working capital. The finance sector seemed to resemble a casino rather than the dull caricature of the city pre-1979. The economic picture steadily darkened during 2007–08 and then rapidly worsened when Lehman Brothers, a huge US-headquartered investment bank, went bankrupt in September 2008. The global economy went into free-fall, and commentators were soon describing events in the same breath as the 1929 Wall Street Crash. Gordon Brown took it upon himself to coordinate the global response, which for the most part was a triumph for his leadership. Brown activated the G20 as a means of bringing as many of the major economies along as possible, including China and some emerging economies who were by no means sympathetic to Western-style capitalism. Ultimately, Brown's domestic response involved two key pillars: recapitalisation of stricken banks with huge taxpayer bailouts and central bank 'quantitative easing' (QE), a means of injecting liquidity into the economy to avoid the deflation of previous crises.

In so far as market forces were at work in the British economy before 2008, the response to the crash managed to wildly distort them, at least until the time of writing. Ultra-low interest rates and QE kept the economy afloat and prevented a recession turning into a depression, but the economy only barely recovered during the 2010s. The situation was made worse by the Conservative–Liberal Democrats' austerity policies during the decade, encouraged by academics and commentators fixated on debt-to-GDP and deficit-to-GDP ratios in the aftermath of the huge bank bail outs. If the patient was the British economy, it survived after experiencing a near-death trauma, but was only kept going by heavy and consistent doses of medication.

The economic policies during and after the crash succeeded in their primary aims, a total collapse was averted, and unemployment, although reaching 8.5% in 2011, did not climb to the levels seen in other downturns.[2] Nevertheless, although fewer people lost jobs than in previous recessions, the recovery was less marked, and income and living standards stagnated for many. Public services, meanwhile, started to come under strain during the 2010s owing to austerity-driven lack of funding.[3] QE also led to criticism. Although the policy—central bank bond and asset buying as a means of injecting liquidity—has provided monetary stability, critics point to the uneven distribution of the impact of QE, favouring mainly the wealthy and capital owners and being directed towards profits.[4] Therefore, we have seen a situation of heavy intervention in the economy to prop up failing firms, leaving the taxpayer with a monumental bill to pay, and further stabilisation measures that have seemingly enriched the better-off while much of the rest of British society has endured stagnating living standards. In hindsight, this would prove fertile conditions for populism.

Devolution

One policy area that has continued during the 2010s has been the trend towards, or at least rhetoric of, empowerment and devolution. John Major launched the Citizen's Charter in 1991 that provided rights and accountability in terms of public services. It was derided as ineffective at the time, but was a harbinger of later reforms. New Labour offered choice in public services, supposedly empowering NHS patients and parents in education. In the political sphere, the Blair government offered referendums on devolved power and then established devolved administrations in Scotland, Wales and London. When David Cameron became leader of the Conservative Party in opposition in 2005, he sought to combine these various initiatives to devolve power. Furthering the devolution agenda was, perhaps, unusual for a Conservative leader. His predecessors had opposed devolved governments in Wales and Scotland. Cameron, however, was mainly interested in English devolution, including more city mayors as well as his close ally George Osbourne's 'Northern Powerhouse' project of devolving more responsibilities to cities in northern England. This was to be matched partly when the Conservatives formed a coalition government with the Liberal Democrats in 2010, who themselves were proponents of 'localism'. Cameron even agreed to an independence referendum in Scotland in 2014, although, having kept the union together by a 55% to 45% margin, the prime minister scored a spectacular own goal in its aftermath by promising "English votes for English laws", thereby fanning the flames of Scottish *and* English nationalism.[5]

David Cameron's Conservatives offered to radically redistribute power in the UK with the much maligned 'Big Society'. A somewhat slippery concept, the Big Society had a libertarian, anti-government core, using the language of devolving and redistributing power. Cameron and his associates, including George Osbourne, MP Oliver Letwin, peer Daniel Finkelstein and advisors such as Steve Hilton, sought to orientate the Big Society around the provision of public services by seemingly any organisation or group that could not be labelled the 'state'. The high watermark of the Big Society was the 2010 Conservative Party's general election manifesto. The Big Society would empower social enterprises, charities, voluntary groups, community organisers and active neighbourhood groups to provide services and further "the progressive aims of reducing poverty, fighting inequality, and increasing general well-being".[6] Yet the idea ran into the ground after the Conservatives took office. Widespread budget cuts might have seemed to have created the space for more involvement for the voluntary sector in providing services, but reductions in their funding reduced the capacity to do so.[7] Moreover, when reform packages were initiated, such as Secretary of State for Health Andrew Lansley's NHS reorganisation, dispersal of accountability and power provoked confusion and more layers of bureaucracy.[8] As a result, the Big Society proved disappointing when compared with its lofty aims before the 2010 election. Nevertheless, the trend towards greater devolution continued during the 2010s, the newly established English mayoralties attracting nationally known political figures such as Andy Burnham in Manchester; Boris Johnson and Sadiq Khan in London; and former managing director of John Lewis, Andy Street, in Birmingham. As well as the Conservative–Liberal Democrat coalition's support of decentralising political power, the 'Blue Labour' project, which had some influence during Ed Miliband's leadership of the Labour Party, advocated localism.[9] All major parties now support greater devolution, including in England. More devolution is, in some ways, a response to the 2016 Brexit referendum, which showed some correlation between levels of support for 'Leave' and lower levels of devolved power.

Populism

A feature of British, and world, politics in the years after the 2008 financial crash has been the rise of populist parties, politicians and policies. Populism can emanate from the right, often including nationalism and anti-immigrant sentiment, or the left, frequently focusing on economic inequality. Sometimes, the two strands even share key policy proposals. The coalition that initially formed in Italy in

2018, between the left populist Five Star Movement—founded in 2009 in the financial crisis and the resulting Eurozone sovereign debt crisis—and the right populist Lega—a much older party that adopted a more nationwide populist stance under the leadership of Matteo Salvini—might have seemed unorthodox, but only survived at all because there was a significant amount of policy overlap. Populists alight on familiar themes: they represent the 'authentic' voice of the 'people' and juxtapose this with out-of-touch, arrogant and corrupt elites. For contemporary populists, the elites, and by implication the status quo, usually represent a version of liberalism. The left rails against economic liberalism, and the right opposes social liberalism. Both see globalisation as a core problem and a trend encouraged by ruling mainstream parties. In Britain, populism manifested itself on the right as UKIP and the fringe of the Conservative Party, which opposed the European Union and various other trends, including, but not solely, immigration. This was aligned on the Conservative right with vague and nostalgic notions of Britain's, and often England's, past.[10] Right-wing populism in Britain also developed both pro- and anti-trade threads. On the left, populism has mainly flourished within the Labour Party following the election of Jeremy Corbyn as party leader in 2015. Britain's embrace of populism and rejection of the pre-financial-crash orthodoxy can be seen in the 2016 Brexit referendum campaign, which, along with some limited debate over sovereignty, contained anti-immigrant tropes aimed at appealing to voters' worst prejudices. The pro-EU campaign, on the other hand, looked better suited to the politics of the late 1990s in its managerial and technocratic appeals, rather than the hysteria of the 2010s. It was not just Britain, of course: populists of every description—most consequentially, Donald Trump in the US in 2016—have been elected across the world in the previous decade. The culmination of 2010s British populism came during the December 2019 general election, a fitting end to a tumultuous decade, when arch populists Boris Johnson and Jeremy Corbyn faced off against one another.

Many of the trends covered in this book are structural. Nevertheless, agency has also played a huge part in the changes in political economy in Britain. The situation in which the UK found itself at the end of the 2010s, electorally and otherwise, was the result of a long list of individual decisions and contingent factors. It is worth considering David Cameron's decisions to hold referendums on Scottish independence in 2014 and EU membership in 2016. The success and approach of the former seemed to govern strategy towards the latter. Cameron's call for English laws after the 2014 referendum played its part in turbo-charging support for the SNP in Scotland and dramatically changing the UK electoral map in Westminster. In turn, a number of these events boosted support for UKIP and English nationalism more generally, proving crucial to the result in 2016. Ed Miliband's decision to change the threshold for MP nominations for Labour Party leadership elections to 15% instead of the initially planned 20% proved critical for getting Jeremy Corbyn on to the ballot, setting off a whole host of what-ifs. The list goes on. Politics and economics are the sum of all these smaller contingencies, as well as longer-term structural factors. One trend, however, that does seem to have a played a part concerns the changes in political leadership in the

UK, particularly the fashion for inexperience. Steve Richards has identified this as a 'crisis' of leadership, comparing, as one example, the leadership contests in the 2010s with the 1975 Conservative and 1976 Labour races.[11] Whereas, in recent years, leadership contests have seemingly favoured candidates billed as outsiders with little experience, the 1975–76 races included historical figures with years of experience such as Margaret Thatcher, Edward Heath, Willie Whitelaw and Geoffrey Howe for the Conservatives; and James Callaghan, Michael Foot, Roy Jenkins, Tony Benn, Denis Healey and Tony Crosland for Labour. This point regarding the lack of weighty leadership in the UK perhaps needs greater prominence in analyses of recent political history.

Economic trends

Opposition to globalisation has been one of the focal points in the rise of populism in the UK. Whereas, previously, national governments sought ever-lower tariff barriers and greater openness to trade as a means to stimulate growth, the approach appeared to hit the buffers in the 2010s. Despite the calls for a more global trade policy by some Brexiteers after the 2016 referendum, it seems just as likely that Leave supporters wanted less international trade, rather than more. After all, the referendum was a vote to leave the world's largest trading block. In any case, general sentiment towards international and supranational bodies, such as the EU and WTO, has declined owing to their association with globalisation and free trade.

Alongside the backlash against globalisation and the prevailing economic model, discussions about income inequality have moved into the mainstream since the 2008 financial crash. As mentioned earlier in this book, various measures have been used to gauge inequality, including the Gini coefficient, wealth accumulated by the top percentile, whether by the top 10%, 1%, 0.1% or 0.1%. In particular, the bestselling *Capital in the Twenty-First Century*, published in 2013 by French economist Thomas Piketty, gave academic rigour to what had been previously suspected, that income inequality had soared since the advent of the so-called neoliberal era. In fact, Piketty's work showed the fall in inequality in the mid-20th century as an anomaly against the longer sweep of history. Not everyone agreed that inequality was actually a bad thing. Margaret Thatcher herself summed up the economic liberal right's view of inequality as far back as 1975:

> We are all unequal. No one, thank heavens, is like anyone else, however much the Socialists may pretend otherwise. We believe that everyone has the right to be unequal but to us every human being is equally important.[12]

Nevertheless, few politicians declare that they think income inequality is a positive development in the modern era. In Britain, the Gini coefficient fell slightly in the wake of the financial crisis and has stayed more or less stable during the 2010s. Governments and political parties have yet to propose a coherent strategy to curb inequality, but it is noticeable that, after the austerity politics of the 2010–15 coalition government, both Labour and Conservative parties have advocated more public spending and a more interventionist state. One of Boris Johnson's key planks during the 2019 election campaign, seemingly responding to the concerns of Brexit voters, was a 'levelling up' agenda to equalise disparities of wealth and investment in Wales and Northern England. As discussed elsewhere in this book, this approach may require greater devolved powers to satiate local complaints and feelings that certain areas have been 'left behind'.[13]

Economic concentration: the new gilded age

Whereas politics moved in a more collectivist direction during the 2010s, encapsulated by the nationalist right and a left demanding more redistribution, in some respects individualism and liberalism steamed ahead. Patterns of consumption became ever more bespoke, from online shopping to social media to the viewing of films and television. Products in the economic sphere were being increasingly tailored to the individual. The most obvious example of this trend is the rise of giant tech companies. A number of acronyms have emerged such as the FANGs (Facebook, Amazon, Netflix, Google) or GAFAM (Google, Amazon, Facebook, Apple and Microsoft). Although providing benefits for many, the rise of these tech giants has raised questions about monopoly profits and rent-seeking, as well as both employment conditions and the future of work in the new economy.

Antitrust agencies have struggled to cope with the changes in the tech economy, where profits are made and tax is paid, and how omnipotent firms have effectively blocked new entrants to markets previously not fully understood or even categorised.[14] The tactics of the tech giants have been crudely described as "copy, acquire, kill".[15] In recent years, the EU Competition Commission has been particularly active in investigating tech monopolies, bringing cases against Microsoft, Google and Apple. In the 2000s, the EU Competition Directorate charged Microsoft with refusing to provide interoperability with its software packages—essentially imposing a monopoly in this relatively new technology.[16] Google, with a huge preponderance of market share in internet searches, has been fined for abusing its dominant position, and Apple became a focus for the Commission regarding its tax arrangements in Ireland, which were interpreted as state aid.[17] The EU's General Data Protection Regulation, introduced in 2018, was the first concerted attempt to control the use of data and was particularly aimed at tech firms, whose business model has been to trade in data.[18] Nevertheless, the lengthy cases and the relatively minor penalties imposed demonstrate how difficult it is to prevent anti-competitive behaviour by the tech giants, even when the regulator is determined. Some critics, such as Pierre Dardot and Christian Laval, have outlined how the previous view of national economies operating relatively discretely and made up primarily of small- and medium-sized enterprises is no longer relevant in today's globalised system.[19] Dardot and Laval describe the Ordoliberal view of the economy as a "largely defunct myth".[20] This has huge implications in terms of concentration and acting to curb anti-competitive behaviour, because how and where firms operate have become increasingly complex.

The case of big tech is important because these companies are leading the charge into a new economy. The huge profits and market shares these firms have gained, as well as the high profiles of some of the companies' founders and executives—such as Bill Gates, Steve Jobs, Steve Cook, Jeff Bezos and Mark Zuckerburg—have led some to compare the modern era with the 'gilded age' of the late 19th century and early 20th century, or, less flatteringly, characterise it as a new era of "robber barons".[21] Such has been the pace of change, from the advent of personal computers in the 1970s to the rise of the internet in the 1990s, smart phones in the 2000s and the virtual economy of the 2010s, governments and regulators have been playing catch-up.[22] Some strategies for gaining market share and impeding potential rivals, such as mergers and acquisitions, have also been widespread in other sectors of the economy since 2008. As shown in Chapter 4, although concentration in some UK markets has fallen, partly owing to effective regulation, for most sectors the opposite has been true. One study of 250 industries showed that, between 2004 and 2016, almost 60% had become more concentrated.[23] A separate analysis by the Social Market Foundation outlined rent-seeking by large firms in maintaining dominant positions, from 'automatic switching' for utility customers to the use of data by tech firms such as Google, stating "that too many British consumer markets are dominated by big companies who do not have to compete hard to remain on top, meaning that prices are too high and customers get poor service".[24] Even the IMF has criticised the trend, describing an increase in market power in many countries and sectors, as well as a 'winner-takes-most' model.[25]

Some of this is feeding back into politics. Increased concentration is likely to lead to consumers paying higher prices and workers being paid less.[26] Perhaps the best examples of the real-world impact of these trends are patterns in work. Many of the new jobs created in the tech-led economy include fewer rights, zero-hour contracts, productivity monitored by algorithms and customer ratings, as well as the fear that a job will either be outsourced or simply not exist in the future. Taken together, work in the modern economy for many is highly uncertain and insecure. To use the gilded age example from history, anger grew at the turn of the 20th century over giant firms and their practices. This resentment fuelled populism, but ultimately led to some real-world changes and regulations that did curb monopolies. We can observe some similarities in recent years, insofar as rent-seeking is partly driving populism. It remains to be seen whether the second gilded age will be tamed in a similar fashion to the first.

Some of the trends stem from policies initiated over several decades, domestically and internationally. Critics of neoliberalism itself tend to focus primarily on structural causes. The technocratic and apolitical consensus that prevailed in the 1990s and 2000s is now clearly under strain, even in areas such as independent central banks primarily concerned with controlling inflation. In recent years, there have been calls to revise the mandate of the Bank of England to include unemployment and environmental objectives. Critics of inflation targeting by central banks complain about the lack of accountability to voters and that this form of technocracy is anti-democratic. Dani Rodrik, in particular, has identified the flaws or 'paradox' in globalisation in terms of responsiveness to voter concerns.[27]

Meanwhile, numerous countries appear to have abandoned democracy altogether. Populism and authoritarianism have made for a potent combination in countries such as Russia, Turkey and Hungary. Authoritarian leaders such as Viktor Orban openly talk up "illiberal democracy",[28] while others tout the 'Beijing Consensus'[29] or managed 'state capitalism' accompanied by oppressive, illiberal politics.[30]

Conclusion

The era of neoliberalism, as we understood it in the 1979–2007 period, seemed to run out of steam in the 2010s, in part because of the numerous flaws the system caused or exacerbated. Yet, in its earliest formulation, the neoliberals made a number of crucial observations and analyses of capitalist economies that are still pertinent, even in our much-changed world. They can also demonstrate how neoliberalism is failing even on its own terms. Partly this is because neoliberals seem to want to contain politics. One of the early Ordoliberals, Wilhelm Röpke, for instance, set out a familiar approach to political economy, urging "such limitations and safeguards as will prevent liberalism being devoured by democracy".[31] This is a familiar neoliberal theme, pointing the way to a technocratic set of policies to keep democratic forces from overly interfering in markets. Yet neoliberals also sought ways to balance economic and political interests. Another key Ordoliberal, Walter Eucken, as Raphaël Fèvre points out, "understood the problem of 'economic power' as a three-way alternative level of control", quoting Eucken by saying this could mean : "control by state central bodies, control by groups, or control by competition".[32] One of the themes that has run through the examples in this chapter, and study more widely, is that favouring one group over another, even if this is business by running an overly technocratic system of governance, will likely lead to a populist backlash. In the years since the 2008 financial crash, it has become increasingly obvious that these forces and interests need to be rebalanced. Without change, another of Röpke's predictions is possible: "Mass man fights against liberal-democracy in order to replace it by illiberal democracy".[33] Already we have seen how, in recent years, illiberal democracy and authoritarianism have appeared in the ascendency in a number of countries.

Notes

1 Philip G. Cerny, "In the Shadow of Ordoliberalism: The Paradox of Neoliberalism in the 21st Century", *European Review of International Studies*, 3:1 (2016), 78–79.
2 Office for National Statistics, "Unemployment Rate (Aged 16 and Over, Seasonally Adjusted)", 16 June 2020, www.ons.gov.uk/employmentandlabourmarket/peoplenot inwork/unemployment/timeseries/mgsx/lms [accessed 24 June 2020].
3 Institute for Government, "Which Public Services Face the Biggest Pressures Ahead of the Spending Round?", 2020, www.instituteforgovernment.org.uk/publication/publ ic-services-spending-round [accessed 24 June 2020].
4 Larry Elliott, "Britain's Richest 5% Gained Most from Quantitative Easing—Bank of England", 23 August 2012, www.theguardian.com/business/2012/aug/23/britains-riche st-gained-quantative-easing-bank [accessed 24 June 2020].
5 Steve Richards, *The Prime Ministers: Reflections on Leadership from Wilson to May* (London: Atlantic Books, 2019); Kiran Stacey, "David Cameron Pushes for 'English

Votes for English Laws'", *Financial Times*, 27 November 2014, www.ft.com/content/4 66984bc-7644-11e4-a777-00144feabdc0 [accessed 25 June 2020].

6 Conservative Party, "Invitation to Join the Government of Britain: The Conservative Manifesto 2010", 2010, 37, https://conservativehome.blogs.com/files/conservative-m anifesto-2010.pdf [accessed 25 June 2020].

7 Howard Gibson, "Between the State and the Individual: 'Big Society' Communitarianism and English Conservative Rhetoric", *Social and Economics Education*, 14:1 (2015), 40–55.

8 Richards, *Prime Ministers*.

9 Ben Jackson, "Progressivism in British Politics: Some Revisionist Themes", *Political Quarterly*, 88:1 (2017), 69–75.

10 Talking Politics, "Twilight of Democracy", 16 July 2020, www.talkingpoliticspodcast .com/blog/2020/267-twilight-of-democracy [accessed 23 July 2020].

11 Richards, *Prime Ministers*.

12 Margaret Thatcher Foundation (hereafter MTF), MTF 102777, Margaret Thatcher, "Speech to Conservative Party Conference", 10 October 1975.

13 Camilla Cavendish, "Boris Johnson's 'Levelling Up' Agenda Depends on Devolving Power", *Financial Times*, 6 March 2020, www.ft.com/content/db51cd3c-5f05-11ea-80 33-fa40a0d65a98 [accessed 27 June 2020].

14 See: Brian McCullough, *How the Internet Happened: From Netscape to the iPhone* (New York: Liveright, 2018).

15 James Clayton, "Tech Giants Facebook, Google, Apple and Amazon to Face Congress", *BBC News*, 29 July 2020, www.bbc.com/news/technology-53571562 [accessed 6 August 2020].

16 European Commission, "Antitrust: Commission Adapts Nature of Monitoring of 2004 Microsoft Decision", 4 March 2009, https://ec.europa.eu/commission/presscor ner/detail/en/IP_09_349 [accessed 29 June 2020].

17 European Commission, "Antitrust: Commission Fines Google €2.42 Billion for Abusing Dominance as Search Engine by Giving Illegal Advantage to Own Comparison Shopping Service", 27 June 2017, https://ec.europa.eu/commission/ presscorner/detail/en/IP_17_1784 [accessed 29 June 2020]; European Commission, "State Aid: Ireland Gave Illegal Tax Benefits to Apple Worth up to €13 billion", 30 August 2016, https://ec.europa.eu/commission/presscorner/detail/en/IP_16_2923 [accessed 29 June 2020].

18 Laureline Lemoine, "Competition Law: What to Do against Big Tech's Abuse?", *European Digital Rights*, 1 April 2020, https://edri.org/competition-law-what-to-do-a gainst-big-tech-abuse/ [accessed 29 June 2020].

19 Pierre Dardot and Christian Laval, *The New Way of the World: On Neo-Liberal Society* (translated by Gregory Elliott), (London: Verso, 2013), 210.

20 Ibid.

21 Robert Reich, "Facebook, Google and Amazon Are the New Robber Barons. Bust Them Up", *Newsweek*, 11 March 2019, www.newsweek.com/elizabeth-warren-google -facebook-amazon-monopolies-breakup-1358898 [accessed 15 July 2019].

22 Maurice Stucke and Allen Grunes, *Big Data and Competition Policy* (Oxford: Oxford University Press, 2016).

23 *The Economist*, "More Money, More Problems: The British Economy is Becoming More Concentrated and Less Competitive", 26 July 2018, www.economist.com/britain /2018/07/26/the-british-economy-is-becoming-more-concentrated-and-less-competiti ve [accessed 29 June 2020].

24 Social Market Foundation, "Press Release: New 'Minister for Competition' Needed after Brexit, Think-Tank Says", 31 July 2018, www.smf.co.uk/press-release-competi tion-not-concentration/ [accessed 29 June 2020].

25 World Economic Outlook, "Chapter 2: The Rise of Corporate Market Power and Its Macroeconomic Effects", (IMF, April 2019, 55–76), 68, www.imf.org/en/Publi cations/WEO/Issues/2019/03/28/world-economic-outlook-april-2019#Chapter%202 [accessed 14 January 2020].

26 *Economist*, "More money".

27 Dani Rodrik, *The Globalization Paradox: Democracy and the Future of the World Economy* (New York: W.W. Norton, 2011), 231–232.

28 Marc F. Plattner, "Illiberal Democracy and the Struggle on the Right", *Journal of Democracy*, 30:1 (2019), 5–19, 7.

29 Brian Klaas, *The Despot's Accomplice: How the West is Aiding and Abetting the Decline of Democracy* (London: Hurst, 2016), 206–207.

30 For instance, see Joshua Kurlantzick, *State Capitalism: How the Return of Statism Is Transforming the World* (Oxford: Oxford University Press, 2016).

31 Werner Bonefeld, "Crisis, Free Economy and Strong State: On Ordoliberalism", *European Review of International Studies*, 2: 3, (2015), 5–14; Wilhelm Röpke, *Against the Tide* (Vienna: Ludwig von Mises Institute, 1969), 97.

32 Raphaël Fèvre, "Keynes and Eucken on Capitalism and Power", ed. Manuela Mosca, *Power in Economic Thought. Palgrave Studies in the History of Economic Thought* (Basingstoke: Palgrave Macmillan, 2018, 321–347), 337.

33 Röpke, *Against the Tide*, 97.

Conclusion

This study has explored issues and trends around concentration of economic and political power in the so-called neoliberal era. We have predominantly been interested in the decisions taken by the Thatcher, Major and Blair governments that contributed to changes in concentration, while also investigating some key events predating 1979, as well some developments after 2007. Our narrative started with neoliberal insights into concentration and its negative impact on democracy in the 1930s. Although virtually never framed in the same way, British politicians are usually—with some exceptions—keen to say they are both distributing power from the centre and empowering the individual. The issue is a constant one in British politics, if rarely acted upon coherently. This book has attempted to demonstrate how, despite British governments' intermittently attempting to prevent concentration at various points between 1979 and 2007, economic power has, broadly speaking, increasingly accumulated over this time.

The first part looked at theoretical approaches to concentration and the historical perspective in Britain. Neoliberalism, the renewal then resurgence of economic liberal thought during the 20th century, went on something of a journey from the 1930s—when Ordoliberal and Chicago School economists paid particular attention to concentration of power, monopolies and cartels—to the 1970s—where a Chicago School led by Milton Friedman was dominant and much more relaxed about concentration—to the 'End of History' and 'Washington Consensus' peak of the 1990s and early 2000s, in which neoliberalism seemed to denote market fundamentalism. Splits in neoliberalism over concentration and regulation emerged even at conferences such as the 1938 Colloque Walter Lippmann and post-war Mont Pelerin Society meetings. These would be reflected in how politicians absorbed liberal ideas, from those who sought greater oversight of markets to proponents of deregulation and liberalisation with minimal supervision. Of course, neoliberalism was not the only, or for the most part even a remotely popular, ideological framework in Britain during the mid-to-late 20th century. Other viewpoints had some overlap with the more interventionist, Ordoliberal approach, which is why there could be some convergence between political parties on a 'social market economy' model from the mid-to-late 1970s. Regulation of British business developed broadly along social market lines after 1945, being strengthened as a result of the Heath government's 1973 competition legislation.

The New Labour government overhauled the system in 1998, bringing the UK into line with the EU's Competition Directorate and installing the toughest anti-trust, and perhaps most pro-market, framework in British history. Nevertheless, a crucial component of the neoliberal competition model, particularly the type proposed by Ordoliberals, was independence from political decisions. Although Britain did pursue independence in monetary policy from 1997, when Gordon Brown granted operational independence to the Bank of England, a discretionary element was retained in antitrust throughout the entire period. This gave business interests the opportunity to lobby politicians in high-profile merger cases.

The second part looked at long-term trends in economic concentration, focusing both on structural changes and government decision-making. Globalisation looms large over many of the important trends from the 1970s, at times encouraged by UK governments—for instance, relaxing controls on movement of capital as well as trade liberalisation—whereas at other times Britain was forced to respond to systemic shifts in the world economy. Deindustrialisation and a movement towards a service-based economy was seen in many comparable countries during this period. Nevertheless, British governments made a number of decisions that brought about fundamental change, such as shifts in ownership, regional policy and the expansion of higher education. These changes led to wealth and well-paid jobs being increasingly concentrated in London and South East England.

Chapter 4, in particular, examined specific case studies of how British governments dealt with concentration. One example, post-privatisation of the energy markets, showed that determined regulation could reduce concentration and impose competition through mandating new market entrants. Media publishing and broadcasting, on the other hand, showed how the discretionary component to British antitrust regulation could allow concentration to persist. In these industries, it would be technology that reduced the power of the traditional media giants. Studies of a wide range of UK markets, however, demonstrate how concentration, despite the post-1998 British antitrust framework and an activist regulator at the European level, has broadly increased in recent years.

Political concentration was explored in the third part. Political power is often considered to follow economic power. Nevertheless, the picture around political concentration during the Thatcher–Major–Blair period is multifaceted. Conservative governments rhetorically supported individual freedom and liberty but, in some respects, concentrated power towards the political centre. Local authorities were a particular target for the Thatcher government. Typically, the Major government was more emollient, scrapping the divisive, and by-and-large centralising, 'poll tax' and initiating the Citizen's Charter, but it was Tony Blair's government that made the most serious attempt to disperse political power from the centre. The devolution process started in 1997 was subsequently adopted by other parties and has been extended since New Labour left office. Power moved from the centre in other ways during the 1979–2007 era. Globalisation was again a core driver of this, allowing giant multinational firms to form that weakened the position of national governments. Multilateral organisations such as the World Trade Organization, formed in 1995, set out a particular view of and agenda on trade that seemed to undermine national governments' trade and economic policies.

It was European integration, however, that led to the most criticism, particularly on the right, which claimed Britain was surrendering sovereignty as a member of the EU. Devolution had a real impact on British politics from the late 1990s. Complaints about globalisation and multinational bodies are somewhat harder to pin down. Nevertheless, taken together, these changes would play some part in the rise of populism. The EU was clearly a focus for populists in Britain, along with the changes brought about by globalisation. Devolution seemed to partially pacify populism, judging by the map of highest Brexit voting constituencies in 2016, which demonstrated most support in the least devolved areas. But populism was also a driver for devolution in the first instance. By the time a national assembly was established in Scotland in the late 1990s, the Scottish National Party (SNP), which we could also view as populist, was entrenched in Scottish politics. Politics in Scotland did not pan out as its architects intended. Instead of pacifying nationalist demands, devolution has turbocharged the popularity of the SNP, although the reasons for the party's rise to dominance are myriad. In any case, that Labour might have been dispirited in 1997 if its leaders could have foreseen the medium-term impact of Scottish devolution does not mean the policy was misguided, only that democracy produces unpredictable outcomes, and that the party needs to reappraise its strategy in Scotland. Wales took a different devolution path, although at the time of writing Labour has retained electoral primacy there. Taken together, however, the pattern of devolution in the UK since 1997, constant Euroscepticism and growing disquiet with globalisation appear to have fuelled the rise of English nationalism. The implications of this would be felt in UK-wide elections during the 2010s.

In terms of high-level politics, perceptions matter, and these have soured towards politicians—already held in low regard—and political institutions in the modern era. Critics have accused prime ministers—notably Margaret Thatcher and Tony Blair—of accumulating power and operating an increasingly presidential style of government. There is little evidence, however, to suggest the extent of prime ministerial power can be separated from the size of a governing majority. British politics has been engulfed by ever more scandals, both individual and sectoral. This is partly the result of round-the-clock media coverage rather than a particular decay in the British political class in recent years. Nevertheless, the perception has held that the UK has been corrupted by 'elites', exacerbated by notions such as 'regulatory capture' and a 'revolving door' between privileged, well-paid positions. Meanwhile, politics has been singularly unable to broach issues such as growing wealth and income inequality. In short, this combination has proven fertile ground for populists.

Finally, we have looked at a legacy of concentration in the years after 2007. The UK has been hit by two seismic shocks (three, if you add the coronavirus crisis, ongoing at the time of writing): the 2007–08 financial crash and the 2016 Brexit referendum. The financial crisis seemed to signal the beginning of the end for the post-1979 economic model in Britain, although Conservative governments attempted to resuscitate the system using austerity policies in the 2010s. Although greater attention has fallen on some of the themes covered in this study, most notably income inequality, in recent years, concentration within the economy itself has continued and perhaps moved into a new phase, with giant tech firms operating in a new 'gilded age' of rentier capitalism. The democratic response has been increasing doses of populism.

To deem the 1979–2007 period ideologically coherent, as the neoliberal era, is to oversimplify. Nevertheless, a range of polices became politically possible during these decades. Politics, and economic policy, existed within certain parameters. This paradigm is outlined in a number of works,[1] most notably by Peter A. Hall.[2] The impact of commentators, the media and think-tanks can also prove important in setting these policy parameters.[3] The impact of neoliberal ideas could be seen, however unevenly, during the years of Thatcherism. Yet Thatcherite neoliberalism was not consistently pursued in the 1990s and 2000s, or even by the Thatcher government itself. By the time New Labour came to power in 1997, other policy options were possible. As Martin B. Carstensen and Matthias Matthijs have set out, New Labour went about using the available policy tools towards more social democratic goals than its predecessors.[4] Nevertheless, as we have seen, preventing or curtailing concentration of economic power was within the paradigm of neoliberalism, albeit a particular strand of thinking. Antitrust authorities and regulators could have provided oversight to prevent monopolies and cartels, curb anti-competitive behaviour and promote competition. During most of the 1979–2007 period, however, although every government broadly committed itself rhetorically to dispersing power in one respect or another, in reality preventing concentration was usually not high up on the list of priorities. New Labour did a more effective job than its Conservative predecessors of reducing the concentration of economic and political power, devolving power from the centre and setting a robust antitrust framework. Yet these changes have only proven effective, and durable, to a limited extent. Across a broad range of markets and measures, concentration increased from 1979 to 2007 and beyond. The trends were in part due to external factors within the global economy. Nevertheless, with populism on the rise in the 2010s, questions of concentration seem more urgent than ever.

Returning to our initial questions, a number of concluding points can be drawn. First, how did power concentrate during the 1979–2007 period? There were many reasons for the broad trend towards concentration, partly through government decisions and partly through external factors. British governments encouraged the rise of the finance sector, prioritising the borderless movement of capital at the expense of sectors such as heavy industry and manufacturing. In general, British governments were pro-business rather than pro-market, which was reflected in repeated flaws in antitrust policy. Trade union reform rebalanced the labour market and the economy more generally, disempowering many workers. Industries in different parts of the UK rapidly changed, allowing wealth to further accumulate in and around London. External changes were also important, for instance accelerating globalisation, which caused jobs to be lost to other parts of the world, and the emergence of powerful multinational companies.

Second, to what extent did British governments in the period 1979–2007 attempt to disperse economic and political power? Empowerment was a consistent rhetorical theme throughout this period. The Thatcher government sought to spread capital through increasing home ownership and other initiatives such as privatisation, which encouraged share ownership. Competition did increase in some markets owing to deregulation and liberalisation under the Thatcher government and a more effective system of regulation under New Labour. All governments during this era sought empowerment through 'choice' in public services, including in health and education, as well as schemes such as John Major's Citizen's Charter. The Blair government dispersed power from the centre with its far-reaching devolution agenda, a policy continued under its successors. Clearly, governments see dispersing power as both politically popular and a useful policy in its own right. As we have seen, however, it has proven difficult for British governments, despite policies to disperse power, to stop concentration in the longer term. This is primarily owing to the accumulation of wealth and economic power in certain sectors, leading to concurrent political clout.

Third, how can political economy, or theory more generally, explain the actions or results of these governments in relation to power concentration? Without active regulation and even constitutional safeguards, economic (and, therefore, political) power concentrates. Britain is particularly susceptible to concentration of power because it lacks a formal constitution. Concentration weakens democracy and democratic institutions, creating opportunities for populists, who then benefit at the ballot box because the system itself has failed to prevent concentration. In this way, populists can claim that the system is 'rigged' or that 'elites' or the 'establishment' are out of touch with the average voter. This kind of rhetoric reflects the unresponsiveness of a political system.

Finally, how do these trends inform the post-2007 narrative around British politics? We have seen both increasing concentration (alongside rent-seeking) in the economy as well as the backlash of populism. Nevertheless, governments have sought, however clumsily, to broach some of the issues around concentration. Several administrations have claimed to want to rebalance the regional structure of the UK economy. Theresa May, responding to the Brexit referendum, railed against 'citizens of nowhere', an apparent rebuke to the kind of upwardly and geographically mobile person who might have prospered in the British economy between 1979 and 2007. Boris Johnson, focusing on previously safe Labour seats won in Northern England and Wales at the 2019 general election, has set out a 'levelling-up' agenda to rebalance investment and jobs away from the South East. Labour leaders have also made the case against economic concentration. Ed Miliband sought to reduce the power of some of the economy's giants, from media magnates to energy companies. Jeremy Corbyn proposed nationalisation and more redistribution to tackle wealth inequality. Taken together, they almost equate to a coherent programme to reduce concentration. On their own, they are insufficient. Rapid technological change, globalisation and the new economy mean much more flexible policies are required to prevent and curb concentration. Unless policymakers recognise that, in most markets and spheres, concentration of power is harmful to democracy and accountability, attempts by British govern-ments to pursue more equitable policies are likely to be forlorn.

Notes

1 Including by the current author: see Robert Ledger, *Neoliberal Thought and Thatcherism: "A Transition from Here to There?"* (Abingdon: Routledge, 2017), 41–48.
2 Peter A. Hall, "Policy Paradigms, Social Learning, and the State: The Case of Economic Policymaking in Britain", *Comparative Politics*, 25:3 (April 1993), 275–296.
3 Richard Cockett, *Think-Tanks and the Economic Counter-Revolution, 1931–83* (London: Fontana Press, 1995).
4 Martin B. Carstensen and Matthias Matthijs, "Of Paradigms and Power: British Economic Policy Making since Thatcher", *Governance*, 31:3 (July 2018), 431–447.

Bibliography

Manuscript collections

Records of the Board of Trade (PRO: National Archives, Kew, London)
Records of the Cabinet Office (PRO: National Archives, Kew, London)
Records of the Foreign and Commonwealth Office (PRO: National Archives, Kew, London)
Records of the Prime Minister's Office: Correspondence and Papers, 1979–1997 (PRO: National Archives, Kew, London)
The Papers of Baroness Thatcher (Cambridge: Churchill Archives)
The Papers of Sir John Hoskyns (Cambridge: Churchill Archives)
The Papers of Wilhelm Röpke (Cologne: Institut für Wirtschaftspolitik)

Online resources

Archives of the Obama White House, https://obamawhitehouse.archives.gov
European Commission, https://ec.europa.eu/commission/
Margaret Thatcher Foundation, www.margaretthatcher.org
Office of National Statistics, www.ons.gov.uk
Parliamentary Records, Hansard. House of Commons Debates, https://hansard.parliament.uk/
UK Government Legislation, www.legislation.gov.uk

Books

Allen, J., Massey, D., Cochrane, A. *Rethinking the Region: Spaces of Neo-Liberalism* (Abingdon: Routledge, 1998).
Armstrong, K.A., Bulmer, S.J. *The Governance of the Single European Market* (Manchester: Manchester University Press, 1998).
Balls, E. *Speaking Out* (London: Arrow Books, 2016).
Barry, N. *The New Right* (Beckenham: Croom Helm, 1987).
Bealey, F. *Power in Business and the State: An Historical Analysis of Its Concentration* (Abingdon: Routledge, 2001).
Beckett, A. *When the Lights Went Out: Britain in the Seventies* (London: Faber & Faber, 2009).
Bork, R. *The Antitrust Paradox* (New York: Free Press, 1978).

Braudel, F. *Civilization and Capitalism, 15th–18th Century: The Perspective of the World* (Los Angeles, CA: University of California Press, 1992).

Brown, G. *My Life, Our Times* (London: Bodley Head, 2017).

Burgin, A. *The Great Persuasion. Reinventing Free Markets since the Depression* (London: Harvard University Press, 2012).

Burk, K. *The First Privatization. The Politicians, the City, and the Denationalization of Steel* (London: The Historians' Press, 1988).

Burk, K., Cairncross, A. *Goodbye Great Britain* (London: Yale University Press, 1992).

Butler, S.M. *Enterprise Zones. Greenlining the Inner Cities* (London: Heinemann, 1982).

Caldwell, B. *Hayek's Challenge: An Intellectual Biography of F.A. Hayek* (Chicago, IL: Chicago University Press, 2005).

Campbell, A. *The Diaries: The Blair Years* (Reading: Arrow Books, 2008).

Campbell, J. *Margaret Thatcher. Volume Two: The Iron Lady* (London: Pimlico, 2004).

Campbell, J. *Roy Jenkins: A Well-Rounded Life* (London: Jonathan Cape, 2014).

Cini, M., McGowan, L. *Competition Policy in the European Union* (Basingstoke: Macmillan, 1998).

Clegg, N. *Politics* (London: Bodley Head, 2016).

Cockett, R. *Think-Tanks and the Economic Counter-Revolution, 1931–83* (London: Fontana Press, 1995).

Crisell, A. *An Introductory History of British Broadcasting* (London: Routledge, 2002).

Dardot, P., Laval, C. *The New Way of the World: On Neo-Liberal Society* (London: Verso, 2013, translated by Gregory Elliott).

Darling, A. *Back from the Brink. 1,000 Days at Number 11* (London: Atlantic Books, 2012).

Davies, S., Lyons, B. *Mergers and Merger Remedies in the EU: Assessing the Consequences for Competition* (Cheltenham: Edward Elgar, 2007).

Davis, J., Rentoul, J. *Heroes or Villains? The Blair Government Reconsidered* (Oxford: Oxford University Press, 2019).

Denham, A. *Think-Tanks of the New Right* (Abingdon: Routledge, 1996).

Denham, A., Garnett, M. *Keith Joseph* (Chesham: Acumen, 2001).

Dorey, P. *British Conservatism and Trade Unionism, 1945–1964* (Farnham: Ashgate, 2009).

Eagleton-Pierce, M. *Neoliberalism: The Key Concepts* (Abingdon: Routledge, 2016).

Eatwell, R., Goodwin, M. *National Populism: The Revolt against Liberal Democracy* (London: Penguin, 2018).

Ebenstein, A. *Friedrich Hayek, A Biography* (Basingstoke: Palgrave, 2001).

Edgerton, D. *Warfare State: Britain, 1920–1970* (Cambridge: Cambridge University Press, 2005).

Edgerton, D. *The Rise and Fall of the British Nation: A Twentieth-Century History* (London: Penguin, 2018).

Erhard, L. *Prosperity through Competition* (New York: Frederick A. Praeger, translated by Edith Temple Roberts and John B. Wood, 1958).

Freyer, T. *Regulating Big Business: Antitrust in Great Britain and America; 1880–1990* (Cambridge: Cambridge University Press, 1992).

Friedman, M. *Capitalism and Freedom* (Chicago, IL: University of Chicago Press, 1962).

Friedman, M. *Inflation and Unemployment: The New Dimension of Politics. The 1976 Alfred Nobel Memorial Lecture* (London: IEA, Occasional Paper 51, 1977).

Friedman, M. *Why Government Is the Problem* (Stanford, CA: Stanford University Press, 1993).

Friedman, M., Schwartz, A. *A Monetary History of the United States* (Princeton: Princeton University Press, 2015, first published 1963).

Fukuyama, F. *The End of History and the Last Man* (New York: Free Press, 1992).

Fumagalli, C., Motta, M., Calcagno, C. *Exclusionary Practices: The Economics of Monopolisation and Abuse of Dominance* (Cambridge: Cambridge University Press, 2018).

Funnell, W., Jupe, R., Andrew, J. *In Government We Trust. Market Failure and the Delusions of Privatization* (London: Pluto Press, 2009).

Gamble, A. *Hayek. The Iron Cage of Liberty* (Cambridge: Polity Press, 1996).

Gennard, J., Bain, P. *SOGAT: A History of the Society of Graphical and Allied Trades* (London: Routledge, 1995).

Geyer, R., Mackintosh, A., Lehmann, K. *Integrating UK and European Social Policy: The Complexity of Europeanisation* (Oxford: Radcliffe, 2005).

Gregg, S. *Wilhelm Röpke's Political Economy* (Cheltenham: Edward Elgar, 2010).

Hanson, C.G. *Taming the Trade Unions. A Guide to the Thatcher Government's Employment Reforms, 1980–90* (Basingstoke: Macmillan, 1991).

Harris, R. *Not for Turning. The Life of Margaret Thatcher* (London: Bantam Press, 2013).

Hassan, G., Shaw, E. *The Strange Death of Labour Scotland* (Edinburgh: Edinburgh University Press, 2012).

Hayek, F.A. *Choice in Currency. A Way to Stop Inflation* (London: IEA, 1976).

Hayek, F.A. *Social Justice, Socialism & Democracy. Three Australian Lectures by F.A. Hayek* (Turramurra: Centre for Independent Studies, 1979).

Hayek, F.A. *Hayek on Hayek: An Autobiographical Dialogue*, Leif Wenar and Stephen Kresge (eds) (Chicago, IL: University of Chicago, 1994).

Hayek, F.A. *The Constitution of Liberty* (London: Routledge, 2006, first published 1960).

Hayek, F.A. *The Road to Serfdom* (London: Routledge, 2007, first published 1944).

Held, D., McGrew, A. *Globalization/Anti-Globalization* (Cambridge: Policy Press, 2003).

Holmes, M. *The First Thatcher Government, 1979–83* (Brighton: Wheatsheaf, 1985).

Howe, G. *Enterprise Zones and the Enterprise Culture* (London: Bow Group, 1988).

Howe, G. *Conflict of Loyalty* (Basingstoke: MacMillan, 1994).

Klaas, B. *The Despot's Accomplice: How the West Is Aiding and Abetting the Decline of Democracy* (London: Hurst, 2016).

Kurlantzick, J. *State Capitalism: How the Return of Statism Is Transforming the World* (Oxford: Oxford University Press, 2016).

Kynaston, D. *City of London, The History* (London: Chatto & Windus, 2011).

Lawson, N. *The View from No.11: Memoirs of a Tory Radical* (London: Corgi Books, 1993).

Ledger, R. *Neoliberal Thought and Thatcherism: "A Transition from Here to There?"* (Abingdon: Routledge, 2017).

MacCulloch, A., Rodger, B.J. *Competition Law and Policy in the EU and UK* (Abingdon: Routledge, 1999).

Mason, P. *Postcapitalism* (London: Allen Lane, 2015).

Matthijs, M. *Ideas and Economic Crises in Britain from Attlee to Blair 1945–2005* (Abingdon: Routledge, 2011).

McCullough, B. *How the Internet Happened: From Netscape to the iPhone* (New York: Liveright, 2018).

Mercer, H. *Constructing a Competitive Order: The Hidden History of British Antitrust Policies* (Cambridge: Cambridge University Press, 1995).

Middlemas, K. *Power, Competition and the State: Volume 2* (Basingstoke: Palgrave Macmillan, 1990).

Mierzejewski, A.C. *Ludwig Erhard. A Biography* (London: University of North Carolina Press, 2004).

Mirowski, P., Plehwe, D. (eds), *The Road from Mont Pelerin. The Making of the Neoliberal Thought Collective* (Harvard: Harvard University Press, 2009).

Moore, C. *Margaret Thatcher: The Authorized Biography, Volume Two: Everything She Wants* (London: Allen Lane, 2015).

Moore, C. *Margaret Thatcher: The Authorized Biography, Volume Three: Herself Alone* (London: Allen Lane, 2019).

Mosca, M. (ed) *Power in Economic Thought. Palgrave Studies in the History of Economic Thought* (Basingstoke: Palgrave Macmillan, 2018).

Mudde, C., Kaltwasser, C.R. *Populism: A Very Short Introduction* (Oxford: Oxford University Press, 2017).

Müller, J.W. *What Is Populism?* (London: Penguin, 2016).

Müller-Armack, A. *Genealogie der Sozialen Marktwirtschaft* (Genealogy of the Social Market Economy) (Stuttgart: Haupt, 1981).

Nicholls, A.J. *Freedom with Responsibility: The Social Market Economy in Germany, 1918–1963* (Oxford: Oxford University Press, 1994).

Nichter, L.A. *Richard Nixon and Europe: The Reshaping of the Postwar Atlantic World* (Cambridge: Cambridge University Press, 2015).

Parker, D. *The Official History of Privatization. Volume 1: The Formative Years 1970–87* (London: Routledge, 2009).

Parkinson, C. *Right at the Centre* (London: Weidenfeld & Nicolson, 1992).

Patel, K.K., Schweitzer, H. *The Historical Foundations of EU Competition Law* (Oxford: Oxford University Press, 2013).

Piketty, T. *Capital in the Twenty-First Century* (Cambridge: Harvard University Press, 2014).

Rawnsley, A. *The End of the Party: The Rise and Fall of New Labour* (London: Penguin, 2010).

Richards, S. *The Rise of the Outsiders: How Mainstream Politics Lost Its Way* (London: Atlantic Books, 2018).

Richards, S. *The Prime Ministers: Reflections on Leadership from Wilson to May* (London: Atlantic Books, 2019).

Rodrik, D. *The Globalization Paradox: Democracy and the Future of the World Economy* (New York: W.W. Norton, 2011).

Röpke, W. *The Social Crisis of Our Time* (London: William Hodge, 1950, first published in 1941, translated from the German by Annette and Peter Schiffer Jacobsohn).

Röpke, W. *A Humane Economy: The Social Framework of the Free Market* (Chicago, IL: Henry Regnery, 1960, translated by Elizabeth Henderson, first published 1958).

Röpke, W. *Against the Tide* (Vienna: Ludwig von Mises Institute, 1969).

Röpke, W. *Two Essays by Wilhelm Röpke: The Problem of Economic Order. Welfare, Freedom and Inflation* (London: University Press of America, 1987, first published 1951 and 1957).

Ruddy, D. *Theodore the Great: Conservative Crusader* (Washington, DC: Regnery History, 2016).

Sachs, J. *Poland's Jump to the Market Economy* (Cambridge: MIT Press, 1994).

Skousen, M. *Vienna & Chicago. Friends or Foes? A Tale of Two Schools of Free-Market Economics* (Washington, DC: Capital Press, 2005).

Sloman, P. *The Liberal Party and the Economy, 1929–1964* (Oxford: Oxford University Press, 2015).

Smith, A. *The Wealth of Nations, Books I–III* (London: Penguin, 1986, first published in 1776).

Spicka, M.E. *Selling the Economic Miracle: Economic Reconstruction and Politics in West Germany, 1949–1957* (Oxford: Berghahn, 2000).

Standing, G. *The Corruption of Capitalism: Why Rentiers Thrive and Work Does not Pay* (London: Biteback, 2016).

Stucke, M., Grunes, A. *Big Data and Competition Policy* (Oxford: Oxford University Press, 2016).

Thatcher, M. *The Path to Power* (London: Harper Collins, 1995).

Thompson, N.W. *Political Economy and the Labour Party: The Economics of Democratic Socialism, 1884–2005* (Abingdon: Routledge, 2006).

Thornley, C., Coffey, D. *Globalization and Varieties of Capitalism: New Labour, Economic Policy and the Abject State* (Basingstoke: Palgrave Macmillan, 2009).

Turner, R.S. *Neoliberal Ideology. History, Concepts and Policies* (Edinburgh: Edinburgh University Press, 2008).

Vinen, R. *Thatcher's Britain. The Politics and Social Upheaval of the 1980s* (London: Simon and Schuster).

Viscusi, W.K., Harrington Jr., J.E., Vernon, J.M. *Economics of Regulation and Antitrust* (Cambridge: MIT Press, 2005).

Wilks, S.R.M. *In the Public Interest: Competition Policy and the MMC: Competition Policy and the Monopolies and Mergers Commission* (Manchester: Manchester University Press, 1999).

Williamson, A. *Conservative Economic Policymaking and the Birth of Thatcherism, 1964–1979* (Basingstoke: Palgrave Macmillan, 2015).

Woodward, N. *The Management of the British Economy, 1945–2001* (Manchester: Manchester University Press, 2004).

Young, L. *The Enterprise Years: A Businessman in the Cabinet* (London: Headline, 1991).

Chapters

Biebricher, T., Vogelmann, F. "Introduction", in T. Biebricher, F. Vogelmann (eds), *The Birth of Austerity: German Ordoliberalism and Contemporary Neoliberalism* (London: Rowman & Littlefield, 2017, 1–22).

Booth, P. "More Regulation, Less Regulation or Better Regulation?", in P. Booth (ed), *Verdict on the Crash. Causes and Policy Implications* (London: IEA, 2009, 157–170).

Buchanan, J.M. "Rent Seeking and Profit Seeking", in J.M. Buchanan, R.D. Tollison G. Tullock (eds), *Toward a Theory of the Rent-Seeking Society* (College Station, TX: Texas A&M University Press, 1980).

Büthe, T. "The Politics of Competition and Institutional Change in European Union: The First Fifty Years", in S. Meunier, K.R. McNamara (eds), *Making History: European Integration and Institutional Change at Fifty* (Oxford: Oxford University Press, 2007, 175–194).

Campos, N.F., Coricelli, F. "How Does European Integration Work? Lessons from Revisiting the British Relative Economic Decline", in N.F. Campos, F. Coricelli (eds), *The Economics of UK–EU Relations: From the Treaty of Rome to the Vote for Brexit* (Basingstoke: Palgrave Macmillan, 2017, 47–78).

Denver, D. "From Hegemony to Ignominy: Elections and Public Opinion under John Major", in K. Hickson, B. Williams (eds), *John Major: An Unsuccessful Prime Minister? Reappraising John Major* (London: Biteback, 2017, 3–20).

Eucken, W. "What Kind of Economic and Social System?", in A. Peacock, H. Willgerodt (eds), *Germany's Social Market Economy: Origins and Evolution* (Basingstoke: Macmillan, 1989, first published in *Ordo Jahrbüch*, 1, 1948, 27–45).

Exley, S. "Education Policy", in K. Hickson, B. Williams (eds), *John Major: An Unsuccessful Prime Minister? Reappraising John Major* (London: Biteback, 2017, 231–247).

Fèvre, R. "Keynes and Eucken on Capitalism and Power", in M. Mosca (ed), *Power in Economic Thought. Palgrave Studies in the History of Economic Thought* (Basingstoke: Palgrave Macmillan, 2018, 321–347).

Finlay, R. "Thatcherism, Unionism and Nationalism: A Comparative Study of Scotland and Wales", in B. Jackson, R. Saunders (eds), *Making Thatcher's Britain*, (Cambridge: Cambridge University Press, 2012, 165–179).

Garnett, M. "Foreign and Defence Policy", in K. Hickson, B. Williams (eds), *John Major: An Unsuccessful Prime Minister? Reappraising John Major* (London: Biteback, 2017, 269–286).

Gertenbach, L. "Economic Order and Political Intervention: Michel Foucault on Ordoliberalism and Its Governmental Rationality", in T. Biebricher, F. Vogelmann (eds), *The Birth of Austerity: German Ordoliberalism and Contemporary Neoliberalism* (London: Rowman & Littlefield, 2017, 239–260).

Haldane, A. "Targeting Inflation: The United Kingdom in Retrospect", in M.I. Bléjer, A. Ize, A.M. Leone, S. Ribeiro da Costa Werlang (eds), *Inflation Targeting in Practice: Strategic and Operational Issues and Application to Emerging Economies* (IMF, 2000, 52–59).

Jackson, B. "The Think-Tank Archipelago: Thatcherism and Neoliberalism", in B. Jackson, R. Saunders, *Making Thatcher's Britain* (Cambridge: Cambridge University Press, 2012, 43–61).

Kuenzler A., Warlouzet, L. "National Traditions of Competition Law: A Belated Europeanization through Convergence?", in K.K. Patel, H. Schweitzer (eds), *The Historical Foundations of EU Competition Law* (Oxford: Oxford University Press, 2013, 89–124).

Lawson, N. "Foreword", in *Big Bang 20 Years On. New Challenges Facing the Financial Services Sector. Collected Essays* (London: CPS, 2006, i–v).

Letwin, W.L. "The English Common Law Concerning Monopolies", in R.A. Epstein (ed), *Contract—Freedom and Restraint: Liberty, Property, and the Law* (Abingdon: Routledge, 2000, 93–124).

Martin, S. "Dispersion of Power as an Economic Goal of Antitrust Policy", in M. Mosca (ed), *Power in Economic Thought. Palgrave Studies in the History of Economic Thought* (Palgrave Macmillan, 2018, 251–290).

McGlynn C., McDaid, S. "'72 Hours to Save the Union': John Major and Devolution", in K. Hickson, B. Williams (eds), *John Major: An Unsuccessful Prime Minister? Reappraising John Major* (London: Biteback, 2017, 91–105).

Michie, R. "City and Government: Changing Relationship", in R. Michie, P. Williamson (eds), *The British Government and the City of London in the Twentieth Century* (Cambridge: Cambridge University Press, 2011, 31–56).

Mirowski, P. "Postface: Defining Neoliberalism", in P. Mirowski, D. Plehwe (eds), *The Road from Mont Pelerin. The Making of the Neoliberal Thought Collective* (Harvard: Harvard University Press, 2009, 417–446).

OECD, "A Global or Semi-Global Village? (1990s to Today)", in J.Y. Huwart and L. Verdier (eds), *Economic Globalisation: Origins and Consequences* (Paris: OECD, 2013, 48–67).

Parr, H. "European Integration", in M. Beech, K. Hickson, R. Plant (eds), *The Struggle for Labour's Soul: Understanding Labour's Political Thought Since 1945* (Abingdon: Routledge, 2018, 159–171).

Pilbeam, P. "Social Morality", in K. Hickson, B. Williams (eds), *John Major: An Unsuccessful Prime Minister? Reappraising John Major* (London: Biteback, 2017, 215–230).

Plehwe, D. "Introduction", in P. Mirowski, D. Plehwe (eds), *The Road from Mont Pelerin. The Making of the Neoliberal Thought Collective* (Harvard: Harvard University Press, 2009, 1–44).

Plehwe, D., Walpen, B.J.A., Neunhöffer, G. "Introduction: Reconsidering Neoliberal Hegemony", in D. Plehwe, B.J.A. Walpen, G. Neunhöffer (eds), *Neoliberal Hegemony: A Global Critique* (Abingdon: Routledge, 2007, 1–24).

Powell, M. "New Labour and Social Justice", in M. Powell (ed), *Evaluating New Labour's Welfare Reforms* (Bristol: Policy Press, 2002, 19–38).

Ramirez, S.M., Van de Scheur, S. "The Evolution of the Law on Articles 85 and 86 EEC [Articles 101 and 102 TFEU]: Ordoliberalism and Its Keynesian Challenge", in K.K. Patel, H. Schweitzer (eds), *The Historical Foundations of EU Competition Law* (Oxford: Oxford University Press, 2013, 19–53).

Saunders, R. "Thatcherism and the Seventies", in B. Jackson, R. Saunders (eds), *Making Thatcher's Britain* (Cambridge: Cambridge University Press, 2012, 25–42).

Schnapper, P. "New Labour, Devolution and British Identity: The Foreign Policy Consequences", in O. Daddow, J. Gaskarth (eds), *British Foreign Policy* (Palgrave Macmillan, 2011, 48–62).

Seaton, J., McNicholas, A. "It Was the BBC Wot Won It. Winning the Peacock Report for the Corporation, or How the BBC Responded to the Peacock Committee", in T. O'Malley, J. Jones (eds), *The Peacock Committee and UK Broadcasting Policy* (Basingstoke: Palgrave Macmillan, 2009, 121–145).

Streit, M.E., Wohlgemuth, M. "The Market Economy and the State. Hayekian and Ordoliberal Conceptions", in P. Koslowski (ed), *The Theory of Capitalism in the German Economic Tradition* (London: Springer, 2000, 224–260).

Watrin, C. "Alfred Muller-Armack—Economic Policy Maker and Sociologist of Religion", in P. Koslowski (ed), *The Theory of Capitalism in the German Economic Tradition* (London: Springer, 2000, 192–220).

Williams, B. "Social Policy", in K. Hickson, B. Williams (eds), *John Major: An Unsuccessful Prime Minister? Reappraising John Major* (London: Biteback, 2017, 197–214).

Wolmar, C. "Transport Policy", in K. Hickson, B. Williams (eds), *John Major: An Unsuccessful Prime Minister? Reappraising John Major* (London: Biteback, 2017, 181–196).

Young, B. "Is Germany's and Europe's Crisis Politics Ordoliberal and/or Neoliberal?", T. Biebricher, F. Vogelmann (eds), *The Birth of Austerity: German Ordoliberalism and Contemporary Neoliberalism* (London: Rowman & Littlefield, 2017, 221–238).

Journals and Research Papers

Audickas, L., Cracknell, R., Loft, P. "UK Election Statistics: 1918–2019: A Century of Elections", Briefing Paper CBP7529, House of Commons Library, 27 February 2020.

Aydina, U., Thomas, K.P. "The Challenges and Trajectories of EU Competition Policy in the Twenty-First Century", *Journal of European Integration*, 34:6 (2012), 531–547.

Baldi, G. "Europeanising Antitrust: British Competition Policy Reform and Member State Convergence", *British Journal of Politics and International Relations*, 8:1 (2006), 503–518.

Bell, T., Tomlinson, D. "Is Everybody Concentrating? Recent Trends in Product and Labour Market Concentration in the UK", Resolution Foundation, July 2018, www .resolutionfoundation.org/app/uploads/2018/07/Is-everybody-concentrating_Recent-tr ends-in-product-and-labour-market-concentration-in-the-UK.pdf

Boas, T., Gans-Morse, J. "Neoliberalism: From New Liberal Philosophy to Anti-Liberal Slogan", *Studies in Comparative International Development*, 44:2 (June 2009), 137–161.

Bockman, J. "Socialist Globalization against Capitalist Neocolonialism: The Economic Ideas behind the New International Economic Order", *Humanity: An International Journal of Human Rights, Humanitarianism, and Development*, 6:1 (2015), 109–128.

Bonefeld, W. "Adam Smith and Ordoliberalism: On the Political Form of Market Liberty", *Review of International Studies*, 39:2 (July 2012), 233–250.

Bonefeld, W. "Crisis, Free Economy and Strong State: On Ordoliberalism", *European Review of International Studies*, 2:3 (2015), 5–14.

Branston, J.R., Cowling, K., Tomlinson, P.R. "Profiteering and the Degree of Monopoly in the Great Recession: Recent Evidence from the US and the UK", *Journal of Post Keynesian Economics*, 37:1 (2014), 135–162.

Brownill, S., O'Hara, G. "From Planning to Opportunism? Re-examining the Creation of the London Docklands Development Corporation", *Planning Perspectives*, 30:4 (2015), 537–570.

Callaghan, J., "The Plan to Capture the British Labour Party and Its Paradoxical Results, 1947–91", *Journal of Contemporary History*, 40:4 (2005), 707–725.

Carstensen, M.B., Matthijs, M. "Of Paradigms and Power: British Economic Policy Making since Thatcher", *Governance*, 31:3 (July 2018), 431–447.

Cerny, P.G. "In the Shadow of Ordoliberalism: The Paradox of Neoliberalism in the 21st Century", *European Review of International Studies*, 3:1 (2016), 78–9.

Cowling, K., Tomlinson, P.R. "Globalisation and Corporate Power", *Contributions to Political Economy*, 24:1 (2015), 33–54.

CPS, *Why Britain Needs a Social Market Economy* (Chichester: Barry Rose, 1975).

Crafts, N. "Creating Competitive Advantage: Policy Lessons from History", University of Warwick Working Papers, No. 91 (2012).

Crane, D.A. "The Tempting of Antitrust: Robert Bork and the Goals of Antitrust Policy", *Antitrust Law Journal*, 79:3 (2014), 835–53.

Daddow, O. "Margaret Thatcher, Tony Blair and the Eurosceptic Tradition in Britain", *British Journal of Politics and International Relations*, 15:2 (2013), 210–227.

Frank, A.G. "No End to History! History to No End?", *Social Justice*, 17:4 (1990, 7–29).

Friedman, M. "Neoliberalism and Its Prospects", *Farmand* (February 1951), 89–93.

Gaber, I. "The Lobby in Transition", *Media History*, 19:1 (2013), 45–58.

Gay, O. "Voting Systems: The Jenkins Report", Research Paper 98/112, 10 December 1998, (House of Commons Library).

Gibson, H. "Between the State and the Individual: 'Big Society' Communitarianism and English Conservative Rhetoric", *Social and Economics Education*, 14:1 (2015), 40–55.

Hall, P.A. "Policy Paradigms, Social Learning, and the State: The Case of Economic Policymaking in Britain", *Comparative Politics*, 25:3 (April 1993), 275–296.

Hartwich, O.M. *Neoliberalism: The Genesis of a Political Swearword* (St Leonards: CIS Occasional Papers, 114, July 2009).

Hobolt, S.B. "The Brexit Vote: A Divided Nation, a Divided Continent", *Journal of European Public Policy*, 23:9 (2016), 1259–1277.

Holland, E.E. "Using Merger Review to Cure Prior Conduct: The European Commission's GE/Honeywell Decision", *Columbia Law Review*, 103:1 (2003), 74–110.

Iakhnis, E., Rathbun, B., Reifler, J., Scotto, T.J. "Populist Referendum: Was 'Brexit' an Expression of Nativist and Anti-Elitist Sentiment?" *Research & Politics*, 5:2 (April 2018, 1–7).

Jackson, B. "At the Origins of Neoliberalism: The Free Economy and the Strong State, 1930–1947", *The Historical Journal*, 53:1 (March 2010), 132–139.

Jackson, B. "Freedom, the Common Good, and the Rule of Law: Lippmann and Hayek on Economic Planning", *Journal of the History of Ideas*, 73:1 (2012), 47–68.

Jackson, B. "Currents of Neo-Liberalism: British Political Ideologies and the New Right, c. 1955–1979", *English Historical Review*, 131 (2016), 823–850.

Jackson, B. "Progressivism in British Politics: Some Revisionist Themes", *Political Quarterly*, 88:1 (2017), 69–75.

Keohane, N., Broughton, N. "The Politics of Housing", *Hot House* (Social Market Foundation, and National Housing Federation, 2018), www.smf.co.uk/wp-content/uploads/2013/11/Publication-The-Politics-of-Housing.pdf

Lavalette, M., Mooney, G. "The Struggle against the Poll Tax in Scotland", *Critical Social Policy*, 9:26 (September 1989), 82–100.

Ledger, R. "The Road to Pergau Dam: Aid Policy, Ideology and the Thatcher Government", *Diplomacy & Statecraft*, 30:1 (2019), 50–69.

Lever, J. "The Development of British Competition Law: A Complete Overhaul and Harmonization", (WZB Discussion Paper, No. FS IV 99-4, Wissenschaftszentrum Berlin für Sozialforschung, 1999).

Mercer, H. "The Abolition of Resale Price Maintenance in Britain in 1964: A Turning Point for British Manufacturers?', London School of Economics, (Working Papers in Economic History 39/98, 1998).

Middleton, R. "Brittan on Britain: 'The Economic Contradictions of Democracy' Redux", *The Historical Journal*, 54:4 (2011), 1141–1168.

Molitor, B. "Schwäche der Demokratie" ("The Weakness of Democracy"), *ORDO. Jahrbuch für die Ordnung von Wirtschaft und Gesellschaft* ("The Ordo Yearbook of Economic and Social Order", Stuttgart: Gustav Fischer Verlag, Band 34, 1983, 17–38).

Motta, M., Tarantino, E. "The Effect of Horizontal Mergers, When Firms Compete in Prices and Investments", *Open Access Working Paper Series Mannheim* 17–01 (2017, 1–45).

Plattner, M.F. "Illiberal Democracy and the Struggle on the Right", *Journal of Democracy*, 30:1 (2019), 5–19.

Powell, A. "Labour Market Statistics: UK Regions and Countries", House of Commons Briefing Paper (No. 7950, 9 March, 2020).

Preston, V. "'Big Bang': Chronology of events", *Contemporary British History*, 13:1 (1999), 95–99.

Price, E. "A Cultural Exchange: S4C, Channel 4 and Film", *Historical Journal of Film, Radio and Television*, 33:3 (2013), 418–433.

Raffe, D., Biggart, A., Fairgrieve, J., Howieson, C., Rodger, J., Burniston, S. "Thematic Review of the Transition from Initial Education to Working Life", (OECD, July 1998), 38.

Rhodes, C. "Financial Services: Contribution to the UK Economy", House of Commons Briefing Paper (6193, 31 July 2019).

Ringe, A. "Background to Neddy: Economic Planning in the 1960s", *Contemporary British History*, 12:1 (1998), 82–98.

Robertson, S.L. "Globalising UK Higher Education", *Globalisation Societies and Education*, 8:2 (2012), 191–203.

Robinson, C. *Competition in Electricity? The Government's Proposals for Privatizing Electricity Supply* (London: IEA, 1988).

Rodrik, D. "Populism and the Economics of Globalization", Working Paper 23559, National Bureau of Economic Research (Cambridge, Massachusetts, July 2017).

Rollings, N. "Cracks in the Post-War Keynesian Settlement? The Role of Organised Business in Britain in the Rise of Neoliberalism Before Margaret Thatcher", *Twentieth Century British History*, 24:4 (2013), 637–659.

Rollings, N., Warlouzet, L. "Business History and European Integration: How EEC Competition Policy Affected Companies' Strategies", *Business History*, 62:6 (2018), 1–26.

Rutherford, T. "Energy Prices", House of Commons Library, Briefing Paper No. 04153, 9 February 2018.

Scott, A. "The Evolution of Competition Law and Policy in the United Kingdom", LSE Working Papers (9/2009).

Shapiro, C. "Antitrust in a Time of Populism", *International Journal of Industrial Organization*, 61 (2018), 714–748.

Thompson, H. "How the City of London Lost at Brexit: A Historical Perspective", *Economy and Society*, 46:2 (2017), 211–228.

Tomlinson, J. "Homogenisation and Globalisation", *History of European Ideas*, 20:4–6 (1995), 891–897.

UK Department for Business, Energy & Industrial Strategy. "Energy Trends: September 2016, Special Feature Article—Competition in UK Electricity Markets", 29 September 2016.

UK House Price Index, "House Price Statistics January 1991–March 2018", *Land Registry* (2020), www.landregistry.data.gov.uk.

Williamson, J. "The Strange History of the Washington Consensus", *Journal of Post Keynesian Economics*, 27:2 (2005), 195–206.

World Economic Outlook, "The Rise of Corporate Market Power and Its Macroeconomic Effects" (IMF, April 2019, 55–76).

Zahariadis, N. "The Rise and Fall of British State Ownership: Political Pressure or Economic Reality?" *Comparative Politics*, 31:4 (1999), 445–63.

Newspapers and online articles

Abrams, F. "Blair: 'I Think I'm a Pretty Straight Sort of Guy'", *Independent*, 17 November 1997, www.independent.co.uk/news/blair-i-think-im-a-pretty-straight-sort-of-guy-1 294593.html

Aldred, J. "The Long Read: Socialism for the Rich': The Evils of Bad Economics", *The Guardian*, 6 June 2019, www.theguardian.com/inequality/2019/jun/06/socialism-for -the-rich-the-evils-of-bad-economics

Arsenault, C. "Globalization Worsens Food Price Shocks for Importers—Researchers— TRFN", *Reuters*, 12 May 2015, www.reuters.com/article/us-food-climatechange-poli tics/globalization-worsens-food-price-shocks-for-importers-researchers-trfn-idUS KBN0NX24D20150512

Balls, E., Stansbury, A. "Twenty Years On: Is There Still a Case for Bank of England Independence?", *Vox EU*, 1 May 2017, https://voxeu.org/article/twenty-years-there-still-case-bank-england-independence

Barkham, P. "Setting Britain's Interest Rates", *The Guardian*, 10 February 2000, www.theguardian.com/world/2000/feb/10/qanda.interestrates

BBC News, "Hague: 'Last Chance to Save Pound'", 31 January 2001, http://news.bbc.co.uk/2/hi/uk_news/politics/1146210.stm

BBC News, "Ed Balls 'Deeply Sorry' Over Banking Crisis", 12 September 2011, www.bbc.com/news/uk-politics-14888933

BBC News, "Secret Papers Reveal Push to 'Trailblaze' Poll Tax in Scotland", 30 December 2014, www.bbc.com/news/uk-scotland-scotland-politics-30610043

BBC News, "EU Referendum: The Result in Maps and Charts", 24 June 2016, www.bbc.com/news/uk-politics-36616028

BBC News, "Chris Grayling Says Rail Industry 'Has Failed Passengers'", 30 May 2018, www.bbc.com/news/uk-england-44299902

BBC News, "What Has Happened to Energy Since Privatisation?", 16 May 2019, www.bbc.com/news/business-48284802

Blair, T. "Full Text of Tony Blair's Speech on Education", *The Guardian*, 23 May 2001, www.theguardian.com/politics/2001/may/23/labour.tonyblair

Blair, T. "Full text: Tony Blair's Speech on Compensation Culture", *The Guardian*, 26 May 2005, www.theguardian.com/politics/2005/may/26/speeches.media

Blair, T. "2005 Labour Party Conference Speech", *The Guardian*, 27 September 2005, www.theguardian.com/uk/2005/sep/27/labourconference.speeches

Blair, T. 'Labour's Task Is not to Make Itself Feel Better—It's to Win Power', *The Guardian*, 11 January 2020, www.theguardian.com/commentisfree/2020/jan/11/labour-task-not-make-itself-feel-better-its-about-winning

Blitz, R. "Brexit, Black Wednesday and Lessons in Trading the Pound", *Financial Times*, 15 September 2017, www.ft.com/content/7f68b50a-9a16-11e7-b83c-9588e51488a0

Bowcott, O. "John Major Had a 'Full Gloat' after Defeating Rebels on Maastricht", *The Guardian*, 24 July 2018, www.theguardian.com/politics/2018/jul/24/john-major-full-gloat-defeating-rebels-maastricht-european-union

Brown, G. "A Modern Agenda for Prosperity and Social Reform", *Speech to the Social Market Foundation*, 3 February 2003, www.smf.co.uk/wp-content/uploads/2004/05/Publication-A-Modern-Agenda-for-Prosperity-and-Social-Reform-Gordon-Brown.pdf

Carter, H. "Police Take Fresh Look at Sons of Glyndwr", *The Guardian*, 11 March 2004, www.theguardian.com/uk/2004/mar/11/helencarter

Carvel, J. "North–South, East–West Wealth Divides in Survey", *The Guardian*, 10 November 2005, www.theguardian.com/money/2005/nov/10/northsouthdivide.uknews

Cavendish, C. "Boris Johnson's 'Levelling Up' Agenda Depends on Devolving Power", *Financial Times*, 6 March 2020, www.ft.com/content/db51cd3c-5f05-11ea-8033-fa40a0d65a98

Chakrabortty, A. "The Super-Rich Have Made Britain into a Nation of Losers", *The Guardian*, 6 August 2019, www.theguardian.com/commentisfree/2019/aug/06/britain-super-rich-wealthy

Chee, F.Y. "Apple Spars with EU as \$14 Billion Irish Tax Dispute Drags On", *Reuters*, 18 September 2019, www.reuters.com/article/us-eu-apple-stateaid/apple-spars-with-eu-as-14-billion-irish-tax-dispute-drags-on-idUSKBN1W31FE

Clayton, J. "Tech Giants Facebook, Google, Apple and Amazon to Face Congress", *BBC News*, 29 July 2020, www.bbc.com/news/technology-53571562

Coman, J. "Margaret Thatcher: 20 Ways that She Changed Britain", *The Guardian*, 14 April 2013, www.theguardian.com/politics/2013/apr/14/margaret-thatcher-20-changes-britain

Corfe, S., Gicheva, N. "Concentration not Competition: The State of UK Consumer Markets", Social Market Foundation, October 2017, www.smf.co.uk/wp-content/uploads/2017/10/Concentration-not-competition.pdf

Coughlan, S. "The Symbolic Target of 50% at University Reached", *BBC News*, 26 September 2019, www.bbc.com/news/education-49841620

Daily Post, "Gwynfor Was Thinking of Martyrdom'", 9 November 2005, www.dailypost.co.uk/news/north-wales-news/gwynfor-was-thinking-of-martyrdom-2902456

Douglas, T. "Analysis: Murdoch and Media Ownership in UK", *BBC News*, 22 December 2010, www.bbc.com/news/uk-12062176

Eaton, G. "The Conservatives Are in Crisis because 'Popular Capitalism' Is no Longer Possible", *New Statesman*, 30 May 2018, www.newstatesman.com/politics/economy/2018/05/conservatives-are-crisis-because-popular-capitalism-no-longer-possible

The Economist, "Mr Butskell's Dilemma", 13 February 1954.

The Economist, "Foxconn and Labour Laws: Using Globalisation for Good", 24 February 2012.

The Economist, "Market Power: Big, Bad Amazon", 20 October 2014.

The Economist, "Internet Monopolies: Everybody Wants to Rule the World", 27 November 2014.

The Economist, "Political Power Follows Economic Power", 3 February 2016.

The Economist, "Like America, Britain Suffers from a Lack of Competition", 26 July 2018.

The Economist, "More Money, More Problems: The British Economy Is Becoming More Concentrated and Less Competitive", 26 July 2018.

The Economist, "An Economic Theory of Everything: The IMF Adds to a Chorus of Concern about Competition", 4 April 2019.

The Economist, "The Rich v the Rest: A Rare Peep at the Finances of Britain's 0.01%", 29 June 2019.

The Economist, "The Sweet Hereafter: Cheer Up, Sacked MPs. A Big Payday Awaits", 12 December 2019.

Elliott, L. "Britain's Richest 5% Gained Most from Quantitative Easing – Bank of England", *The Guardian*, 23 August 2012, www.theguardian.com/business/2012/aug/23/britains-richest-gained-quantative-easing-bank

Energy UK, "Powering Europe", June 2015, www.energy-uk.org.uk/publication.html?task=file.download&id=5334

Fay, S. 'What Comes after the Ken and Eddie Show?', *The Independent*, 16 February 1997, www.independent.co.uk/news/what-comes-after-the-ken-and-eddie-show-1278965.html

Ferguson, D. "Twenty Years on—The Winners and Losers of Britain's Property Boom", *The Guardian*, 23 January 2016, www.theguardian.com/money/2016/jan/23/britain-property-boom-losers-winners-housing-market-renting

Freedland, J. "Enough of This Cover-Up: The Wilson Plot Was Our Watergate", *The Guardian*, 15 March 2006, www.theguardian.com/commentisfree/2006/mar/15/comment.labour1

Gani, A. "Clause IV: A Brief History", *The Guardian*, 9 August 2015, www.theguardian.com/politics/2015/aug/09/clause-iv-of-labour-party-constitution-what-is-all-the-fuss-about-reinstating-it

Giugliano, F., Fleming, S., Jones, C. "Central Banks: Peak Independence", *Financial Times*, 8 November 2015, www.ft.com/content/f0664634-7cd4-11e5-98fb-5a6d472 8f74e

Greenslade, R. "It's the Sun Wot's Switched Sides to Back Blair", *The Guardian*, 18 March 1997, www.theguardian.com/politics/1997/mar/18/past.roygreenslade

The Guardian, "The Guardian View on the Bank of England: Independence and Accountability", 4 May 2017, www.theguardian.com/commentisfree/2017/may/04/the-guardian-view-on-the-bank-of-england-independence-and-accountability

The Guardian, "The Guardian View on Rail Privatisation: Going Off the Tracks", 5 December 2017, www.theguardian.com/commentisfree/2017/dec/05/the-guardian-view-on-rail-privatisation-going-off-the-tracks

Hancock, D. "A Channel for Wales", *EMC Seefour*, 1 January 2002, web.archive.org/web /20090304205140/http://www.transdiffusion.org/emc/seefour/wales.php

Hutton, W. "'Neoliberal' Is an Unthinking Leftist Insult. All It Does Is Stifle Debate", *The Observer*, 29 December 2019, www.theguardian.com/commentisfree/2019/dec/29/neol iberal-is-unthinking-leftist-insult-all-it-does-it-stifle-debate

Kaufmann, E. "Rochester and UKIP: We Shouldn't Leap to the Conclusion that this By-Election Is a Bellwether for 2015", *LSE British Politics and Policy Blog*, 21 November 2014, https://blogs.lse.ac.uk/politicsandpolicy/rochester-and-ukip-we-s houldnt-leap-to-the-conclusion-that-this-by-election-is-a-bellwether-for-2015/

Kedward, K. "Why It's Time to Abandon the Myth of Central Bank Independence", Open Democracy, 1 April 2019, www.opendemocracy.net/en/oureconomy/central-bank-i ndependence-myth-its-time-abandon-it/

Kinsley, M. "Greenspan Shrugged", *The New York Times*, 14 October 2007, www.nytime s.com/2007/10/14/books/review/Kinsley-t.html

Kollewe, J. "Canary Wharf Timeline: From the Thatcher Years to Qatari Control", *The Guardian*, 28 January 2015, www.theguardian.com/business/2015/jan/28/canary-wh arf-timeline-london-building-docklands-thatcher

Lemoine, L. "Competition Law: What to Do against Big Tech's Abuse?", *European Digital Rights*, 1 April 2020, https://edri.org/competition-law-what-to-do-against-big -tech-abuse/

Lyons, J. "Ukip Are Closet Racists, Says Cameron", *Independent*, 4 April 2006, www.indepe ndent.co.uk/news/uk/politics/ukip-are-closet-racists-says-cameron-6104699.html

MacAskill, A., White, L. "British Taxpayers Face 27 Billion Pound Loss from Bank Bailout", *Reuters*, 23 November 2016, https://uk.reuters.com/article/uk-britain-eu-budget-banks/british-taxpayers-face-27-billion-pound-loss-from-bank-bailout-idUK KBN13I1FJ

Macintyre, D. "The Cash-for-Questions Affair: Major Rocked as Payments Scandal Grows: Minister Resigns over 'Cash for Questions' PM Reveals He Knew of Allegations by Harrods Owner Three Weeks Ago", *Independent*, 21 October 1994, www.independent .co.uk/news/the-cash-for-questions-affair-major-rocked-as-payments-scandal-grows -minister-resigns-over-cash-for-1444057.html

Mance, H. "Britain Has Had Enough of Experts, Says Gove", *Financial Times*, 3 June 2016, www.ft.com/content/3be49734-29cb-11e6-83e4-abc22d5d108c

Mason, R., Syal, R. "Chris Grayling Criticised for Blaming Rail Delays on 'Militant Unions'", *The Guardian*, 10 January 2018, www.theguardian.com/politics/2018/jan/10 /chris-grayling-criticised-for-blaming-rail-delays-on-militant-unions

Mathewson, G. "Goodwin's Undoing", *Financial Times*, 25 February 2009, www.ft.com/ content/dbcc20aa-02a0-11de-b58b-000077b07658

Neate, R. "Big Four Accountancy Firms Should Break Up, Say MPs", *The Guardian*, 2 April 2019, www.theguardian.com/business/2019/apr/02/big-four-accountancy-firms -should-break-up-say-mps

O'Carroll, L. "Leveson Report: Key Points", *The Guardian*, 29 November 2012, www.t heguardian.com/media/2012/nov/29/leveson-report-key-points

Office of Fair Trading, "Assessment of Market Power: Understanding Competition Law", 2004, https://assets.publishing.service.gov.uk/government/uploads/system/uploads/ attachment_data/file/284400/oft415.pdf

Office of National Statistics, "The History of Strikes in the UK", 21 September 2015, www .ons.gov.uk/employmentandlabourmarket/peopleinwork/employmentandemployee types/articles/thehistoryofstrikesintheuk/2015-09-21

Office for National Statistics, "Changes in the Economy since the 1970s", 2 September 2019, www.ons.gov.uk/economy/economicoutputandproductivity/output/articles/c hangesintheeconomysincethe1970s/2019-09-02

Office for National Statistics, "Unemployment Rate (Aged 16 and Over, Seasonally Adjusted)", 16 June 2020, www.ons.gov.uk/employmentandlabourmarket/peoplenot inwork/unemployment/timeseries/mgsx/lms

Ofgem, 'State of the Energy Market 2019', 3 October 2019, www.ofgem.gov.uk/publicat ions-and-updates/state-energy-market-2019

Orellana Pérez, F.A., Pérez Herrero, P. "The Shadow of Nationalism in the New Populist Proposals in Europe", *The Conversation*, 19 May 2019, https://theconversation.com/th e-shadow-of-nationalism-in-the-new-populist-proposals-in-europe-117127

Ortiz-Ospina, E., Beltekian, D. "Trade and Globalization", *Our World in Data*, October 2018, https://ourworldindata.org/trade-and-globalization

Parker, G. "A Fiscal Focus", *Financial Times*, 7 December 2009, www.ft.com/content/5 f0bf460-e36d-11de-8d36-00144feab49a

Peck, T. "Ken Clarke: David Cameron May Have 'Done Some Sort of Deal' with Rupert Murdoch", *Independent*, 23 November 2017, www.independent.co.uk/news/uk/politics /ken-clarke-rupert-murdoch-deal-2010-election-rebekah-brooks-a8072456.html

Pfeifer, S. "UK Energy 'Challengers' Face Tough Times", *Financial Times*, 11 February 2018, www.ft.com/content/bbee8de6-0ce5-11e8-839d-41ca06376bf2

Pickard, J. "Chris Grayling Takes Flak for Southern Rail Strikes", *Financial Times*, 13 December 2016, www.ft.com/content/8495a28a-c132-11e6-9bca-2b93a6856354

Raikes, L., Lockwood, R. "Revealed: North Set to Receive £2,389 Less per Person than London on Transport", *IPPR*, 19 August 2019, www.ippr.org/news-and-media/press-r eleases/revealed-north-set-to-receive-2-389-less-per-person-than-london-on-transport

Rawnsley, A. "The Damaging Questions Keep Coming", *The Guardian*, 14 September 2003, www.theguardian.com/politics/2003/sep/14/tonyblair.iraq

Reich, R. "Facebook, Google and Amazon Are the New Robber Barons. Bust Them Up", *Newsweek*, 11 March 2019, www.newsweek.com/elizabeth-warren-google-facebook- amazon-monopolies-breakup-1358898

Robinson, N. "Economy: There Is No Alternative (TINA) Is Back", *BBC News*, 7 March 2013, www.bbc.com/news/uk-politics-21703018

Rogers, S. "How Britain Changed under Margaret Thatcher. In 15 Charts", *The Guardian*, 8 April 2013, www.theguardian.com/politics/datablog/2013/apr/08/britain-changed -margaret-thatcher-charts

Rosenbaum, M. "Local Voting Figures Shed New Light on EU Referendum", *BBC News*, 6 February 2017, www.bbc.com/news/uk-politics-38762034

Seymour, R. "A Short History of Privatisation in the UK: 1979–2012", *The Guardian*, 29 March 2012, www.theguardian.com/commentisfree/2012/mar/29/short-history-of -privatisation

Shuttleworth, K. "Electoral Systems across the UK", Institute for Government, 1 July 2020, www.instituteforgovernment.org.uk/explainers/electoral-systems-uk

Sim, P. "Who Is Nicola Sturgeon? A Profile of the SNP Leader", *BBC News*, 26 May 2017, www.bbc.com/news/uk-scotland-25333635

Sivaev, D. "Enterprise Zones: The Forgotten Legacy of Lady Thatcher", Centre for Cities, 22 April 2013, www.centreforcities.org/blog/enterprise-zones-the-forgotten-legacy-of- lady-thatcher/

Social Market Foundation, "Press Release: New "Minister for Competition" Needed after Brexit, Think-Tank Says', 31 July 2018. www.smf.co.uk/press-release-competition-not -concentration/

Sparrow, A., Mulholland, H., Partington, R., Wintour, P. "More than 50 MPs Flipped Second Home, New Expenses Figures Show", *The Guardian*, 10 December 2009, www .theguardian.com/politics/2009/dec/10/mps-expenses-50-flipped-homes

Spero, J. "Chris Grayling Blames Network Rail for Timetable Chaos", *Financial Times*, 23 May 2018, www.ft.com/content/63eed0d8-5ea7-11e8-9334-2218e7146b04

Stacey, K. "David Cameron Pushes for 'English Votes for English Laws'", *Financial Times*, 27 November 2014, www.ft.com/content/466984bc-7644-11e4-a777-00144fe abdc0

Stevenson, R. "Blair Intervened over F1 Tobacco Ban Exemption, Documents Show", *The Guardian*, 12 October 2008, www.theguardian.com/politics/2008/oct/12/tonyblair -labour

Summers, D. "Labour's Attempts to Reform the House of Lords", *The Guardian*, 27 January 2009, www.theguardian.com/politics/2009/jan/27/house-of-lords-reform

Sweeney, P. "'A Great Future Prime Minister Lost to This Country': On the Legacy of John Smith", *New Statesman*, 13 May 2019, www.newstatesman.com/politics/staggers /2019/05/great-future-prime-minister-lost-country-legacy-john-smith

Taylor-Gooby, P., Leruth, B. "Why British People Don't Trust the Government Any More—And What Can Be Done about It", *The Conversation*, 31 January 2018, https ://theconversation.com/why-british-people-dont-trust-the-government-any-more-and -what-can-be-done-about-it-89627

Tempest, M. "Treasury Papers Reveal Cost of Black Wednesday", *The Guardian*, 9 February 2005, www.theguardian.com/politics/2005/feb/09/freedomofinformation.uk1

Topham, G. "Completion of London's Thameslink Rail Project Delayed Until December 2019", *The Guardian*, 23 November 2017, www.theguardian.com/uk-news/2017/nov /23/thameslink-rail-completion-delayed-london-december-2019

Townsend, M. "How the Battle of Lewisham Helped to Halt the Rise of Britain's Far Right", *The Guardian*, 13 August 2017, www.theguardian.com/uk-news/2017/aug/13/ battle-of-lewisham-national-front-1977-far-right-london-police

Treanor, J. "Balls Intervenes on LSE to Remove Fears of a US Takeover", *The Guardian*, 14 September 2006, www.theguardian.com/business/2006/sep/14/politics.economicpo licy

US Department of Justice, "Herfindahl–Hirschman Index", 31 July 2018, www.justice.gov /atr/herfindahl-hirschman-index

Wearden, G. "Wall Street and FTSE 100 Suffer Worst Week since 2008—As It Happened", *The Guardian*, 28 February 2020, www.theguardian.com/business/live/2020/feb/28/

british-airways-easyjet-coronavirus-stock-markets-ftse-dow-global-recession-business
-live

Webber, E. "The Rise and Fall of the GLC", *BBC News*, 31 March 2016, www.bbc.com/
news/uk-england-london-35716693

Wigglesworth, R. "US Stocks' Record Bull Run Brought to Abrupt End by Coronavirus",
Financial Times, 12 March 2020, www.ft.com/content/6b987f46-644f-11ea-b3f3-fe
4680ea68b5

Wilby, P. "Paul Dacre of the Daily Mail: The Man Who Hates Liberal Britain", *New
Statesman*, 2 January 2014, www.newstatesman.com/media/2013/12/man-who-hates-l
iberal-britain

Wood, Z. "Sainsbury's–Asda Merger Blocked by Competition Watchdog", *The Guardian*,
25 April 2019, www.theguardian.com/business/2019/apr/25/sainsburys-asda-merger-b
locked-by-competition-watchdog

Woodward, W. "Spin and Scandal: How New Labour Made the News", *The Guardian*,
13 June 2007, www.theguardian.com/media/2007/jun/13/politicsandthemedia.pressan
dpublishing

Podcasts

BBC Radio Wales, "Gwynfor Evans Hunger Strike, 1980", Welsh Experience: Gwynfor
Evans, 3 May 2011, www.bbc.co.uk/programmes/p00gpzsf

Talking Politics, "Moneyland", 26 September 2018, www.talkingpoliticspodcast.com/blog
/2018/117-moneyland

Talking Politics, "Monopoly and Muckraking", 29 December 2019, www.talkingpoliticsp
odcast.com/blog/2019/211-monopoly-and-muckraking

Talking Politics, "Twilight of Democracy", 16 July 2020, www.talkingpoliticspodcast
.com/blog/2020/267-twilight-of-democracy

Index

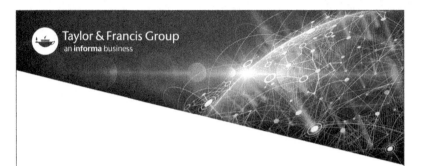

Printed in the United States
By Bookmasters